SIMPLY ELEGANT

Caviar and Crème Fraîche on Puff-Pastry Squares, page 43

SIMPLY ELEGANT

QUICK RECIPES
FOR STYLISH ENTERTAINING

American Express Publishing Corporation
New York

Editorial Director: Judith Hill
Assistant Editors: Jacqueline Bobrow and Susan Lantzius
Copy & Production Editor: Terri Mauro
Recipe Consultant: Judith Sutton
Wine Editor: Richard Nalley
Designer: Nina Scerbo
Photographer: Ellen Silverman
Food Stylist: Deborah Mintcheff
Prop Stylist: Betty Alfenito
Illustrator: Karen Scerbo
Production Manager: Yvette Williams-Braxton

Marketing Director: Mary V. Cooney
Marketing/Promotion Manager: Roni Stein
Operations Manager: Ilene Polen-Lacombe

Cover Photos: Belgian Endive Leaves with Herbed Chèvre, page 15 (front);
Poached Pears in Cassis with Kir Sorbet and Lemon Pound Cake, page 249 (back)

AMERICAN EXPRESS PUBLISHING CORPORATION
©1995 American Express Publishing Corporation

Published by American Express Publishing Corporation
1120 Avenue of the Americas, New York, New York 10036

Library of Congress Catalog Card Number: 95-76117

ISBN 0-916103-26-9

Manufactured in the United States of America

Contents

Cipollini in Marsala Glaze, page 207

FOREWORD

I spend more time dreaming about giving dinner parties than anyone could ever imagine. I mull over ideal menus, perfect pairings, great desserts. I think about who I would invite, bringing together people who would never meet otherwise (but should), balancing old friends and new acquaintances.

When time allows, I actually do throw small dinner parties. I start by pulling my favorite cookbooks from the shelf and scattering them on my bed. Sitting cross-legged, surrounded by these friendly volumes, I try to find unusual recipes that can be accomplished in a reasonable amount of time. And I always cook something I've never attempted before (a potentially dangerous endeavor, but it has worked out so far). The most recent addition to my small library of favorites is this book, *Simply Elegant*.

I know I'm partisan, but *Simply Elegant* is everything I want in a cookbook. The menus serve eight, a perfect number. It's small enough to allow me to talk to everyone and big enough for spirited conversation. The recipes are innovative without being tricky or tortuously complicated. There are variations to give me choices and plan-ahead information in case I suddenly decide to be organized. I'm not one to set my menu weeks in advance and stick to it, but I do read those tips avidly, envious of others who can shop and cook days beforehand.

Most of all, though, these are recipes I can trust. Every one has been tested; the book department's kitchen is side-by-side with the magazine's, both plunked in the middle of a mid-Manhattan office building. Judith Hill, the editor of the book, and her talented team pour their love and energy into developing the recipes from scratch, and it shows. Judy takes the guesswork out of cooking, and so I know I'll get it right every time I entertain. What could be better?

DANA COWIN
Editor in Chief
Food & Wine Magazine

Polenta Lasagne, page 161

WINE AND COMFORT

Serving wine to guests is a time-honored act of generosity and hospitality, a message that says: Relax, let the smile spread.

Among the pleasures of the table, a wine is almost always something new, something best chosen—and offered—in the spirit of exploration. It is true that the most basic, industrial-strength wines can be relied upon to vary little from month to month, year to year; that is their goal. But what a limitation! If you are willing to move up a notch, there are literally thousands of more savorable, aromatic, evening-enhancing wines around, many of them still easily affordable.

Such a surfeit of riches can be confusing, but don't be intimidated, be elated. No one, not even James Bond, not even the Baroness de Rothschild, knows everything about wine, and no one expects you to, either. Experiment, enjoy, seek out what you like. If you know a little something about the bottle you're serving before you pour it, you won't hit many clunkers, and you will open yourself up to lots of pleasant surprises.

Finding a comfort level with wine doesn't mean reaching a point where you think, "Now, lucky guests, you will be awed by the exquisitely calibrated perfection of my wine selection." It means, "Let's try this, I think we'll enjoy it."

The wine pairings that accompany the following recipes are suggestions for a place to start in wine shopping. Your own pleasure meter will lead you on from there.

RICHARD NALLEY

HORS D'OEUVRES

BELGIAN ENDIVE LEAVES WITH HERBED CHEVRE

For an appealing combination, top crisp endive leaves with a mixture of fresh goat cheese, scallion and parsley. The chopped walnuts round out the flavor of the tangy cheese but can be omitted if you're in a rush. Since the saltiness of cheese varies from one producer to the next, you should taste the topping for salt before adding any; you may find that none is needed.

MAKES ABOUT 30 LEAVES

6   ounces mild goat cheese, such as Montrachet, at room temperature

3   tablespoons heavy cream

1   scallion including green top, minced

1   tablespoon minced fresh parsley

1/8   teaspoon salt (if needed)

Large pinch fresh-ground black pepper

2   large heads Belgian endive, leaves separated

1/4   cup walnuts, chopped fine (optional)

In a medium bowl, combine the cheese, cream, scallion, parsley, salt, if needed, and pepper. Beat with a wooden spoon until smooth and creamy. Mound or pipe about 1½ teaspoons of the mixture onto each endive leaf. Sprinkle the walnuts, if using, on top.

MAKE IT AHEAD
You can prepare the cheese mixture hours in advance. Top the leaves up to an hour or two ahead. Keep, loosely covered with damp paper towels, in the refrigerator.

VARIATION

BELGIAN ENDIVE LEAVES WITH ROQUEFORT AND WALNUTS

Roquefort replaces the goat cheese, and walnuts are stirred into the creamy filling for this easy alternative.

MAKES ABOUT 30 LEAVES

6   ounces Roquefort or other blue cheese, at room temperature

2   tablespoons heavy cream

1/4   cup walnuts, chopped fine

1   tablespoon minced fresh parsley

Large pinch fresh-ground black pepper

2   large heads Belgian endive, leaves separated

In a medium bowl, combine the cheese, cream, walnuts, parsley and pepper. Beat with a wooden spoon until smooth and creamy. Mound about 1½ teaspoons of the mixture onto each endive leaf.

MUSHROOMS FILLED WITH BOURSIN CHEESE

Broiled just before serving, mushrooms stuffed with this well-known herb-and-garlic-flavored French cream cheese make meltingly delicious mouthfuls. It's hard to believe how quick and easy they are to make.

MAKES 32 STUFFED MUSHROOMS

32 medium mushrooms (about 10 ounces),
    stems removed

1   6-ounce package garlic-and-herb
    Boursin cheese, at room temperature

1. Fill the cavity of each mushroom with about a teaspoon of the cheese, mounding it slightly. Put the stuffed mushrooms on a baking sheet.

2. Just before serving, broil the mushrooms, about 5 inches from the heat, until browned on top and heated through, about 3 minutes. The mushrooms should be just barely cooked. If cooked too long, they will begin to release water. Serve immediately.

—NICKY MAJOR
MAJOR THE GOURMET

MAKE IT AHEAD
This hors d'oeuvre can be assembled hours ahead of time. Put the stuffed mushrooms on a baking sheet, cover them with plastic wrap and refrigerate. Broil just before serving, allowing perhaps a minute more if they're thoroughly chilled.

BOCCONCINI MARINATED IN SPICED OLIVE OIL

Bocconcini means "little mouthfuls." Toss these delightful marble-size balls of fresh mozzarella cheese with a red-pepper, garlic and parsley-flavored olive oil.

MAKES 3 CUPS

- 1 pound fresh mozzarella cheese, either bocconcini or 1 large ball
- ½ cup olive oil
- 1 clove garlic, minced
- 1 tablespoon chopped flat-leaf parsley
- ¾ teaspoon dried red-pepper flakes
- ¼ teaspoon salt

1. Drain the mozzarella. If using a large ball of cheese instead of bocconcini, cut it into ¾-inch cubes.

2. In a medium bowl, combine the remaining ingredients. Add the mozzarella and let marinate at room temperature, stirring occasionally, for at least 2 hours. The flavors get stronger the longer the cheese marinates. Drain and serve at room temperature with toothpicks for spearing.

MAKE IT AHEAD
Make these up to a day ahead and refrigerate. Bring to room temperature before serving. The flavor is good even after two or three days, but the cheese softens too much from standing in the oil. At this point, use it for cooking. Toss it with pasta or into risotto. It also makes a great grilled-cheese sandwich.

POLENTA SQUARES WITH PESTO

Nothing could be easier than these golden pesto-topped squares. If you have time, you can cut the polenta into rounds or other shapes using small cookie or canapé cutters.

MAKES 64 SQUARES

3 cups water

1¼ teaspoons salt

1 cup coarse or medium cornmeal

4 tablespoons butter, at room temperature

¼ cup grated Parmesan cheese

6 tablespoons Pesto alla Genovese, page 275, or store-bought pesto, at room temperature

MAKE IT AHEAD
The polenta can be made days ahead. And the pesto can be put together well in advance, even weeks before serving if you freeze it. Or you can simply choose one of the many good brands now available in supermarkets.

1. Oil an 8-inch-square cake pan. In a medium saucepan, bring the water and salt to a boil. Add the cornmeal in a slow stream, whisking constantly. Reduce the heat to moderate. Simmer, stirring frequently with a wooden spoon, until the polenta is very thick and pulls away from the sides of the pan, about 20 minutes.

2. Stir in the butter and Parmesan. Spread the polenta evenly in the prepared pan. Refrigerate to set, about 30 minutes.

3. Heat the broiler. Unmold the polenta and cut into 1-inch squares. Put the squares on a baking sheet and place under the broiler until warmed through, 3 to 5 minutes. Spoon about ¼ teaspoon pesto onto each square and serve.

PARMESAN, BLACK-PEPPER AND PINE-NUT BISCUITS

Bursting with the flavors of cheese and black pepper and studded with pine nuts, these crisp little rounds are positively addictive. Just shape the dough into a log, chill and then slice and bake.

MAKES ABOUT 4 DOZEN BISCUITS

½   cup pine nuts

6   tablespoons unsalted butter, at room temperature

1   cup grated Parmesan cheese

1   cup plus 2 tablespoons flour

½   teaspoon salt

1   teaspoon fresh-ground black pepper

1   large egg, beaten to mix

1. In a small frying pan, toast the pine nuts over moderately low heat, stirring frequently, until golden brown, about 4 minutes. Or toast in a 350° oven for about 6 minutes. Let cool.

2. In a large bowl, mix the butter and Parmesan. Add the pine nuts. In a medium bowl, whisk together the flour, salt and pepper. Add to the cheese mixture and stir just until blended. Add the egg and stir just until blended.

3. Shape the dough into a log about 1¼ inches in diameter and roll up in waxed paper or plastic wrap. Refrigerate until the dough is firm, about 2 hours.

4. Heat the oven to 350°. Cut the log of dough into ¼-inch slices and put the slices, about 1 inch apart, on two ungreased baking sheets. Bake until the biscuits are golden brown, about 15 minutes. Transfer them to a rack to cool.

MAKE IT AHEAD
Baked biscuits keep well for several days in an airtight container. You can refrigerate the log of raw dough for two days before baking or freeze it for up to a month.

QUICK MIX

There's no need to sift dry ingredients together. Instead, borrow a chef's trick and whisk them. Just a few strokes will combine the ingredients thoroughly.

Cheddar Pecan Biscuits

Cheddar cheese and pecans are a perfect duo for these cocktail biscuits. Roquefort and walnuts are another natural combination and make a delicious variation. These are the same kind of savory cookie as the Parmesan, Black-Pepper and Pine-Nut Biscuits, opposite page, but use slightly different proportions.

MAKES ABOUT 4 DOZEN BISCUITS

7   tablespoons unsalted butter, at room temperature

¼   pound sharp cheddar cheese, grated fine (about 1 cup)

½   cup pecans, chopped

1   cup plus 1 tablespoon flour

¾   teaspoon salt

⅛   teaspoon cayenne

    Pinch paprika

1   large egg yolk

2   tablespoons heavy cream

1. In a large bowl, mix the butter and cheese. Add the pecans. In a medium bowl, whisk together the flour, salt, cayenne and paprika. Add to the cheese mixture and stir just until blended. Combine the egg yolk and cream and add them to the dough. Stir just until blended.

2. Shape the dough into a log about 1¼ inches in diameter and roll up in waxed paper or plastic wrap. Refrigerate until the dough is firm, about 2 hours.

3. Heat the oven to 350°. Cut the log of dough into ¼-inch slices and put the slices, about 1 inch apart, on ungreased baking sheets. Bake until the biscuits are golden brown, about 15 minutes. Transfer them to a rack to cool.

MAKE IT AHEAD
See Parmesan, Black-Pepper and Pine-Nut Biscuits, opposite page.

VARIATION

Roquefort Walnut Biscuits

Substitute crumbled Roquefort cheese for the cheddar, and cream it into the butter. Use walnuts instead of pecans. Reduce the cream to 1½ tablespoons.

CHEDDAR LACE

No one will believe that these lacy crisps are nothing but melted cheese. Making them is like watching a bit of magic.

MAKES ABOUT 30 CRISPS

¼ pound cheddar cheese, cut into ½-inch cubes

1. Heat the oven to 350°. Arrange the cheese cubes about 3 inches apart on non-stick baking sheets. Bake until the cheese is crisp, 10 to 15 minutes. If the cheese browns, it will taste bitter, but if it is not cooked enough, it will be chewy rather than crisp.

2. With a metal spatula, carefully transfer the cheese crisps to paper towels to cool. Serve them warm or at room temperature.

MAKE IT AHEAD Except in very humid weather, these crisps keep for a few days. Layer them in an airtight container, with a piece of waxed paper between each layer, and store at room temperature.

SMOKED SALMON WITH HERBS AND CREME FRAICHE

Serve this elegant but unfussy spread with firm black bread or with toast. Use whatever soft-leaved herbs, such as basil or parsley, that you like.

MAKES ABOUT 1⅓ CUPS

½ pound sliced smoked salmon, cut into ¼-inch squares

6 tablespoons crème fraîche, more if needed

¾ teaspoon lemon juice

1½ tablespoons mixed chopped fresh herbs, such as chervil, tarragon and chives

⅛ teaspoon salt

⅛ teaspoon fresh-ground black pepper

In a medium bowl, combine all the ingredients.

MAKE IT AHEAD You can make the salmon spread hours in advance. Cover and refrigerate. If it dries out a bit, simply add another tablespoon of crème fraîche. The toast can be made ahead, too, as long as the day is not humid. Just set the toasted bread aside at room temperature, and it will be fine for a few hours.

Feta and
Black-Olive Wedges

When shepherd's bread is sandwiched with melted cheese, scallions, oregano, ground black pepper and olives, it makes a great hors d'oeuvre that disappears quickly. An excellent version of this bread, a round Middle Eastern flat bread also called lavash, is now available in most supermarkets. It's usually about fourteen inches in diameter and is sold in pairs, folded together in plastic bags.

MAKES 24 WEDGES

- 1   14-inch-round shepherd's bread
- 2   tablespoons olive oil
- 2½ ounces feta cheese, crumbled (about ½ cup)
- ¼   cup black olives, such as Niçoise or Kalamata, pitted and chopped
- 2   scallions including green tops, chopped
- ½   teaspoon dried oregano
- ⅛   teaspoon fresh-ground black pepper

MAKE IT AHEAD
You can have your ingredients ready to go—cut, chopped or crumbled. But wait to assemble and broil these just before serving. The whole recipe takes only minutes.

1. Heat the broiler. Cut the bread in half. Put one piece on a baking sheet and brush with half the oil. Broil the bread until it is beginning to brown, about 2 minutes.

2. Turn the browned bread over and sprinkle with the cheese, olives, scallions, oregano and pepper. Top with the second piece of bread and brush with the remaining oil. Broil until the bread is brown and the cheese is beginning to melt, about 2 minutes. Transfer to a cutting board and press gently all over with a wide metal spatula. Cut the bread in half lengthwise, then cut each half into 12 wedges.

Slice the filled shepherd's bread into wedges by shifting the angle of your knife after each cut.

BLACK OLIVES WITH FENNEL SEEDS AND FRESH FENNEL

Good-quality olives are now sold in most specialty-food stores. Make them even more interesting with a double dose of fennel. The seeds have a stronger flavor than the bulb, but fresh fennel provides an agreeable crunch.

MAKES ABOUT 3 CUPS

- 2 teaspoons fennel seeds
- 2 cups black olives, such as Niçoise or Kalamata, slightly crushed
- 1 fennel bulb, cut into thin slices
- 2 sprigs fresh rosemary, each broken into 3 pieces
- 1 tablespoon olive oil
- 4 teaspoons red-wine vinegar

1. In a small frying pan, toast the fennel seeds over moderately high heat, shaking the pan, until fragrant, about 30 seconds.

2. In a medium bowl, combine the fennel seeds, olives, sliced fennel, rosemary, oil and vinegar. Let the olives and fennel marinate at least 2 hours.

MAKE IT AHEAD
You can put this together a day before serving. Or you can combine everything except the fresh fennel up to a week ahead, and slice and add it a day in advance.

TO CRUSH OLIVES

Put the olives in a heavy plastic bag. Set the bag on your work surface and smack it a few times with the bottom of a medium saucepan. This will crack open the olives so that the flavorings can penetrate. Don't get carried away, though. If you hit the olives too hard, the pits may splinter.

GRILLED SCALLOPS WITH SALSA VERDE

A bowl of zesty, brilliant-green salsa surrounded by grilled scallops makes an attractive dish that's uncommonly delicious. The scallops are great served hot, warm or at room temperature. So you can prepare this hors d'oeuvre ahead or at the last minute, depending on your schedule. Shrimp is a fine alternative to the scallops, and the dipping sauce also works well with raw vegetables.

SERVES 8

1	3-inch piece French baguette or bread equivalent, crusts removed
1¼	cups flat-leaf parsley leaves
1	tablespoon capers
3	anchovy fillets
2	tablespoons minced onion
1	clove garlic, minced
2½	teaspoons red-wine vinegar
¾	teaspoon salt
	Fresh-ground black pepper
½	cup plus 2 tablespoons olive oil
¾	pound bay scallops, or sea scallops cut in half horizontally

1. Soak the bread in a bowl of water until the bread is moist throughout, and squeeze to remove as much water as possible. In a blender, puree the bread, parsley, capers, anchovies, onion and garlic with the vinegar, ½ teaspoon of the salt and ¼ teaspoon pepper. With the blender running, add ½ cup of the oil in a thin stream.

2. Light the grill or heat the broiler. Stick a toothpick into each scallop. Brush with the remaining 2 tablespoons oil and sprinkle with ⅛ teaspoon pepper and the remaining ¼ teaspoon salt. Grill or broil the scallops, turning once, until just done, about 3 minutes.

3. Spoon the salsa verde into a small serving bowl set on a platter and arrange the scallops around it. Serve the scallops hot, warm or at room temperature.

MAKE IT AHEAD
The salsa keeps for several days. If you want to serve the scallops at room temperature, make them early, cool, cover and refrigerate. Take them out about thirty minutes before serving so that they're not too cold to have any flavor.

Spicy Scallop Salsa in Cucumber Cups

Crisp cucumber provides a refreshing contrast to the chile-pepper heat of the scallop salsa here. Use a long, thin-skinned English cucumber (the kind that is sold shrink-wrapped) rather than the standard kind, which is often seedy.

MAKES 16 CUCUMBER CUPS

1 English cucumber, peeled and cut into 16 pieces

1 tablespoon olive oil

1 small dried red chile

1 clove garlic, crushed

2 tablespoons finely diced red bell pepper

1 tablespoon minced onion

¼ pound sea scallops, cut into ¼-inch dice

½ teaspoon salt

Pinch sugar

1 tablespoon lime juice

1 tablespoon chopped cilantro

1. With a small spoon, scoop out enough of the seeds and flesh from each piece of cucumber to make a shallow cup. Place the "cups" upside down on a paper-towel-lined plate and refrigerate.

2. In a medium nonstick frying pan, heat the oil over moderately high heat. Add the chile and cook until very lightly browned, about 1 minute. Remove and discard. Add the garlic and cook until golden brown, 2 to 3 minutes. Remove and discard. Add the bell pepper and onion and cook, stirring occasionally, until soft, about 4 minutes. Add the scallops and cook, stirring, until just done, about 2 minutes. Stir in the salt and sugar. Transfer the salsa to a bowl and let cool. Stir in the lime juice and cilantro. Cover and refrigerate for at least 30 minutes.

3. Spoon the salsa into the cucumber cups and serve.

—Grace Parisi

MAKE IT AHEAD
Both the cucumber cups and the salsa can be prepared hours ahead and chilled until you're ready to assemble and serve.

Scoop out the center of each piece of cucumber, being careful not to go through the bottom.

Fresh-Cod Brandade

Made with fresh fish rather than dried salt cod, this creamy puree has a lighter flavor than the traditional version of the Provençal classic. Sprinkling the toast with pepper after baking it is a simple trick that adds another dimension to the combination; or you can serve the brandade with both plain and peppered toast to give your guests a choice.

SERVES 8

½ baking potato (about ¼ pound), peeled and quartered

1 clove garlic, crushed

1 pound cod fillet

¾ teaspoon salt

⅛ teaspoon fresh-ground black pepper

¾ cup olive oil

3 tablespoons grated Parmesan cheese

Peppered Toast, page 279

1. Put the potato and garlic in a medium saucepan of salted water. Bring to a boil and simmer until tender, about 15 minutes. Drain.

2. Meanwhile, in a medium nonstick frying pan, bring ¼ inch of water to a simmer over moderately high heat. Add the cod, cover, reduce the heat and simmer until just done, 10 to 12 minutes. Drain and transfer to a bowl.

3. Add the potato and garlic to the cod and mash with a fork. With an electric mixer, beat at low speed until smooth. Beat in the salt and pepper. With the mixer at medium speed, gradually add the oil. Transfer the brandade to a 1½-quart gratin or shallow baking dish.

4. Heat the broiler. Sprinkle the cheese over the brandade. Broil until golden brown on top, 3 to 5 minutes. Serve with the toast.

MAKE IT AHEAD
You can make the brandade a day ahead and even put it in the gratin dish and sprinkle with the cheese, all ready to reheat. Cover with plastic wrap and refrigerate. If you don't have time to bring it to room temperature before reheating, give it the full five minutes under the broiler, and check to be sure it's hot in the center before serving.

Is It Hot Yet?

When reheating this dish, you don't have to spoil its appearance by sticking your finger into it to see whether or not it's warmed through. Just slide a knife or fork into the center, leave it for about fifteen seconds and then touch it. If it's hot, so is the food.

VIETNAMESE SPRING ROLLS WITH SHRIMP AND AVOCADO

Packed with fresh vegetables, shrimp, cilantro and mint, and served with a spicy Asian dipping sauce, these rolls make a light hors d'oeuvre that fills your mouth with flavor. Because these take some time to roll, we suggest serving them the way the Vietnamese often do: Arrange all of the ingredients on a platter and have your guests make their own. The platter is stunning, and the process fun. Roll the first one yourself to show your guests how. If you want to make the rolls in advance, be sure to cut them in half before serving so that the colorful filling shows.

MAKES 18 ROLLS

- 3 ounces cellophane noodles*
- 3 carrots, grated
- 2 teaspoons sugar
- 1/2 pound medium shrimp
- 1 avocado, preferably Hass
- 1 1/2 teaspoons lime juice
- 1/8 teaspoon salt
- 1/2 head Bibb lettuce
- 18 6-inch rice-paper rounds*
- 3/4 cup cilantro sprigs
- 1/2 cup fresh mint leaves
  Nuoc Cham Dipping Sauce, recipe follows

*Available at Asian markets

1. In a medium bowl, cover the noodles with very hot water and leave until softened, about 20 minutes. Drain well and dry on paper towels. With kitchen scissors, snip the noodles into 2-inch lengths.

2. In a medium bowl, combine the carrots and sugar. Let sit 10 minutes to soften.

3. In a medium pot of boiling, salted water, cook the shrimp until just done, about 2 minutes. Drain. When cool enough to handle, peel and slice in half lengthwise.

4. Cut the avocado into 1/4-inch slices. In a medium bowl, combine the avocado, lime juice and salt.

5. Separate the lettuce leaves, remove the tough part of the ribs and cut the leaves in half lengthwise.

6. Fill a medium bowl with water. Dip each rice-paper round to completely cover. Shake off excess water. Arrange the rounds, overlapping, on a platter. Cover with damp paper towels. Let soften at least 5 minutes.

7. To serve, arrange all the ingredients on a platter and accompany with the Nuoc Cham sauce. To form the rolls, put a rice-

paper round on a plate or napkin. Layer all the ingredients down the center of the rounds using a cilantro sprig, 3 shrimp halves, a slice of avocado, about a tablespoon each of the carrots and noodles, 2 mint leaves and a piece of lettuce. Starting with the edge closest to you, roll the rice paper over the filling. Fold in the sides and continue rolling. The rice paper should stick to itself so that you can form a tight roll. If it doesn't stick, moisten it with a little water.

MAKE IT AHEAD

You can either prepare the filling ingredients and arrange them on a platter or assemble the rolls up to three hours ahead. Cover the filling ingredients or spring rolls with damp paper towels and refrigerate. It's best to soak the rice-paper rounds just before using. The dipping sauce is good for a day or two.

NUOC CHAM DIPPING SAUCE

MAKES ABOUT 1 ³/₄ CUPS

½ cup Asian fish sauce (nam pla or nuoc mam)*

¼ cup lime juice (from about 2 limes)

1 tablespoon rice-wine vinegar or white vinegar

½ cup sugar

2 cloves garlic, minced

1 tablespoon chopped fresh mint

1 teaspoon dried red-pepper flakes

1 cup warm water

*Available at Asian markets

Combine all of the ingredients and stir until the sugar is dissolved. Serve at room temperature.

THE DREADED DOUBLE DIP

You'll want some sauce on each bite of your spring roll. If the thought of eight people dipping into a communal bowl after each bite appalls you, there are a couple of solutions. You can either put the dipping sauce in small individual bowls, or you can provide plates (not a bad idea in any case) and put a spoon in the sauce so that everyone can transfer a bit of it to a plate and dip their own spring roll in it.

SKEWERED SHRIMP MARINATED IN LIME-AND-BASIL VINAIGRETTE

Presented in a bowl of pale-green vinaigrette, these zesty shrimp on skewers are a tempting hors d'oeuvre. We've included a second vinaigrette made with sherry vinegar, scallions and soy sauce, which is a good alternative to the lime and basil combination. Or offer a choice and serve them side by side.

MAKES 36 SHRIMP

36 medium shrimp
¾ cup lime juice (from about 6 limes)
3 tablespoons grainy mustard
⅛ teaspoon sugar
1¾ teaspoons salt
¾ cup olive oil
⅓ cup chopped fresh basil
10 scallions including green tops, cut into thin slices

1. In a large pot of boiling, salted water, cook the shrimp until just done, about 2 minutes. Drain and, when the shrimp are cool enough to handle, peel.

2. In a medium bowl, whisk the lime juice with the mustard, sugar and salt. Add the oil slowly, whisking. Stir in the basil and scallions.

3. Thread each shrimp onto a 6-inch skewer. Pour the vinaigrette into a shallow bowl. Add the shrimp, with the ends of the skewers sticking out of the bowl.

MAKE IT AHEAD
Cooked shrimp keep nicely, well wrapped and refrigerated, for several days. The vinaigrette should be put together just a couple of hours before using, or the basil and scallions will discolor and the raw garlic in the variation will begin to taste stale.

VARIATION

SHERRY-VINEGAR, SCALLION AND SOY VINAIGRETTE

Make in the same way as the above vinaigrette using these ingredients.

½ cup sherry vinegar
¼ cup chili sauce
2 tablespoons grainy mustard
2 tablespoons soy sauce
⅛ teaspoon salt
½ cup olive oil
1 clove garlic, minced
10 scallions including green tops, cut into thin slices

Shrimp and Guacamole in Mini-Pitas

Avocado and shrimp are always a great combination. You can be sure everyone will like these charming miniature sandwiches. Choose Hass avocados or another variety from California for the best flavor.

MAKES 24 MINI-SANDWICHES

24 small shrimp

2 avocados, preferably Hass

¼ cup plus 1 tablespoon chopped cilantro, plus additional leaves for garnish

2 tablespoons lime juice

1 teaspoon salt

  Pinch fresh-ground black pepper

1 teaspoon olive oil

24 mini-pitas, about 2 inches across

1. In a large pot of boiling, salted water, cook the shrimp until just done, about 2 minutes. Drain and, when the shrimp are cool enough to handle, peel. Cover and refrigerate.

2. In a medium bowl, combine the avocados, ¼ cup of the cilantro, the lime juice, ¾ teaspoon of the salt and the pepper. Mash with a fork until smooth.

3. In a medium bowl, toss the boiled shrimp with the remaining 1 tablespoon cilantro, the oil and the remaining ¼ teaspoon salt.

4. Cut the top third off each mini-pita to make a pocket. Spoon the guacamole into the pita pockets, put a shrimp in each, with the tail peeking out, and garnish with cilantro leaves.

MAKE IT AHEAD
All the components of these pitas can be prepared a day ahead, but they should not be assembled until shortly before serving. Cook and peel the shrimp, cover well and refrigerate. Make the guacamole. Cover it with plastic wrap, pressing the wrap directly on the surface of the guacamole, and refrigerate. If the surface darkens slightly, stir the guacamole just before assembling the pitas.

Colorful Guacamole

Forget those tricks you've heard about how to keep guacamole green—such as saving the avocado pit and leaving it in the guacamole. Exposure to air makes the flesh of the avocado discolor; so oxygen is what you want to avoid. Covering guacamole with plastic wrap placed directly on the dip's surface keeps it as airtight as possible.

TUNA TARTARE

Fresh raw tuna is chopped and mixed with shallots, herbs and seasonings. Even those who find sushi a bore love this combination. Small pieces of toast are the ideal accompaniment.

MAKES ABOUT 2¹/₂ CUPS

- 1   tablespoon olive oil
- 1   teaspoon lemon juice or white-wine vinegar
- 2   tablespoons minced shallot
- 2   tablespoons chopped fresh chives or scallion tops
- 2   tablespoons chopped fresh parsley
- 1   teaspoon salt
- ¹/₈   teaspoon fresh-ground black pepper
- 1   1-pound piece tuna steak, skinned

1. In a medium bowl, combine the oil, lemon juice, shallot, chives, parsley, salt and pepper.

2. Cut the tuna into thin slices. Stack the slices and cut them lengthwise into strips. Gather the strips together and cut them crosswise. Chop until the pieces are fine. Add the fish to the bowl and stir until it forms a mass.

3. Pack the tuna into a small bowl. Invert the bowl onto a serving platter to unmold the tuna tartare. Arrange the pieces of toast around the edge of the plate. Alternatively, serve the tuna in a bowl.

MAKE IT AHEAD
The tuna absolutely must be impeccably fresh. Buy it on the day you're going to serve it. You can combine the other ingredients hours ahead and mix with the tuna shortly before serving.

VARIATION

SESAME SOY TUNA TARTARE

Make this Asian-flavored version as above but with these ingredients.

- 2   teaspoons cooking oil
- ¹/₄   teaspoon Asian sesame oil
- 2   teaspoons soy sauce
- ¹/₂   teaspoon lemon juice or white-wine vinegar
- 2   tablespoons minced shallot
- 1¹/₂   tablespoons chopped cilantro
- ¹/₂   teaspoon salt
- ¹/₈   teaspoon fresh-ground black pepper
- 1   1-pound piece tuna steak, skinned

BUTTERED PECANS

A little salt and some butter are just enough to transform plain pecans. Though these are the easiest of hors d'oeuvres, guests always feel you've gone to extra trouble, rather than just opening a can of nuts.

MAKES 2 CUPS

2 cups pecan halves

1 tablespoon butter

¼ teaspoon salt

In a medium frying pan, toast the pecans over moderately low heat, stirring frequently, until golden brown, about 5 minutes. Add the butter and salt and cook 1 minute longer. Let cool. Alternatively, toast the nuts in a 350° oven for about 8 minutes. Add the butter and salt and toss until the butter is melted. Bake 2 minutes longer. Let cool.

MAKE IT AHEAD
The oil in nuts can turn rancid. So store them in the refrigerator to keep them fresh. These toasted nuts are especially handy to have around. They keep for weeks. Just bring them back to room temperature before setting them out to accompany drinks.

VARIATION

PEPPERED CASHEWS

Cashews have so much natural oil that no butter is needed to toast them to a golden brown. The bite of pepper is the perfect foil for their richness.

2 cups cashews

½ teaspoon fresh-ground black pepper

¼ teaspoon salt

In a medium frying pan, toast the cashews over moderately low heat, stirring frequently, until golden brown, about 5 minutes. Add the pepper and salt and cook 1 minute longer. Let cool. Alternatively, toast the nuts in a 350° oven for about 8 minutes. Add the pepper and salt and toss until the nuts are coated. Bake 2 minutes longer. Let cool.

MUSSELS ON THE HALF-SHELL WITH CILANTRO

Even though this hors d'oeuvre is made with just a handful of ingredients, it's filled with flavor. Choose small mussels, if you can find them, for a sweeter taste and more elegant look.

MAKES 4 DOZEN MUSSELS

- 4 dozen mussels, scrubbed and debearded
- ¼ cup olive oil
- ¼ cup finely chopped cilantro
- 2 tablespoons minced shallot
- ½ teaspoon salt
- ½ teaspoon fresh-ground black pepper

1. Discard any mussels that have broken shells or that do not clamp shut when tapped. Pour 1 inch of water into a large pot. Add the mussels to the pot. Cover, raise the heat to high and bring to a boil. Cook, shaking the pot occasionally, just until the mussels open, about 3 minutes. Remove the open mussels. Continue to cook, uncovering the pot as necessary to remove the mussels as soon as their shells open. Discard any that do not open.

2. Heat the broiler. In a small bowl, combine the oil, cilantro, shallot and salt.

3. Pull off and discard the top shells of the mussels. Arrange the mussels on a baking sheet. Spoon the cilantro mixture over them and sprinkle with the pepper. Broil just until heated through, 1 to 2 minutes.

MAKE IT AHEAD
Cook the mussels a day ahead if you like; either keep them in the shells or pull off the top shells, put the mussels on a baking sheet and cover tightly with plastic wrap before refrigerating. The topping can be stirred together several hours in advance. Then you have only a few minutes of work before serving. If the mussels have been refrigerated, broil an extra minute or so to heat them through.

ROMESCO DIP

Red peppers, ground almonds and a bit of bread form the base for this Catalan sauce best known in Spain as an accompaniment to fish. We find that the sauce makes an excellent dip for raw vegetables as well. Hard-cooked eggs and toast fingers are delicious with it, too. We tested the recipe in both a food processor and a blender and found that the blender was more successful in turning the mixture into a smooth, emulsified puree.

MAKES 2 CUPS

¾ cup olive oil

½ cup blanched almonds

1 ½-inch piece French baguette or bread equivalent

1 red bell pepper, chopped

1 tomato, seeded and cut into chunks

3 cloves garlic, chopped

1½ tablespoons red-wine vinegar

2 teaspoons paprika

1¼ teaspoons salt

½ teaspoon fresh-ground black pepper

¼ teaspoon dried red-pepper flakes

1. In a small frying pan, heat ¼ cup of the oil over moderately low heat. Add the almonds and cook, stirring frequently, until golden brown, about 5 minutes. With a slotted spoon, transfer the almonds to a bowl. Add the bread to the pan and brown on both sides, about 2 minutes. Remove the bread and add it to the almonds.

2. Raise the heat to moderate and add the bell pepper. Cook, stirring occasionally, until the pepper begins to soften and brown, about 5 minutes. Add the tomato and garlic and cook, stirring occasionally, until the garlic is soft and just beginning to brown, about 2 minutes. Add the mixture to the bread and almonds and leave to cool completely.

3. In a blender, puree the almond mixture with the vinegar, paprika, salt, black pepper and red-pepper flakes. With the blender running, add the remaining ½ cup oil in a thin stream. Serve the dip with crisp vegetables.

MAKE IT AHEAD
Covered and refrigerated, the dip keeps perfectly for several days. You can prepare the vegetables in advance, too, though not so far ahead. Several hours or at most a day before serving, cut up the vegetables, put them in a bowl, cover with damp paper towels and then loosely with plastic wrap, and refrigerate.

ANCHOÏADE PROVENCALE

Bright green with parsley, tangy with lemon juice and pungent with anchovies and garlic, this dip or spread is a favorite in the south of France. Serve it with raw vegetables or spread it on little pieces of toast. It also makes a great accompaniment to shrimp.

MAKES 1¼ CUPS

3   2-ounce tins anchovy fillets in oil, drained

4   cloves garlic

1   cup flat-leaf parsley leaves

8   fresh basil leaves (optional)

½   teaspoon herbes de Provence, or a mixture of dried thyme, rosemary, marjoram, oregano and savory

¼   cup lemon juice

     Pinch salt

¾   cup olive oil

1. In a blender, puree the anchovies, garlic, parsley, basil and herbes de Provence with the lemon juice and salt.

2. With the blender running, add the oil in a thin stream. Cover and chill for at least 1 hour.

MAKE IT AHEAD
Anchoïade lasts for several days, covered and refrigerated. You can prepare most vegetables up to a day ahead of time (see Romesco Dip, opposite page).

CAVIAR AND CREME FRAICHE ON PUFF-PASTRY SQUARES

Perfect for special celebrations, these whimsical squares of thin pastry topped with crème fraîche and speckled, à la Jackson Pollock, with caviar, chives and hard-cooked egg are a natural with Champagne.

MAKES 32 SQUARES

1	5-ounce sheet frozen puff-pastry dough, thawed
1¼	cups crème fraîche
1	ounce osetra or sevruga caviar
2	ounces salmon caviar
1	hard-cooked egg
1	tablespoon chopped fresh chives

1. Heat the oven to 400°. On a floured surface, roll out the puff-pastry dough to a 12-by-16-inch rectangle. Put the pastry on a baking sheet and chill for 30 minutes.

2. Prick the chilled pastry every inch or so with a fork. Bake in the middle of the oven until golden brown on the surface, about 10 minutes. Put a heavy baking sheet on top of the pastry. Reduce the oven temperature to 325° and bake until the pastry is cooked through, about 10 minutes longer. Remove the top baking sheet and let the pastry cool completely on the baking sheet.

3. Spread the crème fraîche in an even layer over the pastry. Scatter the black caviar over half of the pastry and the salmon caviar over the other half. Push the egg through a sieve. Scatter the sieved egg and the chives over all the caviar. Refrigerate just 10 minutes to set the topping.

4. Using a serrated knife, trim the edges and then cut the pastry into 2-inch squares. Serve at once.

MAKE IT AHEAD
Cook the pastry up to eight hours ahead and set it aside at room temperature. With the pastry baked and the toppings ready, these squares are a snap to put together just before serving. Don't assemble ahead of time, or the pastry will get soggy.

PUFFLESS PUFF PASTRY

Sometimes you want the layered flakiness of puff pastry in a compact form. These squares are a case in point. If you let the pastry rise, it's hard to cut and harder to eat with one hand. A chef's trick that keeps the pastry flat is to put a heavy baking sheet on top of the pastry once it has formed a crust. Use a heavy sheet or a regular light one weighed down with an ovenproof pot.

TOMATO AND BLACK-OLIVE CROSTINI

Ripe summer tomatoes and salty black olives benefit from virtually any herb, fresh or dried. If you have fresh herbs in your garden, choose what you fancy, or use the combination that we suggest here.

MAKES ABOUT 24 CROSTINI

1	pound tomatoes (about 2), seeded and chopped
¼	cup black olives, such as Niçoise or Kalamata, pitted and chopped
1	tablespoon olive oil
1	teaspoon red-wine vinegar
1	tablespoon chopped fresh basil
½	teaspoon chopped fresh thyme, or ¼ teaspoon dried
½	teaspoon chopped fresh marjoram, or ¼ teaspoon dried
½	teaspoon chopped fresh oregano, or ¼ teaspoon dried
½	teaspoon salt
¼	teaspoon fresh-ground black pepper
	Crostini, page 278

MAKE IT AHEAD

You can prepare the tomato, olive and herb mixture a few hours before serving the hors d'oeuvre. As a matter of fact, if you're using dried herbs instead of fresh, they'll be better after a long soak.

1. In a medium bowl, combine the tomatoes and olives with the oil, vinegar, basil, thyme, marjoram, oregano, salt and pepper.

2. Just before serving, top each of the crostini with a few spoonfuls of the tomato mixture.

ROASTED-EGGPLANT AND MANCHEGO-CHEESE CROSTINI

Tiny cubes of eggplant and red bell pepper are roasted together in a hot oven until brown and then tossed with red-wine vinegar and nutty manchego. This Spanish cheese is made from sheep's milk and is sold in most cheese shops. If it's not available in your area, try substituting another sheep's-milk cheese, such as feta.

MAKES 24 CROSTINI

1 eggplant (about 1¼ pounds), cut into ¼-inch dice

1 red bell pepper, cut into ¼-inch dice

1 teaspoon salt

2 ounces manchego or feta cheese, cut into ¼-inch dice

2 tablespoons red-wine vinegar

1 tablespoon chopped flat-leaf parsley

⅛ teaspoon fresh-ground black pepper

Crostini, page 278

1. Heat the oven to 400°. Generously brush a baking sheet with olive oil. Spread the eggplant and red bell pepper on the baking sheet and sprinkle the vegetables with ½ teaspoon of the salt.

2. Bake the vegetables in the oven, stirring occasionally, until they are soft and brown, about 35 minutes. The vegetables may stick to the baking sheet during cooking; be sure to loosen them with a wooden spoon or spatula so that they don't burn. Transfer the roasted eggplant and bell pepper to a bowl and leave them to cool.

3. When the vegetables are cool, stir in the cheese, vinegar, parsley, the remaining ½ teaspoon salt and the pepper. Pile a few spoonfuls of the eggplant mixture on each crostini.

■ MAKE IT AHEAD
Cook the eggplant and bell pepper and toss with the other ingredients up to a day before serving.

CROSTINI WITH WHITE-BEAN SALAD

The sweet and sour tang of balsamic vinegar and the perfume of tarragon make this bean salad special. Some of the beans are mashed so that the mixture will hold together well enough to pile on top of toast.

MAKES ABOUT 1¹/₂ CUPS

1   19-ounce can cannellini beans, drained and rinsed

3   tablespoons seeded, chopped tomato

2   teaspoons balsamic vinegar

2   teaspoons minced shallot

2   teaspoons minced fresh tarragon, or ³/₄ teaspoon dried

2   teaspoons chopped flat-leaf parsley

¹/₂   teaspoon salt

¹/₈   teaspoon fresh-ground black pepper

   Crostini, page 278

1. Put the beans in a medium bowl and mash about half of them with a fork. Stir in the tomato, vinegar, shallot, tarragon, parsley, salt and pepper.

2. Top the crostini with the bean mixture, or serve the mixture in a bowl with the crostini alongside.

MAKE IT AHEAD
The white-bean salad is fine when made a day ahead. In fact, the tarragon flavor will just intensify. Wait to add the tomato, though, until just a few hours before serving the hors d'oeuvre.

VARIATIONS

■ Tarragon makes this white-bean salad a bit unusual, but if it's not one of your favorite herbs, use another. Basil, rosemary and thyme all work well. Use the same quantity of soft-leaved herbs like basil, but less of the tougher leaves, about ¹/₂ teaspoon fresh or ¹/₄ teaspoon dried.

■ If tomatoes are not in season, simply omit them or substitute diced red bell pepper, either raw or roasted.

PROSCIUTTO-AND-HERB CROSTINI

Cut the crostini into hors d'oeuvre-size servings after you top them with the parsley and prosciutto. That way, you can make these easy but elegant toasts even more quickly.

MAKES 24 CROSTINI

Crostini, page 278

2   tablespoons chopped flat-leaf parsley

3   ounces thin-sliced prosciutto

1. Sprinkle the crostini with the chopped parsley.

2. Arrange the prosciutto on the slices of toast, covering them completely. Cut into squares or rectangles.

MAKE IT AHEAD
Put these crostini together a couple of hours before serving, if you like. Cover loosely with plastic wrap and keep at room temperature.

CHICKEN KABOBS WITH SPICY MANGO SAUCE

The gingery marinade imparts such a delicious flavor to these chicken kabobs that they're good even on their own. Served with an easy chile-spiked mango dipping sauce, they're really addictive.

MAKES 24 KABOBS

2 tablespoons tamari or dark soy sauce

1 tablespoon Worcestershire sauce

1 tablespoon molasses

1 tablespoon cooking oil

2 teaspoons lime juice

2 teaspoons grated fresh ginger

4 teaspoons sugar

¼ teaspoon dried red-pepper flakes

⅛ teaspoon salt

1 pound boneless, skinless chicken breasts, cut into ¾-inch cubes

1 mango, peeled and chopped (see "Cutting Mangos," page 84)

1 clove garlic, minced

½ teaspoon minced jalapeño pepper

3 tablespoons rice-wine vinegar or cider vinegar

1. In a medium glass or stainless-steel bowl, combine the tamari, Worcestershire sauce, molasses, oil, lime juice, ginger, 1 teaspoon of the sugar, the red-pepper flakes and salt. Add the chicken and toss to coat. Cover and marinate in the refrigerator for at least 1 hour.

2. In a shallow dish, soak 24 six-inch wooden skewers in water for at least 30 minutes.

3. Make the dipping sauce: In a medium stainless-steel saucepan, combine the mango, garlic, jalapeño, the remaining 3 teaspoons sugar and the vinegar and bring to a simmer over moderately low heat. Cook, stirring occasionally, until the mango is soft, about 15 minutes. Transfer to a food processor or blender and pulse or blend briefly to a coarse puree. Let cool.

4. Heat the broiler. Drain the chicken and thread 2 pieces onto each skewer. Put the skewers on a baking sheet and broil, turning once, until golden brown on both sides, about 5 minutes in all. Serve with the dipping sauce.

—GRACE PARISI

MAKE IT AHEAD
The dipping sauce keeps perfectly in the refrigerator for several days. Serve it cold or at room temperature. You can marinate the chicken a few hours ahead and be all set to thread it on skewers and broil.

49

SOY AND LIME MARINATED CHICKEN

Make these juicy, spicy, tangy chicken strips with just a few simple ingredients.
Cook for only three minutes so that they stay moist.

MAKES ABOUT 24 KABOBS

- 2 tablespoons cooking oil
- 2 tablespoons soy sauce
- 2 tablespoons lime juice
- 2 teaspoons finely grated onion
- 1½ teaspoons grated fresh ginger
- 2 teaspoons sugar
- Pinch dried red-pepper flakes
- ¾ pound boneless, skinless chicken breasts
- 2 tablespoons sesame seeds (optional)
- 3 scallion tops, cut into 1½-inch lengths

1. In a medium bowl, combine the oil, soy sauce, lime juice, onion, ginger, sugar and red-pepper flakes.

2. Cut the chicken crosswise into ¼-inch slices, holding the blade on a diagonal so that the slices will be about 1½ inches wide (see photo, page 141). Add to the soy-sauce mixture. Cover and marinate in the refrigerator at least 30 minutes and up to 1 hour.

3. Meanwhile, in a small frying pan, toast the sesame seeds, if using, over moderate heat, stirring frequently, until light brown, about 3 minutes.

4. Heat the broiler. Set one piece of scallion on top of each slice of chicken and secure with a toothpick. Put the chicken on a baking sheet. Broil the chicken on both sides until just done, about 3 minutes in all. Sprinkle a pinch of sesame seeds, if using, on top of the scallion and serve.

MAKE IT AHEAD
The marinade can be prepared a day ahead. Though you can marinate the chicken and ready it for cooking a few hours before your guests arrive, we suggest broiling the kabobs shortly before serving them.

PORK SATAY WITH SPICY PEANUT DIPPING SAUCE

This Thai favorite can also be made with chicken or beef instead of pork; use boneless chicken breasts or thighs, or steak sliced across the grain. For a sweet undertone, you can add the optional coconut milk to the spicy dipping sauce—but it's good either way.

MAKES 24 KABOBS

¼ cup packed cilantro leaves

1 small jalapeño pepper, seeded and chopped

1 clove garlic, chopped

3 tablespoons cooking oil

2 teaspoons lime juice

1 teaspoon salt

¾ pound boneless pork loin

1 cup natural peanut butter

1 scallion including green top, chopped

¼ teaspoon finely chopped fresh ginger

2 tablespoons canned unsweetened coconut milk (optional)

4 teaspoons soy sauce

¼ teaspoon dried red-pepper flakes

1 teaspoon sugar

½ cup hot water, more if needed

1. In a blender, puree the cilantro, jalapeño and garlic with the oil, lime juice and ¾ teaspoon of the salt.

2. Cut the pork into slices about ¼ inch thick. Stack the slices and cut them into 1-inch-wide strips about 3 inches long.

3. Put the pork in a glass dish, pour the cilantro mixture over the top and toss to coat. Cover and let marinate at room temperature for 30 minutes to 1 hour.

4. In a shallow dish, soak 24 six-inch wooden skewers in water for at least 30 minutes.

5. In a blender, puree the peanut butter, scallion and ginger with the coconut milk, if using, the soy sauce, red-pepper flakes, sugar and the remaining ¼ teaspoon salt. With the blender running, gradually add the hot water and blend until smooth. If the sauce seems too thick, blend in an additional 1 or 2 tablespoons of hot water.

6. Heat the broiler. Remove the strips of pork from the marinade and thread 1 strip onto each of the skewers. Put the skewers on a baking sheet and broil, turning once, until the pork is just done, 3 to 4 minutes. Serve the pork with the peanut dipping sauce. ➤

Prepare the dipping sauce up to a day in advance; before serving, heat it just until warm. You can make the marinade early in the day and even slice the pork, but don't combine them more than an hour ahead; the acid of the lime juice will start to "cook" the meat.

SATAYS

Satays, or satés, are understandably popular snacks in Southeast Asia. Malaysia and Thailand both claim them as their own, but Indonesia stakes strong claims, too. Satays are small pieces of meat, chicken, fish or shellfish threaded on short skewers and grilled or broiled. They're often soaked in a spicy soy marinade first and served with a dipping sauce, the most common being the thick, spicy peanut one we offer here.

🍇 SERVING WINE WITH HORS D'OEUVRES

An aperitif is like a first impression, a chance to set the tone for what's to come. It is also a dividing line, separating the efforts of the day from the rewards of the evening.

Nothing so instantly makes a statement of welcome as a glass of Champagne or fine-quality sparkling wine; it's like being handed a notice that the evening will be special. You may wish to note that although French wine-country hosts from Bordeaux to the Rhône virtually never serve a bottle from outside their region, the great exception is Champagne, universally offered as an aperitif. For your own guests, expect to spend around ten dollars and up for a good bottle of *méthode champenoise* wine, made by the classic techniques. A word about serving cheap sparkling wine at a dinner party: Don't.

In warm-weather months, the emphasis is on refreshment and relaxation, and light, chilled white wines are always appropriate before dinner. Homemade sangria sets a party mood and feels especially appropriate when your hors d'oeuvres have a Spanish flavor, such as the Romesco Dip, page 40, or the Grilled Scallops with Salsa Verde, page 27. Surprise choices—though very traditional in their native settings—are a chilled, dry sercial Madeira and a rather exotic-tasting white port, which can be served as the Portuguese do, on the rocks with a wedge of lime or a splash of soda. Try this with the Chicken Kabobs with Spicy Mango Sauce, page 49.

In cooler months, the welcome should be invigorating, if not literally warming (as with mulled wine). An excellent and easy-to-find choice is a medium-sweet, nutty amontillado sherry, always a good match with nuts, such as the Buttered Pecans or Peppered Cashews, page 37. If pâté is being served, a dessert wine such as Sauternes, late-harvest riesling or Beaumes-de-Venise is a classic matchup. The Roquefort and Walnut Biscuits, page 21, would be perfect, too, with a sweet wine.

You may also want to sample flavored wine aperitifs, an age-old tradition in Europe but often a surprise to Americans. These aperitifs include vermouth and various branded products such as Lillet and Dubonnet.

—RICHARD NALLEY

First Courses

ASPARAGUS SOUP WITH SALMON CAVIAR

On a warm day, serve this springtime soup cold, rather than hot, for a refreshing first course. The salmon caviar seems to add a touch of luxury even though it's not terribly expensive. If it tastes rather strong, rinse it briefly in cold water.

WINE RECOMMENDATION
Asparagus is a famously tough wine match, but a concentrated, well-balanced Alsatian riesling or pinot blanc will pull it off with style.

SERVES 8

- 3 pounds asparagus
- 9 cups Chicken Stock, page 276, or canned low-sodium chicken broth
- 2¾ teaspoons salt
- 4 tablespoons butter
- 2 leeks, white and light-green parts only, split lengthwise, cut crosswise into thin slices and washed well
- ⅓ cup basmati or other long-grain rice
- 2 tablespoons chopped fresh parsley
- ¼ teaspoon fresh-ground black pepper
- 1 teaspoon lime or lemon juice
- ½ cup crème fraîche or sour cream
- 3 ounces salmon caviar

1. Snap the tough ends off the asparagus and discard them. Cut the tips into two or three slices. Cut the stems into 1-inch pieces. Bring the stock to a boil with 1 teaspoon of the salt. Add the asparagus tips and cook until just done, about 5 minutes. Remove with a slotted spoon or strainer and rinse with cold water. Drain thoroughly and set aside. Reserve the stock.

2. In a large pot, melt the butter over moderately low heat. Add the leeks. Cook, stirring occasionally, until soft, about 5 minutes. Add the reserved stock and the rice. Bring to a simmer and cook, partially covered, until the rice is almost tender, about 20 minutes. Add the asparagus stems and the remaining 1¾ teaspoons salt and cook until just done, about 5 minutes.

3. In a blender, puree the soup with the parsley. Strain the soup back into the pot, pressing the vegetable puree through the sieve with a spoon or ladle.

4. Add the asparagus tips and reheat. Stir in the pepper and lime juice and ladle into individual bowls. Top each serving with a dollop of crème fraîche and some of the salmon caviar.

—KATHERINE ALFORD

MAKE IT AHEAD
Complete the soup through step three a day or two before serving. Store the asparagus tips separately so that they don't loose their bright-green color. Reheat and finish the soup shortly before serving.

CORN CHOWDER WITH ROASTED POBLANOS AND CRAB

Thanks to roasted poblano chiles and a handful of fresh cilantro leaves, this soup has a lovely pale-green hue. Because of the color, guests will be pleasantly surprised by the fresh corn flavor, which comes through clearly. If you make the soup with out-of-season corn, strain out the chewy skins.

SERVES 8

- 8 ears corn
- 2 poblano chiles
- 2 tablespoons cooking oil
- 2 onions, chopped
- 1 carrot, chopped
- 2 cloves garlic, chopped
- 1 quart Chicken Stock, page 276, or canned low-sodium chicken broth
- 2 cups water
- 1/4 cup loosely packed cilantro leaves, plus extra leaves for serving
- 1/2 cup heavy cream
- 1 3/4 teaspoons salt
- 1/4 teaspoon fresh-ground black pepper
- 1 teaspoon butter
- 1/2 pound lump crab meat, picked free of shell

1. Using a sharp knife, cut the corn kernels from the cobs. Put the kernels in a bowl. With a table knife, scrape the "milk" from the cobs into the bowl.

2. Roast the chiles over an open flame or broil 4 inches from the heat, turning with tongs until charred all over, about 10 minutes. When the chiles are cool enough to handle, pull off the skin. Remove the stems and seeds. Cut lengthwise into very thin strips. Cut the strips crosswise into 1-inch lengths.

3. In a large pot, heat the oil over moderately low heat. Add the onions, carrot and garlic and cook, stirring occasionally, until the onions are translucent, about 5 minutes. Add the corn, three-quarters of the roasted poblano chiles, the stock and water. Bring to a boil. Reduce the heat and simmer, stirring occasionally, until all the vegetables are soft, about 30 minutes.

4. In a blender, puree the soup with the cilantro in batches. Return the soup to the pot and add the cream, salt and pepper. Bring just back to a boil.

5. Meanwhile, in a small frying pan, heat the butter over moderate heat. Add the crab and cook, stirring, just until warmed through.

6. Ladle the soup into shallow bowls. Arrange a small pile of crab in the center of each bowl and top with the remaining poblano strips and the extra cilantro leaves.

—Grace Parisi

▪ MAKE IT AHEAD

If you like, you can make the soup a day in advance. Simply reheat it before serving and top with the crab meat and other garnishes.

THE GREAT POBLANO

The poblano possesses a piquant flavor that, for many, makes it the ultimate chile pepper. It's the medium-sized, thick-fleshed variety familiar from its use in chiles rellenos. Taste to be sure, but generally, these shiny, dark-green chiles are not too hot. They're also not always easy to find, though they are worth looking for. If you can't locate them, use another mild to moderately hot pepper.

FENNEL-AND-MUSHROOM SALAD WITH SHAVED PARMESAN

Thin slices of crisp fennel and earthy mushrooms are tossed with a pepper-spiked lemon vinaigrette for a light and refreshing first course. The salad is topped with large shavings of Parmesan cheese. Two ounces of Parmesan should be enough for eight salads, but it's easier to make thin shavings from a larger piece of cheese.

WINE RECOMMENDATION
A chenin blanc (including French Vouvray) has the moderate sweetness to balance out the acidity of the lemon vinaigrette and the fruitiness to throw sparks with the earthy, peppery flavors of the dish.

MAKE IT AHEAD
You can prepare the ingredients several hours ahead. Wrap the mushrooms in dry paper towels, put them in a plastic bag and refrigerate. Cover the greens with a damp paper towel and refrigerate. Then just toss everything together at the last minute.

SERVES 8

1   ¼-pound piece Parmesan cheese
1   fennel bulb, cut into very thin slices
    Lemon Pepper Vinaigrette, page 274
½   pound mixed salad greens (about 3 quarts)
5   ounces mushrooms, cut into thin slices

1. With a vegetable peeler, shave off about half of the Parmesan in thin slices and set aside. About 5 minutes before tossing the salad, combine the fennel with about half of the vinaigrette and let soften slightly.

2. Just before serving, toss together the fennel, greens, mushrooms and the remaining vinaigrette. Divide the salad among eight plates and top each serving with a few slices of Parmesan.

WARM PORTOBELLO AND BASIL SALAD

Portobello mushrooms are so big and meaty that they're often compared to steak. And, like steak, they're wonderful grilled or broiled.

WINE RECOMMENDATION
Go red on this one. A fruity, spicy dolcetto from Piemonte or a Côtes du Rhône captures the meaty savor.

MAKE IT AHEAD
You can toss the mushrooms with the oil and garlic several hours in advance and set aside at room temperature. Grill them and assemble the salad shortly before serving.

SERVES 8

- 3 pounds portobello mushrooms, stems removed
- 8 tablespoons olive oil
- 4 cloves garlic, minced
- 3 tablespoons chopped fresh basil
- 1½ teaspoons salt
- ⅛ teaspoon fresh-ground black pepper
- 6 ounces mixed salad greens (about 9 cups)

1. Light the grill or heat the broiler. Put the mushrooms in a large bowl, drizzle with 6 tablespoons of the oil, add the garlic and toss. Grill or broil about 5 inches from the heat, turning three or four times, until softened and lightly browned, 8 to 10 minutes. Return the mushrooms to the bowl. Add the basil, salt and pepper and toss gently.

2. Mound the salad greens on individual plates. Slice the mushrooms, return them to the bowl and toss them with the remaining 2 tablespoons oil. Arrange on top of the greens.

GREEN-BEAN SALAD WITH SHIITAKE MUSHROOMS

This tasty salad makes a tempting, light first course—just the thing to serve before a substantial main dish.

WINE RECOMMENDATION
Look for an herbal-inflected New World sauvignon/fumé blanc or a sémillon with a note of fruitiness.

SERVES 8

1½	pounds haricots verts or standard green beans
1	tablespoon olive oil
⅓	pound shiitake mushrooms, stems removed and caps sliced
½	teaspoon chopped fresh thyme, or ⅛ teaspoon dried
1	shallot, minced
¼	cup Classic Vinaigrette, page 274
½	teaspoon salt
8	radicchio leaves

1. In a large pot of boiling, salted water, cook the beans until tender, about 10 minutes. Drain, rinse with cold water and drain thoroughly. Pat dry with paper towels.

2. In a large frying pan, heat the oil over moderate heat. Add the mushrooms and thyme and cook, stirring occasionally, until the mushrooms are brown, about 5 minutes. Add the shallot and cook, stirring, until soft, about 2 minutes longer.

3. In a large bowl, toss the green beans, mushrooms, vinaigrette and salt. Put one radicchio leaf on each of eight plates and arrange the salad in the leaves.

—Stephanie Lyness

MAKE IT AHEAD
Sauté the mushrooms and boil the beans a day or two in advance, if you like. Store them separately in the refrigerator and let them come to room temperature before serving. Don't dress the salad until shortly before serving or the beans will lose their bright-green color.

ARTICHOKE SALAD
WITH CAPER VINAIGRETTE

In this updated first course, we've "deconstructed" the artichokes for an elegant presentation that's easy to eat. Don't be put off by the anchovy paste in the vinaigrette. It adds a delicious but subtle undertone to the dressing, and even those who think they don't like anchovies will be won over.

WINE RECOMMENDATION
Both the artichoke and the vinaigrette make this appetizer a challenging match, but the idea is to find a wine with high acidity—such as a red barbera from Piemonte or a white Orvieto or sauvignon blanc (preferably a European one)—to complement the acidity in the dressing and to contrast with the sweetness of the artichoke.

SERVES 8

8   medium artichokes

1   lemon, cut in half

3   tablespoons lemon juice

1   tablespoon plus 2 teaspoons anchovy paste

1   tablespoon Dijon mustard

¾   teaspoon salt

½   teaspoon fresh-ground black pepper

1½ cups olive oil

2   cloves garlic, minced

3   tablespoons minced capers

3   tablespoons chopped fresh basil

¼   pound mixed salad greens (about 1½ quarts)

1. Cut the stem off one of the artichokes. Cut off the top third of the leaves and rub the cut surfaces with a lemon half to prevent darkening. Repeat with the remaining artichokes. Steam or boil until the bases of the artichokes are tender when pierced with a small knife, 35 to 40 minutes. Let cool.

2. In a medium bowl, whisk the lemon juice with the anchovy paste, mustard, salt and pepper. Add the oil slowly, whisking. Whisk in the garlic, capers and basil.

3. Pull the cone of small, pale-green leaves out of the center of each artichoke and discard. Pull off any tough outer leaves and discard them. Remove the remaining artichoke leaves and reserve. With a teaspoon, scrape the furry chokes from the bottoms of the artichokes. Cut the bottoms into eight wedges each, put them in a bowl and toss with about a third of the caper vinaigrette.

4. Arrange the artichoke leaves, points out, to form a circular border on eight large plates. Mound the lettuce in the center and

64

put the dressed artichoke bottoms on top. Drizzle the remaining vinaigrette over the leaves.

—STEPHANIE LYNESS

MAKE IT AHEAD

You can cook the artichokes a day or two ahead and refrigerate them. Get the cooked artichokes ready early on the day you plan to serve them and refrigerate the leaves and cut-up bottoms separately. Make the vinaigrette hours in advance; whisk to blend just before using.

CHOOSING ARTICHOKES

Artichokes have two seasons. From late March to early May, they're at their peak; in June, supply dwindles, and then in the fall, artichokes begin to reappear in markets. Frost sometimes speckles the outer leaves of this later harvest with light-brown spots, but the blemishes are purely superficial and don't ruin the vegetable's flavor. On the contrary, some people think that because these artichokes have matured slowly, they have more flavor than those available in the spring. Do be wary of blackened or wrinkled leaves, an indication that the artichokes are old and dried out. Look for artichokes that feel heavy for their size and have tightly closed petals and at least an inch or two of stem. Keep artichokes in the refrigerator in an airtight container or in sealed plastic bags so that they don't dry out.

Provencal Vegetable Terrines with Chevre

A muffin pan is a convenient mold for these individual terrines that combine Provençal vegetables with creamy goat cheese. Use the small eggplant slices that just fit in the bottom of the molds, saving the larger ones for the tops.

Go geographical with a white Côtes du Rhône or an exotic viognier. If you're feeling flush, try a Hermitage Blanc instead of the former, or an (equally pricey) French Condrieu in place of the latter.

SERVES 8

2 small eggplant (about 1 pound each), cut into ¼-inch slices

4 tablespoons olive oil

1 teaspoon salt

Fresh-ground black pepper

1 red bell pepper, chopped

1 zucchini, chopped

1 small fennel bulb, cut into thin slices

⅓ cup sun-dried tomatoes, cut into thin slices

2 cloves garlic, minced

½ teaspoon chopped fresh rosemary, or ¼ teaspoon dried

1 teaspoon chopped fresh thyme, or ½ teaspoon dried

2 tablespoons dry bread crumbs

1 6½-ounce log mild goat cheese, such as Montrachet

1 tablespoon grated Parmesan cheese

¼ pound mixed salad greens (about 1½ quarts)

Sherry Scallion Vinaigrette, page 274

1. Heat the oven to 450°. Brush both sides of the eggplant slices with 2 tablespoons of the oil and season with ¼ teaspoon of the salt and ¼ teaspoon pepper. Cook the eggplant in the oven until soft and beginning to brown, about 15 minutes.

2. In a baking dish, combine the bell pepper, zucchini, fennel, sun-dried tomatoes and garlic. Stir in the remaining 2 tablespoons oil, the rosemary, thyme, the remaining ¾ teaspoon salt and ⅛ teaspoon pepper. Cook in the oven, stirring occasionally, until the vegetables are soft and golden and beginning to caramelize, about 35 minutes. Remove. Reduce the oven temperature to 350°.

3. Brush eight cups of a standard muffin pan with oil. Dust with the bread crumbs and turn upside down to remove the excess. Crumble the goat cheese. Lay one eggplant slice, brown-side down, in the bottom of each muffin cup. Sprinkle half the goat cheese over the eggplant. Top with the caramelized vegetables and the remaining

goat cheese. Sprinkle with the Parmesan and top each terrine with an eggplant slice. Press lightly to pack the vegetables together.

4. Bake the terrines until bubbling around the sides, about 20 minutes. Let rest 10 minutes before unmolding. Toss the greens with the vinaigrette and divide among eight plates. Run a small knife around the edge of each terrine. Place a baking sheet over the muffin pan. Invert and tap a few times on a solid surface. Carefully lift the muffin pan straight up, off the terrines. Top each bed of greens with a terrine.

—GRACE PARISI

MAKE IT AHEAD
You can assemble these terrines up to two days in advance. Keep them covered in the refrigerator. Be sure the muffin pan is not aluminum, or the vegetables may discolor in the refrigerator. Either let the terrines come to room temperature before baking or add a few extra minutes to their cooking time.

ANTIPASTO WITH MARINATED CARROTS

For this colorful antipasto, the only element you need to prepare yourself is the marinated carrots. All the other components come from an Italian market. Choose your favorite oil-cured or brined olives, both black and green. If you find ripe, juicy tomatoes, add them to the array; but if the only ones you see are the no-taste winter variety, skip them. There's plenty on the plate already.

 WINE RECOMMENDATION A glass of Champagne or *méthode champenoise* sparkling wine will pair remarkably well with these tidbits and lend an air of elegance to their simplicity.

SERVES 8

- 2 pounds carrots, cut into 1½-by-¼-inch sticks
- 2 tablespoons olive oil, plus more for drizzling
- 1 tablespoon red-wine vinegar
- 2 cloves garlic, minced
- ⅛ teaspoon dried thyme
- ½ teaspoon salt
- ⅛ teaspoon fresh-ground black pepper
- ¼ pound thin-sliced prosciutto
- ½ pound black olives
- ½ pound green olives
- ½ pound fresh mozzarella, sliced
- 2 tomatoes, sliced (optional)
- 8 large basil leaves

1. In a medium saucepan of boiling, salted water, cook the carrots until they are just barely tender, 7 to 10 minutes. Drain.

2. In a medium bowl, combine the 2 tablespoons oil, the vinegar, garlic, thyme, salt and pepper. Add the warm carrots and toss to coat. Let cool; then refrigerate for at least 2 hours.

3. Arrange the carrots, prosciutto, olives and mozzarella on individual plates. Top the mozzarella with the tomatoes, if using, and the basil leaves. Drizzle a little oil over the tomatoes and mozzarella and serve.

MAKE IT AHEAD The carrots can be prepared several days in advance. You can purchase all the other ingredients two or three days ahead; keep the prosciutto tightly wrapped in plastic so that it doesn't dry out. If you like, you can assemble the antipasto about 30 minutes before serving. Cover each plate with plastic wrap and leave at room temperature.

BAKED RADICCHIO AND GOAT-CHEESE PARCELS

For this unusual appetizer, slices of chèvre are wrapped in radicchio leaves and baked just until the cheese is warm and melted. The slight bitterness of the lettuce is the perfect foil for the creamy filling. You could try serving this as a cheese course, too.

WINE RECOMMENDATION
The fruity sweetness of a young pinot noir is a lively contrast to the somewhat austere flavors of this dish.

SERVES 8

- 4 medium heads radicchio
- 2 tablespoons olive oil
- 1 tablespoon balsamic vinegar
- ⅛ teaspoon salt
- Pinch fresh-ground black pepper
- 2 11-ounce logs mild goat cheese, such as Montrachet
- ½ pound spinach, stems removed, leaves washed and cut into thin strips

1. Carefully remove six large outer leaves from each of the heads of radicchio. Slice the remaining radicchio into thin strips. In a large pot of boiling water, blanch the whole leaves just until softened, about 30 seconds. Pat the leaves dry with paper towels.

2. In a medium bowl, whisk the oil, vinegar, salt and pepper. Heat the oven to 350°. Cut the goat cheese into 24 slices. Put a slice in the center of a blanched radicchio leaf and gently press the cheese into a mound. Fold the sides of the leaf over the cheese and put the parcel seam-side down on a baking sheet. Repeat with the remaining leaves and cheese. Bake until the goat cheese is softened, about 5 minutes.

3. Add the radicchio strips and spinach to the dressing and toss. Arrange the greens in the centers of eight salad plates. Arrange three goat-cheese parcels pinwheel fashion on each salad and serve.

MAKE IT AHEAD
Make the dressing days ahead, if you like. You can prepare the goat-cheese parcels hours ahead and put them on the baking sheet. Cover with plastic wrap and refrigerate. Cut up the spinach and radicchio, combine, cover with damp paper towels and refrigerate.

FETTUCCINE WITH WALNUT AND MASCARPONE SAUCE

It's hard to believe that just a few ingredients simply prepared result in such an elegant dish. The heat of the just-cooked fettuccine is enough to reheat the sauce. Don't risk cooking it again, or the mascarpone may separate.

 WINE RECOMMENDATION
A fine Italian white-wine match here would be an arneis from Piemonte or a sauvignon blanc from Friuli. A pinot gris from Oregon or Alsace (it may be called tokay d'Alsace) will add a note of exoticism.

SERVES 8

3 tablespoons butter

1½ cups walnuts, chopped coarse

1 large clove garlic, minced

¾ pound mascarpone cheese

¾ teaspoon salt

⅛ teaspoon fresh-ground black pepper

1 pound fettuccine, plain or spinach

½ cup grated Parmesan cheese

1. In a medium frying pan, melt the butter over moderately low heat. Add the walnuts and cook, stirring, until golden brown, about 4 minutes. Add the garlic and cook until soft but not brown, about 1 minute.

2. Reduce the heat to low. Add the mascarpone and heat, stirring, just until melted and smooth, about 2 minutes. Add the salt and pepper.

3. In a large pot of boiling, salted water, cook the pasta until just done, about 12 minutes. Reserve ½ cup of the pasta water. Drain the pasta.

4. Toss the pasta, sauce and Parmesan. If the sauce seems too thick, add some of the reserved pasta water. Serve immediately.

—ERICA DE MANE

MAKE IT AHEAD
You can assemble the ingredients and cook the walnuts and garlic a few hours ahead. But, as with most pasta dishes, this one should not be finished in advance.

SPAGHETTI WITH PARMESAN AND MIXED SPICY GREENS

Mustard greens, broccoli rabe and escarole, all intensely flavorful, add real punch to this simple pasta. Play around with the proportions of the different greens to suit your taste. Or try other sturdy, robust leaves such as dandelion, collard or kale.

WINE RECOMMENDATION
Try a fruity red with mild tannin such as a Chinon or Bourgueil, cabernet franc–based wines from the Loire. A young Chianti would be delicious as well.

SERVES 8

½   cup pine nuts

⅓   cup olive oil

6   cloves garlic, minced

¾   teaspoon dried red-pepper flakes

¾   pound mixed greens, such as mustard greens, broccoli rabe and/or escarole, tough stems removed and leaves cut into 1½-inch pieces (about 3½ quarts)

¾   teaspoon salt

2   cups Chicken Stock, page 276, or canned low-sodium chicken broth

1   pound spaghetti

1½   cups grated Parmesan cheese, plus more for serving

1. In a small frying pan, toast the pine nuts over moderately low heat, stirring frequently, until the nuts are golden brown, about 4 minutes. Or toast in a 350° oven for 6 minutes.

2. In a large pot, heat the oil over moderately low heat. Add the garlic and red-pepper flakes and cook until the garlic is soft but not brown, about 1 minute. Increase the heat to moderately high, add the greens and salt and cook, stirring, until the greens wilt, 1 to 2 minutes. Add the stock, bring to a simmer and cook 5 minutes longer.

3. In a large pot of boiling, salted water, cook the spaghetti until just done, about 12 minutes. Drain the pasta. Toss with the mixed greens and stock. Add the Parmesan and pine nuts, toss again and serve.

—KATHERINE ALFORD

MAKE IT AHEAD
Toast the pine nuts days in advance, if you like. You can also clean and sauté the greens well ahead, but don't simmer them in the stock until an hour or two before serving.

GRITS WITH WILD-MUSHROOM RAGOUT

In this contemporary version of the familiar Southern dish, grits are treated like their Italian cousin, polenta. Cooked, cooled and cut into wedges, the grits are then browned under the broiler and served with gutsy wild mushrooms.

WINE RECOMMENDATION
These earthy, straightforward flavors will welcome a wine with some flower and perfume, such as a young chardonnay.

SERVES 8

3 cups Chicken Stock, page 276, or canned low-sodium chicken broth

1 cup old-fashioned grits

2 teaspoons salt

1/2 teaspoon dried thyme

4 tablespoons butter

1/4 cup grated Parmesan cheese
Dash Tabasco sauce

1/2 ounce dried porcini mushrooms

2/3 cup boiling water

1 1/2 pounds mixed wild mushrooms, such as shiitake, cremini and portobello

2 cloves garlic, minced

1/2 cup dry white wine

1/2 cup heavy cream, more if needed

3 scallions including green tops, sliced

1 tablespoon olive oil

2 tablespoons chopped flat-leaf parsley

1. Oil a 9-inch-round cake pan. In a medium saucepan, bring the stock to a boil. Add the grits in a slow steam, whisking constantly. Add 1 teaspoon of the salt and the thyme. Reduce the heat to moderate and simmer, stirring frequently with a wooden spoon, until the grits are very thick, about 20 minutes. Remove from the heat and stir in 2 tablespoons of the butter, the Parmesan and Tabasco sauce. Spread the grits in the cake pan in an even layer and refrigerate until firm, at least 30 minutes.

2. Put the dried mushrooms in a small bowl and pour the boiling water over them. Soak until softened, about 20 minutes. Remove the mushrooms and strain their liquid into a bowl through a sieve lined with a paper towel. Rinse the mushrooms well to remove any remaining grit and chop them.

3. If using shiitakes or portobellos, remove the stems. Slice all the fresh mushrooms. In a large frying pan, melt the remaining 2 tablespoons butter over moderate heat. Add the garlic and cook until soft but not brown, about 1 minute. Add the chopped porcini and the fresh mushrooms and cook, stirring occasionally, until brown, about 8 minutes. Add the reserved porcini soaking liquid and the wine. Bring to a boil and cook until reduced by half. Add the cream, scallions and the remaining 1 teaspoon salt and cook until the mixture is thick enough to coat a spoon lightly, about 3 minutes.

4. Heat the broiler. Unmold the grits and cut the round into eight wedges. Put the wedges on a baking sheet and brush with the oil. Broil the grits until brown on top and heated through, about 5 minutes. If the mushroom ragout has thickened, stir in a few tablespoons cream or water. Put the wedges on eight plates. Spoon the ragout over and alongside the wedges and serve sprinkled with the parsley.

—Katherine Alford

MAKE IT AHEAD Both the grits and the mushroom ragout can be made days before serving. At the last minute, just broil the grits and reheat the ragout.

WILD-MUSHROOM RISOTTO

Risotto, made by a uniquely Italian method for cooking rice, is a sophisticated first course for any dinner party. Frequent stirring is required, but you will be rewarded with a creamy dish your guests will truly savor. The rich, earthy flavor of the fresh mushrooms is intensified by dried porcini.

WINE RECOMMENDATION
This is a very wine-versatile dish. Since it's cooked with white wine, you may want to serve the same or a related wine, but a pinot noir or young Chianti would be gorgeous as well.

SERVES 8

½ ounce dried porcini mushrooms

1 cup boiling water

7 to 8 cups Chicken Stock, page 276, or canned low-sodium chicken broth

1 pound mixed wild mushrooms, such as shiitake, cremini and portobello

4 tablespoons olive oil

3 cloves garlic, minced

3 teaspoons salt

2 shallots, minced

3 cups arborio rice, rinsed

1 cup dry white wine

¾ cup grated Parmesan cheese

5 tablespoons butter, at room temperature

2 tablespoons chopped fresh sage, or 2 teaspoons dried

¼ teaspoon fresh-ground black pepper

1. Put the dried mushrooms in a small bowl and pour the boiling water over them. Soak until softened, about 20 minutes. Remove the mushrooms and strain their liquid into a large pot through a sieve lined with a paper towel. Rinse the mushrooms well to remove any remaining grit and chop them. Add the stock to the mushroom soaking liquid and bring to a simmer.

2. If using shiitakes or portobellos, remove the stems. Slice all the fresh mushrooms. In another large pot, heat 2 tablespoons of the oil over moderate heat. Add the chopped porcini and the sliced fresh mushrooms and cook, stirring occasionally, until brown, about 5 minutes. Add the garlic and ½ teaspoon of the salt and cook, stirring, until the garlic is fragrant, about 30 seconds. Put the mushrooms in a bowl.

3. Heat the remaining 2 tablespoons oil in the pot over moderately low heat. Add the shallots. Cook, stirring occasionally, until translucent, about 3 minutes. Add the rice. Stir until the rice begins to turn opaque, about 2 minutes. Add the wine and the remaining 2½ teaspoons salt and cook, stirring constantly, until all the wine has been absorbed.

4. Add about 1 cup of the simmering stock and cook, stirring constantly, until the stock has been completely absorbed. The rice and stock should bubble gently; adjust the heat as needed. Continue cooking the rice, adding the stock 1 cup at a time, allowing the rice to completely absorb the stock before adding the next cup. Cook the rice in this way until tender, about 30 minutes in all. The stock should be thickened by the starch from the rice. You may not need to use all of the liquid. Stir in the mushrooms, cheese, butter, sage and pepper and serve.

—STEPHANIE LYNESS

MAKE IT AHEAD

Traditionally, risotto is cooked at the last minute. However, most of the process can be done ahead of time. Even the finest Italian restaurants will admit to using this trick. Just cook the rice until it is almost done and set it and the few remaining cups of stock aside. Five to ten minutes before you serve, reheat the stock and proceed with the recipe. You'll enjoy that famous creamy texture without the last-minute fuss.

VARIATION

CLASSIC CHEESE RISOTTO

This traditional recipe is still the favorite of many risotto lovers. The subtle but delicious flavor makes it a memorable first course. Omit the porcini and boiling water, the fresh mushrooms, shallots, garlic and sage. Bring 9 cups stock to a simmer. Chop 1 onion fine. In a large pot, heat 2 tablespoons olive oil over moderately low heat. Add the onion and cook, stirring occasionally, until translucent. Add the rice and cook the risotto as directed, using $2\frac{1}{2}$ teaspoons salt. Stir in 1 cup grated Parmesan cheese with the butter and the pepper.

LEFTOVERS?

It's not likely you'll have any leftover risotto, but in case you do, here is a delicious way to enjoy it all over again. Simply form the cool risotto into small pancakes and dip into lightly beaten egg, then into fresh or dry bread crumbs. Cook the risotto cakes in butter and oil over moderate heat until completely warmed through and golden brown on the outside, ten to fifteen minutes.

CARROT FLANS ON MIXED GREENS

These tasty easy-to-make carrot, pancetta and rosemary flans look elegant on a bed of mixed greens.

WINE RECOMMENDATION
A white Bordeaux or sauvignon blanc/sémillon blend (such as a California "Meritage" type wine) provides the right blend of herbal aromatics and body.

SERVES 8

1¼ pounds carrots (about 8 medium), cut into thin slices

¼ pound pancetta, chopped fine

3 shallots, minced

1¼ teaspoons chopped fresh rosemary, or ½ teaspoon dried

⅔ cup half-and-half

5 large eggs, beaten to mix

1 teaspoon salt

¼ teaspoon fresh-ground black pepper

¼ pound mixed salad greens (about 1½ quarts)

¼ cup Classic Vinaigrette, page 274

1. Heat the oven to 350°. Butter eight 5-ounce ramekins or 6-ounce custard cups. Chill just until the butter is cold. Butter the cups again to ensure easy unmolding. Bring water to a simmer for the water bath.

2. Steam or boil the carrots until very tender, about 20 minutes. In a medium frying pan, cook the pancetta over moderate heat, stirring occasionally, until lightly browned, about 5 minutes. Add the shallots and rosemary. Cook, stirring occasionally, until the shallots are translucent, about 3 minutes.

3. In a food processor, puree the carrots with the half-and-half until smooth. Add the eggs and process again. Add the pancetta-and-shallot mixture, the salt and pepper and pulse to combine but not puree.

4. Divide the mixture among the ramekins. Put the ramekins in a baking dish or roasting pan and pour in enough of the simmering water to reach about halfway up the sides of the ramekins. Cover the dish with a piece of aluminum foil. Carefully transfer to the oven. Bake 28 minutes. The flans will puff slightly and pull away from the sides. Test for doneness by touching the center lightly; the flan should spring back. Remove from the water bath and let stand 5 minutes.

5. Toss the greens with the vinaigrette and divide among eight salad plates. Run a knife around the sides of the ramekins and tap the sides and bottoms to loosen the flans. Unmold them onto the greens and serve.

—STEPHANIE LYNESS

MAKE IT AHEAD
The flan mixture can be prepared a day ahead. Bring to room temperature and stir before pouring into the molds.

CREAMY BROILED OYSTERS WITH BACON

One of our more seductive appetizers—and so simple to prepare. Unless you're an experienced shucker, have your fishmonger open the oysters, saving their bottom shells. You could also serve this as a special hors d'oeuvre (with plenty of cocktail napkins).

WINE RECOMMENDATION
Either a chardonnay or a riesling will blossom with this dish.

SERVES 8

6   strips bacon, chopped

1   cup heavy cream

½   teaspoon salt

⅛   teaspoon fresh-ground black pepper

40 oysters, shucked, cupped bottom shells reserved and well scrubbed

1. In a large frying pan, cook the bacon over moderate heat until crisp. Drain on paper towels. Pour off all the fat from the pan. Add the cream and bring to a simmer over moderately low heat, scraping the bottom of the pan to dislodge any brown bits. Simmer until slightly thickened, 1 to 2 minutes. Add the salt and pepper and transfer to a small bowl.

2. Heat the broiler. Line two large baking sheets with crumpled aluminum foil. Put the reserved oyster shells on the baking sheets, using the foil to steady them. Put an oyster in each shell and spoon ½ teaspoon of the cream over each of the oysters. Sprinkle the bacon over the oysters.

3. Broil the oysters, one baking sheet at a time, until the cream is golden brown in spots and the oysters are heated through, about 2 minutes. (Arrange the first batch of oysters on serving plates while you broil the second batch.) Serve immediately.

MAKE IT AHEAD
You can scrub the oyster shells and arrange them on the foil-lined baking sheets early in the day. Put an oyster in each shell, cover tightly with plastic wrap and refrigerate. You can cook and crumble the bacon and simmer the cream several hours in advance, too. Cover the cream and refrigerate.

WARM SCALLOP SALAD WITH SHIITAKE MUSHROOMS AND PINE NUTS

With its combination of colors and textures, this unusual salad looks beautiful on the plate—and tastes delicious.

WINE RECOMMENDATION
A rich chardonnay, such as a Meursault from Burgundy or a better California bottling, will bring out the warm, almost meaty flavors of the mushrooms and complement the sweetness of the scallops.

SERVES 8

⅓ cup pine nuts

6 tablespoons olive oil

3 red bell peppers, cut into thin strips

½ pound shiitake mushrooms, stems removed and caps sliced

2 cloves garlic, minced

1½ pounds sea scallops, cut in half horizontally

   Salt and fresh-ground black pepper

¼ cup fresh basil leaves, cut into thin strips (optional)

½ cup dry white wine

2 teaspoons lemon juice

6 ounces mixed salad greens (about 9 cups)

1. In a small frying pan, toast the pine nuts over moderately low heat, stirring frequently, until the nuts are golden brown, about 4 minutes. Or toast in a 350° oven for 6 minutes.

2. In a large frying pan, heat 4 tablespoons of the oil over moderate heat. Add the bell peppers and cook, stirring occasionally, until softened, about 5 minutes. Add the mushrooms and cook, stirring, until brown, about 5 minutes. Add the garlic and cook until soft but not brown, about 1 minute. Raise the heat to moderately high. Add the scallops, 1½ teaspoons salt and ¼ teaspoon pepper and cook, stirring occasionally, until the scallops are opaque, about 3 minutes. Add the basil, if using, and the wine. Simmer until the liquid has reduced to approximately ¼ cup, about 2 minutes.

3. In a large bowl, whisk together the remaining 2 tablespoons oil, the lemon juice, ⅛ teaspoon salt and a pinch of pepper. Add the greens and toss. Divide the greens among individual plates. Top with the scallop mixture and any pan juices and sprinkle the pine nuts over all.

—ERICA DE MANE

MAKE IT AHEAD
You can slice the scallops early on the day you plan to serve them. Put them on a large plate so that they don't stick together, cover with plastic wrap and refrigerate. Cut up the vegetables early in the day, too; cover and refrigerate.

CARIBBEAN SHRIMP WITH CHILE AIOLI AND MANGO PAPAYA SALAD

Jumbo grilled shrimp are matched with a sweet and savory salad of mangos and papaya. A quick aioli flavored with ancho chile complements the two.

WINE RECOMMENDATION
A mildly sweet rosé would match both the flavors and the whimsical presentation of the dish. A chilly beer would taste good, too.

SERVES 8

¼ cup olive oil

4 tablespoons lime juice (from about 2 limes)

4 tablespoons light rum

1 clove garlic, chopped

2 small dried red chile peppers

2 teaspoons sugar

1 teaspoon salt

¾ teaspoon fresh-ground black pepper

24 jumbo shrimp, shelled

3 mangos, peeled and cut into ½-inch dice (see "Cutting Mangos," next page)

1 papaya, peeled, seeded and cut into ½-inch dice

½ red bell pepper, cut into ¼-inch dice

¼ cup chopped red onion

1 large jalapeño pepper, seeded and minced

2 tablespoons chopped cilantro

Ancho-Chile Aioli, next page

1. In a large, shallow glass dish, combine the oil with 2 tablespoons of the lime juice, 2 tablespoons of the rum, the garlic, dried red chiles, 1 teaspoon of the sugar, ½ teaspoon of the salt and ½ teaspoon of the black pepper. Add the shrimp and toss to coat. Cover with plastic wrap and marinate in the refrigerator 2 to 3 hours.

2. Light the grill or heat the broiler. Remove the shrimp from the marinade and cook on both sides until done, about 2 minutes per side. Cool and refrigerate until ready to serve.

3. Reserve ¼ cup of the mango for the chile aioli. In a large glass or stainless-steel bowl, combine the remaining mango, the papaya, bell pepper, onion, jalapeño, cilantro and the remaining 2 tablespoons lime juice, 2 tablespoons rum, 1 teaspoon sugar, ½ teaspoon salt and ¼ teaspoon black pepper. Chill until ready to serve.

4. To serve, arrange the shrimp, mango papaya salad and aioli on individual plates.

—GRACE PARISI

MAKE IT AHEAD
There are three components in this dish, and each can be prepared well in

advance. You can make the chile aioli and the mango papaya salad a day ahead. Keep them in the refrigerator. The shrimp can be marinated and grilled several hours before serving them so that once guests arrive, you'll need only to arrange the plates.

CUTTING MANGOS

There's a trick to removing the flesh from a mango. Stand the unpeeled mango on end and, using a sharp knife, slice down through the skin and flesh, as close as possible to the pit, to remove the flesh in one piece. Repeat on the other side. With the two pieces skin-side down, score the flesh into cubes, taking care not to cut through the skin. Turn the skin "inside out" and slice off the cubes of fruit.

ANCHO-CHILE AIOLI

MAKES ABOUT 3/4 CUP

1   dried ancho chile

½   cup boiling water

¼   cup reserved chopped mango (from the mango papaya salad, previous page)

1   small clove garlic, chopped

½   cup mayonnaise

½   teaspoon lime juice

     Pinch salt

1. Put the ancho chile in a small bowl and pour the boiling water over it. Let soak until softened, about 20 minutes. Stem and seed the chile. Scrape the inside of the chile with a small knife to get the pulp.

2. In a food processor or blender, puree the ancho-chile pulp, the reserved mango and the garlic with the mayonnaise, lime juice and salt.

MUSSELS WITH PANCETTA AND ROSEMARY

Rosemary is an untraditional herb for shellfish, but along with the pancetta, it lends a depth of flavor. Serve the mussels with crusty Italian bread to soak up the fragrant broth.

WINE RECOMMENDATION
A juicy New World sauvignon/fumé blanc will pick up both the mild sweetness of the mussels and the herby quality of the broth.

SERVES 8

- 4 pounds mussels, scrubbed and debearded
- 2 tablespoons butter
- 2 tablespoons olive oil
- ¼ pound pancetta, chopped fine
- 3 tender, inner ribs celery, ribs chopped fine, leaves chopped
- 6 shallots, chopped fine
- 1 teaspoon chopped fresh rosemary, or ½ teaspoon dried
- 2 bay leaves
- 1½ cups dry white wine
- ¼ teaspoon fresh-ground black pepper

1. Discard any mussels that have broken shells or that do not clamp shut when tapped. In a large pot, heat the butter and oil over moderate heat. Add the pancetta and cook until crisp, about 5 minutes. Add the chopped celery ribs, the shallots, rosemary and bay leaves and cook, stirring occasionally, until the vegetables are soft, about 5 minutes.

2. Add the wine, mussels and celery leaves to the pot. Cover, raise the heat to high and bring to a boil. Cook, shaking the pot occasionally, just until the mussels open, about 3 minutes. Discard any that do not open. Add the pepper. Ladle the mussels and broth into bowls.

—ERICA DE MANE

MAKE IT AHEAD
The mussels should be finished just before serving, but you can cook the pancetta and vegetables and have them ready in the pot hours ahead. That way, you'll only need to spend five minutes in the kitchen while the mussels steam open.

CRAB CAKES WITH CHILE REMOULADE

It seems crab cakes will never go out of style. In this recipe, a minimum of other ingredients is added so that the sweet crab flavor comes through clearly.

 WINE RECOMMENDATION This is a classic match for either a chardonnay or a riesling.

SERVES 8

1½ pounds lump crab meat, picked free of shell

1¼ cups dry bread crumbs

4½ tablespoons mayonnaise

1½ tablespoons Dijon mustard

¾ teaspoon Tabasco sauce

1¼ teaspoons salt

Pinch fresh-ground black pepper

¾ cup flour

2 eggs, beaten to mix

Cooking oil, for frying

Chile Remoulade, next page

1. In a medium bowl, combine the crab, ¼ cup of the bread crumbs, the mayonnaise, mustard, Tabasco sauce, salt and pepper. Shape the mixture into sixteen ¾-inch-thick cakes, about ¼ cup each.

2. Dust the cakes with the flour and pat off the excess. Dip each cake into the eggs and then into the remaining bread crumbs.

3. In a large nonstick frying pan, heat about ½ inch of oil over moderate heat. When the oil is hot, add some of the crab cakes and fry until golden brown and crisp, 2 to 3 minutes. Turn the cakes and fry them until golden brown on the other side, about 2 minutes longer. Drain on paper towels. Repeat until all the crab cakes are fried. Serve with the Chile Remoulade.

—GRACE PARISI

MAKE IT AHEAD You can shape the crab mixture into cakes a day in advance, and you can coat them a couple of hours before frying. Crisp crab cakes are really best served shortly after they are cooked, but you can make them a day ahead, if you need to. Just before serving, put the fried cakes on a baking sheet and reheat in a 400° oven. The remoulade will keep for days, covered and refrigerated. ➤

BREAD CRUMBS

Store-bought dry bread crumbs work perfectly for crab cakes; so there's no need to make them yourself. If, however, you have stale bread around, making crumbs is a great way to use it up. Leave slices out at room temperature for about 3 hours. Or dry them in a 300° oven for 15 minutes, turning once. Pulverize in a food processor or blender.

Chile Remoulade

MAKES ABOUT 1 CUP

  2 dried or canned chipotle chiles

½ cup boiling water

  1 cup mayonnaise

  2 teaspoons Dijon mustard

  2 teaspoons lime or lemon juice

⅛ teaspoon salt

1. Put the dried chiles, if using, in a small bowl, cover with the boiling water and let soak 20 minutes. Stem and seed the chiles. Scrape the inside of each chile with a small knife to get the pulp. Or remove the seeds from canned chiles.

2. Put the chiles in a small bowl and stir in the mayonnaise, mustard, lime juice and salt.

Chipotle Chiles

Chipotle, a chile widely used in Mexican and Southwestern cooking, is from an Indian word meaning "smoked chile." The name refers to any smoked chile, though smoked *chile gordo,* a fat, fleshy jalapeño that's been allowed to ripen to a dark red, is the most common. The dried peppers are available in many specialty-food stores and increasingly in supermarkets. Dried, brown and shriveled, this less-than-luscious-looking pepper actually has a delicious, smoky flavor and subtle heat that are great additions to soups, salsas and sauces such as the remoulade at left. Chipotles are also sold canned in adobo sauce.

SMOKED TROUT WITH JICAMA-AND-CARROT SALAD

The combination of smoked trout and jicama, the crunchy Mexican root vegetable, may seem odd, but in fact the crisp, lemon-dressed salad makes a refreshing contrast to the rich smokiness of the fish.

WINE RECOMMENDATION
The smoky fish will highlight the high, delicate fruit notes of an Alsatian or German riesling.

SERVES 8

2   jicama (about 1 pound each), peeled and cut into 2-inch-long matchstick strips

3   carrots, grated

¼   cup chopped flat-leaf parsley

    Lemon Pepper Vinaigrette, page 274

1   teaspoon salt

8   fillets smoked trout, or 4 whole smoked trout

1. In a large bowl, combine the jicama, carrots and parsley. Add the vinaigrette and salt and toss.

2. If using whole trout, lift each fillet off the bone in one piece. Arrange the fillets on salad plates. Mound the salad next to the trout and serve.

MAKE IT AHEAD
The salad can be prepared hours ahead. If using whole trout, remove the fillets from the bones. Cover separately and refrigerate.

GRAVLAX WITH GRAINY-MUSTARD SAUCE

You're sure to impress your guests with home-cured salmon, and they'll never imagine how easy this Swedish favorite is to prepare.

WINE RECOMMENDATION

A fine-quality gewürztraminer will taste like an orchard full of exotic fruit with this combination.

SERVES 8

- 3 pounds center-cut salmon fillet, with skin intact and pinbones removed
- 2 tablespoons peppercorns
- ⅓ cup coarse salt
- ¼ cup sugar
- 1 large bunch dill
- 2 tablespoons vodka
- ¼ cup grainy mustard
- ¼ cup sour cream

1. Cut the salmon crosswise into two equal pieces. Crush the peppercorns with a rolling pin or in a mortar with a pestle. Combine the peppercorns, salt and sugar

2. Lay the salmon on a work surface, skin-side down, and press the salt mixture onto the fish. Put a third of the dill on the bottom of a shallow glass baking dish. Put a piece of the salmon, skin-side down, on the dill. Top with another third of the dill and sprinkle with the vodka. Top with the second piece of salmon, skin-side up, and the remaining dill. Cover with plastic. Set a plate on the salmon and a weight on the

plate (two 28-ounce cans work well). Leave the salmon to cure in the refrigerator for at least 24 hours and up to 3 days. Turn the fish two or three times while it cures and baste it occasionally with the juices.

3. In a small bowl, combine the mustard and sour cream. Discard the dill and pat the fish dry with paper towels. Cut the fish into the thinnest possible diagonal slices. Serve with rye bread and the mustard sauce.

MAKE IT AHEAD

Gravlax must be prepared one to three days in advance. And once cured it will keep for several additional days. You can also slice it early on the day you plan to serve it.

For nice big slices, cut on a sharp diagonal. A scooping motion at the end releases fish from skin.

SMOKED SALMON WITH WATERCRESS AND SUGAR-SNAP SALAD

The green sugar snap peas and watercress and the pink salmon look lovely and springlike. For the prettiest presentation, arrange slices of salmon down the middle of each plate, overlapping the slices as necessary, and then arrange the salad in the center of the salmon. What could be more elegant?

WINE RECOMMENDATION
Either a chardonnay or a fruitier New World sauvignon/fumé blanc will be an ideal companion for this dish.

SERVES 8

½ pound sugar snap peas

¾ pound thin-sliced smoked salmon

1 tablespoon lemon juice

½ teaspoon salt

⅛ teaspoon fresh-ground black pepper

3 tablespoons olive oil

2 bunches watercress (about 5 ounces each), tough stems removed

4 scallions including green tops, cut into thin diagonal slices

1. In a large saucepan of boiling, salted water, cook the snap peas until just barely tender, 1 to 2 minutes. Drain, rinse with cold water and drain thoroughly. Pat dry with paper towels.

2. Arrange the salmon on individual plates, overlapping the slices as necessary. In a large bowl, whisk the lemon juice, salt and pepper. Add the oil slowly, whisking.

Add the snap peas, watercress and scallions and toss. Mound the salad in the center of each plate and serve.

MAKE IT AHEAD
You can cook the snap peas a day ahead and refrigerate. Trim the watercress several hours in advance, cover with damp paper towels and refrigerate. Slice the scallions ahead, too, wrap and refrigerate.

GRILLED QUAIL WITH CUCUMBER RELISH

Guests are always pleased when offered these luxurious little birds. Here the quail are marinated, grilled and then matched with a crisp cucumber relish. You can add a small mound of dressed mixed salad greens to the plate, if you like.

WINE RECOMMENDATION
The quail will accommodate a wide variety of light-to-medium-bodied wines, including such whites as chardonnay and sauvignon blanc, and reds such as Beaujolais or pinot noir.

SERVES 8

- 8 tablespoons lemon juice (from about 2 lemons)
- 6 tablespoons olive oil
- 2 teaspoons chopped fresh rosemary, or ¾ teaspoon dried
- 2 cloves garlic, minced
- 1½ teaspoons salt
- 1¼ teaspoons fresh-ground black pepper
- 8 quail
- 2 cucumbers, peeled, seeded and cut into ¼-inch dice
- 2 scallions including green tops, minced
- 2 tablespoons chopped flat-leaf parsley

1. In a large bowl, combine 6 tablespoons of the lemon juice, 4 tablespoons of the oil, the rosemary, garlic, 1 teaspoon of the salt and 1 teaspoon of the pepper. Add the quail and rub them inside and out with this marinade. Cover and refrigerate for at least 1 hour.

2. In a large bowl, whisk the remaining 2 tablespoons lemon juice, 2 tablespoons oil, ½ teaspoon salt and ¼ teaspoon pepper. Add the cucumbers, scallions and parsley and toss. Cover and refrigerate until ready to serve.

3. Light the grill or heat the broiler. Grill or broil the quail on both sides until just done, about 5 minutes in all. The quail should still be slightly pink inside. Pile the cucumber relish on salad plates and set the quail alongside. Serve while the quail are still hot from the grill and the relish is cold and crisp.

MAKE IT AHEAD
Small birds such as quail should be finished at the very last minute, but they can be prepared and put in the marinade up to three hours before cooking. The cucumber relish, too, can be made a few hours ahead, but don't add the salt until shortly before serving, or it may draw out some of the moisture in the cucumber and make the relish limp and watery.

THAI BEEF SALAD

Asian cooks often use the stems and even the roots of cilantro in cooking. We've added the stems as well as the leaves to the marinade for the steak in this recipe. Unlike those of many herbs, cilantro stems have lots of flavor.

WINE RECOMMENDATION This may be a classic example of when to switch rather than fight—a cold regional beer will be delicious with this spicy dish. Those determined to drink wine may want to try as full-bodied a rosé as they can get.

SERVES 8

1   cup packed chopped cilantro leaves and stems, plus 3 tablespoons minced leaves

4   cloves garlic, minced

10 tablespoons cooking oil

½   teaspoon fresh-ground black pepper

1½ pounds skirt steak

3   tablespoons lime juice (from about 2 limes)

2   teaspoons Asian fish sauce (nam pla or nuoc mam)*

¼   teaspoon dried red-pepper flakes

    Pinch sugar

3   scallions including green tops, cut into thin slices

3   tablespoons chopped fresh mint

¼   teaspoon salt

1   large head romaine lettuce, halved lengthwise and cut crosswise into ¾-inch-strips (about 3 quarts)

    *Available at Asian markets

1. In a blender, puree the 1 cup chopped cilantro and the garlic with 6 tablespoons of the oil and the pepper. Put the steak in a shallow glass dish or stainless-steel pan, pour the cilantro mixture over the meat and turn to coat. Cover and marinate in the refrigerator for at least 2 hours.

2. In a large bowl, whisk the lime juice with the fish sauce, red-pepper flakes and sugar. Slowly add the remaining 4 tablespoons oil, whisking constantly. Whisk in the scallions, the 3 tablespoons minced cilantro and the mint.

3. Light the grill or heat the broiler. Remove the steak from the marinade. Sprinkle with the salt. Grill or broil the steak for 4 minutes. Turn the meat and cook until medium rare, about 4 minutes longer. Transfer the steak to a carving board and leave to rest in a warm spot for about 10 minutes.

4. Add the lettuce to the dressing, toss and mound on individual plates. Cut the steak into very thin diagonal slices (see photo, page 141) and arrange the slices on top of the salad.

MAKE IT AHEAD You can marinate the steak overnight, if you like, and it will just become more flavorful. The salad dressing can be made several hours in advance, but don't add the minced cilantro or mint until tossing the greens. Cut up the lettuce a few hours ahead and keep in the refrigerator covered with a damp paper towel.

SKIRT STEAK VS. FLANK STEAK

Skirt steak and flank steak are frequently confused. Both need marinating and either fast grilling or slow braising for tenderness, and both should be cut across the grain to cut through the fibers so that the slices aren't too chewy. Maybe it's the appearance of skirt steak, a long, thin, narrow and rather ragged-looking strip of meat, that's prevented it from being as common and popular as flank. Actually, it's the juicier and more flavorful of the two.

MAIN COURSES

SALMON IN SCALLION BROTH

A distinctively green scallion broth is a lovely and delicious background for salmon fillets. Be sure not to overcook the fish, or it will be dry and bland. Take it from the oven when the interior is still slightly undercooked; by the time it gets to the table it will be done perfectly.

WINE RECOMMENDATION
The buttery quality and lemony flavor of a California chardonnay or French white Burgundy such as a Meursault highlights the mild sweet-and-salty contrast of this salmon dish.

SERVES 8

- 1 tablespoon butter
- 12 scallions including green tops, chopped
- 1 cup Chicken Stock, page 276, or canned low-sodium chicken broth
- 1 cup water
- 1 teaspoon salt
- ¼ teaspoon fresh-ground black pepper
- 3 pounds skinless salmon fillets, cut into 8 pieces

1. Heat the oven to 450°. In a medium pot, melt the butter over moderately low heat. Add the scallions and cook, stirring occasionally, until wilted, about 3 minutes. Add the stock, water and ½ teaspoon of the salt. Raise the heat and bring to a boil. Reduce the heat and simmer 2 minutes.

2. With a slotted spoon, transfer the scallions to a blender and puree with a few tablespoons of the cooking liquid. Add the remaining liquid and blend until very smooth, about 2 minutes. Return the scallion broth to the pot and add the pepper.

3. Oil a baking sheet. Put the salmon on the baking sheet and sprinkle with the remaining ½ teaspoon salt. Cook in the upper third of the oven until just barely done (it should still be translucent in the center), 5 to 8 minutes. Meanwhile, bring the scallion broth just to a boil. Transfer the salmon to soup plates and pour the broth around the fish.

MAKE IT AHEAD
The scallion broth can be made a day ahead and reheated. You can have the salmon all ready to go and just pop it in the oven five to ten minutes before you want to serve dinner.

SALMON TANDOORI WITH CUCUMBER RAITA

Chicken tandoori is a classic Indian dish of marinated chicken cooked in a clay oven. In this elegant variation, the typical spicy yogurt marinade is an ideal complement to rich salmon. Roasted in a hot oven, the salmon is moist, fragrant and subtly flavored. Tangy Cucumber Raita adds a refreshing note.

WINE RECOMMENDATION
One exotic spice deserves another. Match this salmon with a chilled, medium-to-rich-bodied gewürztraminer from Alsace, Germany's Rheinpfalz region or California.

SERVES 8

1 cup plain yogurt

2 cloves garlic, minced

2 teaspoons grated fresh ginger

1 teaspoon hot paprika

½ teaspoon ground cumin

½ teaspoon ground cardamom

¼ teaspoon cayenne

3 pounds skinless salmon fillets, cut into 8 pieces

½ teaspoon salt

1 tablespoon chopped fresh mint or flat-leaf parsley

Cucumber Raita, page 184

1. In a small bowl, combine the yogurt, garlic, ginger, paprika, cumin, cardamom and cayenne. Put the fish in a glass baking dish or stainless-steel pan and cover completely with the yogurt mixture. Cover and refrigerate for 2 to 3 hours, turning occasionally.

2. Heat the oven to 450°. Oil a baking sheet. Put the salmon on the baking sheet and sprinkle with the salt. Cook in the upper third of the oven until just barely done (it should still be translucent in the center), 5 to 8 minutes. Sprinkle with the mint and serve with the raita.

MAKE IT AHEAD
The yogurt marinade can be prepared a day in advance. Do not marinate the salmon more than three hours ahead, however, or the acidic yogurt may break down the flesh and ruin its texture.

BLACK-PEPPER SEARED TUNA WITH CORN COUSCOUS

Thick tuna steaks with a crisp, peppery crust and juicy, rare center are luscious-looking when sliced and served encircling a mound of Corn Couscous. We love the contrast of the black pepper with the sweetness of the corn.

WINE RECOMMENDATION
The meaty flavor of the tuna and the spice of the black pepper are a casting call for a medium-bodied red with a contrasting fruitiness. Look for a California pinot noir, a French Chinon or even a merlot.

MAKE IT AHEAD
Here's a dish that's as delicious served at room temperature as it is hot. You can cook the tuna and let it sit at room temperature, covered, for up to two hours before serving. At the last minute, slice it and serve with room-temperature couscous.

SERVES 8

3   pounds tuna steaks, about 2 inches thick, cut into 3½-inch pieces

1   tablespoon cooking oil

1   tablespoon fresh-ground black pepper

½   teaspoon salt

Corn Couscous, page 188

1. Light the grill or heat a heavy frying pan until very hot. Brush all sides of the tuna steaks with the oil and sprinkle with the pepper and salt.

2. Sear the tuna on all 4 sides, 1½ minutes per side. Let sit, loosely covered with foil, for 3 minutes. The fish will be rare.

3. To serve, cut the tuna into ¼-inch slices. Put a small mound of the Corn Couscous on each plate, or mound it all on a platter, and arrange the tuna slices, overlapping, around the couscous.

DON'T LIKE RARE TUNA?

Rare tuna is all the rage these days, but if you prefer it more done, simply buy thinner tuna steaks. If the steaks are one-and-a-half inches thick, the tuna will be medium when cooked the time specified in this recipe. Well-done steaks are sure to be dry.

WHOLE COD WITH PARSLEY SAUCE

If you've never steamed a whole fish—or steamed fish at all—you will be amazed by the delicate flavor and wonderful moist texture of this cod. (Ask at the fish market to have the head and tail cut off the fish so it fits into your steamer.) The green parsley sauce takes only minutes to make, and its bright color sets off the snowy-white fish beautifully.

WINE RECOMMENDATION
A fresh young pinot gris from Alsace (also called tokay d'Alsace) or Oregon is perfect for letting the subtle flavors of this recipe shine.

SERVES 8

1   6½-pound cod, cleaned, head, tail and fins cut off

1   large bunch flat-leaf parsley

3   tablespoons lemon juice

¾   cup olive oil

½   teaspoon salt

⅛   teaspoon fresh-ground black pepper

1   scallion including green top, minced

1   tablespoon capers, chopped

1. Rinse the fish and dry with paper towels. Cut two sheets of heavy-duty aluminum foil about 4 inches longer than the fish and stack them. Cut the stems off the parsley, reserving the leaves, and spread the stems on the foil. Lay the fish on the foil and fold up the edges to make a rim, leaving about 1 inch between the fish and the sides of the foil tray.

2. Pour about ¾ inch of water into a fish poacher or steamer (see "Improvising a Steamer," opposite page). Bring to a simmer over moderately high heat. Lift the foil tray by opposite corners and place on the steamer rack. Cover the pot with a lid of heavy-duty foil, not letting it touch the fish. Press the edges of the foil around the pot to seal. Steam the fish until just done, 25 to 30 minutes.

3. Meanwhile, in a food processor or blender, chop the reserved parsley leaves. Add the lemon juice, oil, salt and pepper and puree. Add the scallion and capers and pulse or blend briefly just to combine.

4. Turn off the heat under the steamer and remove the lid. Prick a few holes in the foil tray so that the liquid drains out. Using oven mitts, lift up the tray by opposite corners and transfer to a cutting board. With a table knife, scrape the skin off the top of the fish. Using a slotted spoon or spatula, remove the top fillet in large pieces to a serving platter or individual plates. Starting at the tail end, lift off the bone and discard it. Lift the bottom fillet off the skin and transfer to the platter or plates. Spoon the parsley sauce over the fish and serve.

—STEPHANIE LYNESS

◼ MAKE IT AHEAD

The sauce can be made well ahead of time and refrigerated, but don't add the lemon juice until shortly before serving or the sauce will lose its vibrant green color. You can keep the cod warm in the steamer over low heat, covered loosely with foil, for up to thirty minutes. Or serve the fish at room temperature if you prefer. Steam it early in the day, cool, cover and refrigerate. Remove the cod from the refrigerator about thirty minutes before you're ready to serve it.

IMPROVISING A STEAMER

If you don't have a fish poacher with a rack, a large roasting pan and a wire rack will do the job nicely. In either case, the rack should be well above the bottom of the pan to allow for enough water, about three-quarters of an inch, for the relatively long steaming time. Set the poaching rack or wire rack on two empty tuna cans (both ends removed), two heatproof ramekins or two custard cups positioned at opposite ends of the rack. Even with a poacher, you'll need to make a foil lid, since the pan lid won't fit over the fish.

POACHED HALIBUT
WITH CILANTRO LIME MAYONNAISE

Halibut served at room temperature is a perfect alternative to the ubiquitous poached salmon. The steaks are easy to divide into serving pieces because of a large central bone, and you can poach them in a large, wide pot or deep, wide frying pan if you don't have a fish poacher.

WINE RECOMMENDATION
A California or Australian sauvignon blanc will complement the creaminess of the mayonnaise and pick up the herb flavor of the cilantro.

SERVES 8

3 quarts water

3 onions, sliced

3 ribs celery, cut into thirds

2 tablespoons white vinegar

1 bay leaf

8 peppercorns

1½ teaspoons salt

3 pounds halibut steaks, 1½ inches thick

Cilantro Lime Mayonnaise, next page

1. In a fish poacher or large pot, combine the water, onions, celery, vinegar, bay leaf, peppercorns and salt. Bring to a boil over moderately high heat. Reduce the heat. Simmer, partially covered, for 30 minutes.

2. Add the fish in one layer and bring almost back to a simmer. Let poach, uncovered, until the fish is just done, about 5 minutes. Gently remove the fish and let cool to room temperature. Serve with the Cilantro Lime Mayonnaise.

MAKE IT AHEAD
This is a great dish to prepare in advance since the fish is served cooled. You can poach the halibut and let it sit at room temperature, covered, for up to two hours before serving. Or you can poach the fish earlier in the day, cool, cover and refrigerate. Remove the halibut from the refrigerator about thirty minutes before you're ready to serve it. The Cilantro Lime Mayonnaise can be made hours ahead. ➤

CILANTRO LIME MAYONNAISE

MAKES 2 CUPS

2½ cups lightly packed cilantro leaves

2 eggs

1½ cups plus 2 tablespoons olive oil

2 tablespoons lime juice

2 tablespoons water

1 teaspoon salt

⅛ teaspoon fresh-ground black pepper

1. In a food processor or blender, puree the cilantro with the eggs.

2. With the machine running, add the oil in a thin stream. Add the lime juice, water, salt and pepper and whir to mix.

FOOD PROCESSOR VS. BLENDER

In most cases, either a food processor or blender will do the job. A blender is usually the better choice when you want a velvety-smooth puree. On the other hand, you aren't always looking for a silky texture, and a processor can handle some larger foods that a blender has trouble with. When we prefer one over the other, only that appliance is mentioned. But if you don't have a processor and a blender, use whichever you have. Don't let the lack of a machine keep you from trying a recipe.

HERB-STUFFED TROUT WITH PANCETTA

Pancetta, a version of bacon that is not smoked, has a mild flavor and contrasts well with the trout without overpowering it. If you can find other smallish fish in your area, try this simple preparation with your favorite.

WINE RECOMMENDATION
A meal that tastes like a summer evening should have a wine to match. Try a good-quality rosé from Tavel or Provence.

SERVES 8

8 trout (about ¾ pound each), cleaned

1 teaspoon salt

¼ teaspoon fresh-ground black pepper

8 sprigs fresh thyme, or ½ teaspoon dried

1 lemon, cut into 12 slices, each slice cut in half

2 tablespoons butter, cut into 8 slices

32 thin slices pancetta (about 1¼ pounds)

MAKE IT AHEAD
You can stuff, wrap with pancetta and tie the trout a few hours ahead. Arrange the fish on the baking sheets, cover with plastic wrap and refrigerate. If the trout has had time to chill, you may need to add a minute or two to the cooking time.

1. Rinse the fish and dry with paper towels. Season the fish inside and out with the salt and pepper. Stuff each fish with 1 thyme sprig (or a pinch of dried thyme), 3 pieces of lemon and 1 slice of butter. Wrap 4 slices of pancetta around each fish and tie with kitchen string to keep the pancetta in place.

2. Heat the oven to 425°. Brush two baking sheets with oil. Arrange the fish on the baking sheets. Cook until just done, about 17 minutes. Remove the string and serve.

BROILED SWORDFISH STEAKS
WITH PINEAPPLE-AND-CHILE SALSA

Broiling is the easiest way to prepare firm, juicy swordfish. Pineapple salsa with ancho chiles makes a refreshing and colorful accompaniment.

WINE RECOMMENDATION
The fruitiness and mild tannin of a *cru* Beaujolais or Beaujolais-Villages, served lightly chilled, will embrace the contrasting flavors of this dish.

SERVES 8

- 3 pounds swordfish steaks (about 1 inch thick)
- 2 tablespoons cooking oil
- ½ teaspoon salt
- ⅛ teaspoon fresh-ground black pepper
- 1 tablespoon butter

  Pineapple-and-Chile Salsa, opposite page

1. Heat the broiler. Brush both sides of the swordfish steaks with the oil and sprinkle with the salt and pepper. Put the swordfish on a baking sheet and dot with the butter.

2. Broil 4 inches from the heat for 2½ minutes. Turn and broil the other side until the fish is just done, about 3 minutes longer. Serve accompanied with the Pineapple-and-Chile Salsa.

MAKE IT AHEAD
The salsa can be made early on the day of the dinner and refrigerated. You can also oil, salt and pepper the fish, cover it well and refrigerate. That leaves just about five minutes of cooking time before you serve. Either bring the fish to room temperature before broiling or add an extra minute of cooking time.

Pineapple-and-Chile Salsa

MAKES 2 CUPS

2 dried ancho chiles

1 cup boiling water

½ pineapple, cut into ¼-inch dice

½ red bell pepper, cut into ¼-inch dice

1 small red onion, cut into ¼-inch dice

¼ cup chopped cilantro

¼ cup orange juice

2 tablespoons lime juice

¼ teaspoon ground cumin

¼ teaspoon salt

Pinch fresh-ground black pepper

1. Put the chiles in a bowl and pour the boiling water over them. Let soak until softened, about 20 minutes. Drain, stem and seed the chiles. Press them through a sieve into a medium glass or stainless-steel bowl.

2. Add the remaining ingredients and stir to combine.

ROASTED MONKFISH WITH FRENCH-LENTIL SALAD

Monkfish has only one large central bone with no small pin bones; so it's an easy fish to prepare and to eat. When you buy the fish, ask to have the thin gray membrane on the outside of the fillets removed.

WINE RECOMMENDATION
A young, acidic wine such as a Sancerre, Pouilly-Fumé or California sauvignon/fumé blanc will bring up the sweetness in the fish while standing up to the vinegar component of the dressing.

SERVES 8

8   tablespoons olive oil

5   cloves garlic, minced

¾   teaspoon chopped fresh thyme,
     or ¼ teaspoon dried

1   teaspoon salt
     Fresh-ground black pepper

3½   pounds monkfish fillets, cut crosswise
     into ⅓-inch diagonal slices (see photo,
     page 141)

3   tablespoons red-wine vinegar

1   teaspoon Dijon mustard

1   tablespoon chopped shallot
     French-Lentil Salad, page 209

1. In a large bowl, combine 3 table-spoons of the oil, the garlic, thyme, ¾ teaspoon of the salt and ¼ teaspoon pepper. Add the fish and turn to coat. Cover and let marinate in the refrigerator for at least 1 and up to 4 hours.

2. In a small bowl, whisk the vinegar with the mustard, the remaining ¼ teaspoon salt and a pinch of pepper. Add the remaining 5 tablespoons oil slowly, whisking. Stir the shallot into the vinaigrette.

3. Heat the oven to 450°. Arrange the monkfish on a baking sheet and roast in the oven 3 minutes. Turn the pieces of fish and cook until just done, 1 to 2 minutes longer. Arrange the fish on individual plates, spoon the lentil salad alongside and drizzle the vinaigrette over both fish and lentils.

—GRACE PARISI

MAKE IT AHEAD
The monkfish takes only five minutes to cook. You can marinate it and arrange on the baking sheet a few hours ahead. Cover with plastic wrap and refrigerate. Either let the fish come to room temperature before cooking or add about thirty seconds to the roasting time.

BOILED LOBSTER WITH GINGER BUTTER

Wonderful as lobsters taste served with plain melted butter, they're even better when you flavor the butter with grated ginger, lemon juice and fresh herbs.

WINE RECOMMENDATION
The balanced sweetness and acidity of
a richer-style riesling from Alsace or Germany (look for a wine of *kabinett* or *spätlese*
quality) is a lovely match for the sweetness
of the lobster and the pungency of the
grated ginger.

MAKE IT AHEAD
Though this dish requires very little
preparation, don't forget how long big pots
of water take to come to a boil. Put them on
well before you intend to cook the lobsters.
You can prepare the ginger and herbs several hours in advance. Cover and set aside.
Squeeze the lemon juice, too, and season it
with the salt and pepper. At serving time,
simply melt the butter and add the prepared
ingredients.

SERVES 8

8   lobsters (about 1½ pounds each)

1   pound butter

2   tablespoons plus 2 teaspoons grated
fresh ginger

2   tablespoons lemon juice

¼   cup chopped flat-leaf parsley

¼   cup chopped cilantro

1   teaspoon salt

¼   teaspoon fresh-ground black pepper

1. In two large pots of boiling, salted
water, cook the lobsters until just done,
about 10 minutes after the water returns to
a boil.

2. Meanwhile, melt the butter over
moderate heat in a medium pot. Remove
the pot from the heat and add the remaining ingredients. Serve the lobsters with the
ginger butter.

SPICY SHRIMP BOIL

Since this Southern one-pot meal can be a bit messy to eat, put large bowls on the table for shrimp shells and corncobs and provide extra-large napkins. We find that the unexpected—eating sticky, juicy food with your fingers at a dinner party—makes people let their hair down and have a great time.

WINE RECOMMENDATION
The idea here is something simple, cold and direct, but with the character to stand up to the spicy flavors. Try a Vouvray or California chenin blanc, or do as the natives do—serve ice-cold beer.

SERVES 8

   3 pounds red new potatoes, cut into halves or quarters

   3 onions, cut into ½-inch slices

   ½ lemon, sliced

   1 bay leaf

   6 teaspoons Old Bay Seasoning

   1 teaspoon peppercorns

   ¼ teaspoon cayenne

   ¾ teaspoon dried thyme

   2 quarts water

   8 ears fresh corn, each cut into thirds

   3 pounds medium shrimp

   2 tablespoons chopped fresh parsley

   1. In an 8-quart pot, combine the potatoes, onions, lemon, bay leaf, 4 teaspoons of the Old Bay Seasoning, the peppercorns, cayenne, thyme and water. Bring to a boil. Reduce the heat. Simmer, uncovered, until the potatoes are tender, about 20 minutes.

   2. Raise the heat and add the corn. Cover and cook 3 minutes. Add the shrimp and sprinkle with the remaining 2 teaspoons Old Bay Seasoning. Cover and cook until the shrimp are just done, about 3 minutes. Serve the shrimp boil in large individual bowls, topped with the chopped parsley.

MAKE IT AHEAD
Make the broth and cook the potatoes several hours ahead. Remove the potatoes with a slotted spoon and set aside. Just before serving, bring the broth back to a boil. Add the potatoes and when the liquid returns to a boil, cook the corn for three minutes. Add the shrimp and cook three minutes longer.

OLD BAY SEASONING

Familiar to many cooks in Maryland, where it's used to season blue crab and shrimp, Old Bay Seasoning is a hot spice blend of celery salt, mustard, red pepper, black pepper, bay leaves, cloves, allspice, ginger, mace, cardamom, cinnamon and paprika. It's sold in most supermarkets, but if you prefer to mix your own, start with the list above and combine to your taste.

INDONESIAN RICE WITH GRILLED SHRIMP

A wok full of a marvelous rice mixture, including aromatic spices, lots of black pepper and bits of ham, bacon and leeks, is the base of this festive Indonesian favorite. Skewered, grilled shrimp sit on the rice, and peanuts and coconut top it all off, adding a pleasant crunch and sweetness. The rice is fairly hot, but if you want more heat, as is traditional, add another teaspoon of Asian chili paste toward the end of cooking.

WINE RECOMMENDATION
A cold regional beer is probably the best choice to cohabit with all these spices, but an off-dry gewürztraminer or a hearty, straightforward red like a zinfandel might just click into place as well.

SERVES 8

5 cloves garlic, 2 crushed, 3 minced

8 tablespoons cooking oil

4 cups rice

½ pound pork tenderloin, cut into ¼-inch dice

¼ pound baked ham, cut into ¼-inch dice

3 onions, chopped

2 tablespoons Asian chili paste *

3 tablespoons ground coriander

1½ tablespoons ground cumin

4¼ teaspoons salt

2¼ teaspoons fresh-ground black pepper

5 tablespoons soy sauce

4 slices bacon, cut into ¼-inch strips

3 leeks, white and light-green parts only, split lengthwise, cut crosswise into thin slices and washed well

48 medium shrimp (about 1½ pounds), shelled

1 cup chopped peanuts

1 cup dried, unsweetened coconut

* Available at Asian markets

1. Soak sixteen 6-inch wooden skewers in water for 30 minutes. In a small bowl, combine the crushed garlic with 2 tablespoons of the oil and set aside.

2. In a large pot of boiling, salted water, cook the rice for 10 minutes. Drain and put back in the pot. Cover and let sit for at least 15 minutes.

3. In a wok or large frying pan, heat 1 tablespoon of the oil over moderate heat. Add the pork and ham and cook, stirring frequently, until the pork is just done, about 5 minutes. Remove with a slotted spoon.

4. Heat the remaining 5 tablespoons oil in the wok over moderately high heat. Add the onions. Cook, stirring frequently, until golden brown, about 5 minutes. Reduce the heat to moderate. Add the minced

garlic. Cook, stirring, for 30 seconds. Add the chili paste, coriander, cumin, 4 teaspoons of the salt and 2 teaspoons of the pepper. Cook, stirring, for 30 seconds. Add the soy sauce and bacon. Cook, stirring, for 3 minutes. Add the pork-and-ham mixture and the leeks. Cook, stirring occasionally, until the leeks are translucent, about 8 minutes.

5. Stir in one-quarter of the rice. Add the remaining rice in thirds, stirring after each addition. Reduce the heat. Let the rice mixture steam, uncovered, stirring occasionally, until the rice is tender, about 30 minutes.

6. Light the grill or heat the broiler. Thread 3 shrimp on each skewer, brush the shrimp with the garlic oil and sprinkle them with the remaining ¼ teaspoon salt and ¼ teaspoon pepper. Grill or broil the shrimp, turning once, until just done, about 3 minutes in all. Serve mounds of the rice topped with the shrimp skewers. Pass the peanuts and coconut to sprinkle on top.

MAKE IT AHEAD
Prepare the spicy pork-and-leek mixture several days ahead, if you like. You can boil the rice a couple of hours in advance and thread the shrimp on skewers, oil them and season them. Refrigerate the shrimp but keep the rice at room temperature. About 40 minutes before serving, heat the pork mixture in a wok. Stir in the rice and continue with the recipe.

RANCH-STYLE SHRIMP

Mexican flavors work beautifully with shrimp. The toasted anise and cumin seeds add real depth of flavor to the spicy tomato and jalapeño sauce. You could seed the jalapeño peppers for a milder dish, but we think the level of chile heat is just right.

WINE RECOMMENDATION Mix your own pitcher of sangria by combining a fruity red or white wine with three-quarters of a cup water, sliced fresh fruit (oranges, limes and whatever strikes your fancy), sugar to taste and a splash of soda water. A cold lager beer served with a wedge of lime also catches the mood.

SERVES 8

1 tablespoon anise seeds

1 tablespoon cumin seeds

3 tablespoons cooking oil

12 scallions including green tops, chopped

4 cloves garlic, minced

2¼ pounds plum tomatoes (about 11), chopped

4 jalapeño peppers, sliced into thin rings

1 tablespoon dried oregano

2 teaspoons salt

3 pounds medium shrimp, shelled

2 limes, cut into wedges

1. In a small frying pan, toast the anise seeds and cumin seeds over moderately high heat, shaking the pan, until fragrant, about 1 minute.

2. In a large, heavy frying pan, heat the oil over moderately high heat until very hot but not smoking. Add the scallions and garlic and cook, stirring, until softened, about 2 minutes. Add the tomatoes, jalapeños, oregano, toasted seeds and salt and cook, stirring, until the tomatoes soften, about 3 minutes. Stir in the shrimp and cook, stirring occasionally, until just done, about 3 minutes. Serve with the lime wedges.

—ZARELA MARTINEZ
ZARELA'S

MAKE IT AHEAD Toast the anise seeds and cumin seeds early in the day. You can peel the shrimp in the morning, cover and refrigerate until ready to cook. If you prepare the vegetables ahead, too, it will take you less than ten minutes to get the dish on the table.

POLENTA-STUFFED CORNISH HENS

Cornish hens are split in half and roasted, each atop a mound of rosemary-and-garlic-flavored polenta.

A dry Italian white with character and acidity, such as an arneis or Gavi, would be excellent here, as would a red dolcetto.

SERVES 8

  6 tablespoons olive oil

  2 cloves garlic, crushed

  1 teaspoon chopped fresh rosemary, or $\frac{1}{2}$ teaspoon dried

  3 cups water

  1 teaspoon salt

  1 cup coarse or medium cornmeal

  $\frac{1}{4}$ teaspoon fresh-ground black pepper

  4 Cornish hens (about $1\frac{1}{4}$ pounds each), halved

1. In a small saucepan, heat the oil, garlic and rosemary over moderate heat and cook until the garlic is soft but not brown, about 1 minute. Set aside.

2. In a medium saucepan, bring the water and $\frac{3}{4}$ teaspoon of the salt to a boil. Add the cornmeal in a slow stream, whisking constantly. Reduce the heat to moderate and simmer, stirring frequently with a wooden spoon, until the polenta is very thick and pulls away from the sides of the saucepan, about 20 minutes. Stir in 3 tablespoons of the rosemary oil and $\frac{1}{8}$ teaspoon of the pepper. Scrape the polenta into a medium bowl and chill until firm, about 30 minutes. Stir the remaining $\frac{1}{4}$ teaspoon salt and $\frac{1}{8}$ teaspoon pepper into the remaining rosemary oil and set aside.

3. Heat the oven to 450°. Unmold the polenta onto a work surface and cut it into 8 wedges. Arrange the wedges of polenta on two baking sheets and top each one with a Cornish-hen half. Rub the hens with the reserved rosemary oil. Roast until the birds are golden and crisp on top and cooked through, about 20 minutes. With a wide metal spatula, lift the polenta and hens to a platter or individual plates.

◆ MAKE IT AHEAD
You can make the polenta up to two days ahead. Keep it and the oil reserved for brushing the hens in the refrigerator. If the oil solidifies, simply let it come to room temperature. Once the polenta is set, you can also unmold and cut it in advance.

INDIAN-SPICED CORNISH HENS AND RED LENTILS

You can go all the way with the Indian theme here, serving the hens and lentils with a pilaf and chutney or raita, or steer the meal in a more eclectic direction by adding sautéed sweet potatoes and tiny green beans flavored with lemon zest and a few drops of Tabasco sauce.

WINE RECOMMENDATION
Look for a flavorful wine with a touch of sweetness (particularly if you serve this dish with chutney), such as a gewürztraminer or chenin blanc. A surprise pleasure would be a good-quality sparkling wine with a touch of residual sugar, like most bruts.

SERVES 8

2	tablespoons cooking oil
2¼	teaspoons ground coriander
1½	teaspoons ground cumin
1½	teaspoons turmeric
1½	teaspoons salt
¾	teaspoon fresh-ground black pepper
¼	teaspoon ground cloves
⅛	teaspoon cayenne
4	Cornish hens (about 1¼ pounds each), halved
	Indian-Spiced Red Lentils, page 208
8	cilantro sprigs (optional)

1. Heat the oven to 425°. In a small bowl, combine the oil, coriander, cumin, turmeric, salt, black pepper, cloves and cayenne.

2. Rub the mixture over the Cornish-hen halves and arrange them, skin-side down, on a baking sheet. Cook for 10 minutes. Turn the hens and continue cooking until just done, about 10 minutes longer.

3. Serve the hens with the spiced lentils. Garnish each hen half with a sprig of cilantro, if using.

MAKE IT AHEAD
Rub the hens with the spice mixture and set them on the baking sheet a few hours ahead, if you like. It isn't necessary to cover them. Refrigerate, but either bring back to room temperature before roasting or add a minute or two to the cooking time.

GRILLED CHICKEN BREASTS WITH GREEN-OLIVE TAPENADE

Perfect for summer when you want something simple and light, this chicken is wonderful with focaccia or any chewy bread.

WINE RECOMMENDATION
A red Côtes du Rhône or young Chianti would work with the Mediterranean savor of this dish.

SERVES 8

- 1 cup good-quality green olives, pitted
- 2 cloves garlic
- 3 anchovy fillets, or ¾ teaspoon anchovy paste
- ¾ cup lightly packed flat-leaf parsley leaves
- 1 tablespoon lemon juice
- ¼ teaspoon fresh-ground black pepper
- ½ cup olive oil
- 2 tablespoons water
- ½ teaspoon salt, more if needed
- 8 boneless, skinless chicken breasts (about 3 pounds)

1. In a food processor, combine the olives, garlic, anchovies, parsley, lemon juice and ⅛ teaspoon of the pepper. Work the mixture to a coarse paste. With the machine running, slowly add ¼ cup of the olive oil and the water. Taste for seasoning. The olives and anchovies are salty; so additional salt may not be needed.

2. In a small bowl, combine the remaining ¼ cup oil with the salt and the remaining ⅛ teaspoon pepper. Light the grill or heat the broiler. Brush the chicken breasts with the oil mixture and grill or broil just until done, about 5 minutes per side. Serve the chicken breasts with the olive tapenade alongside.

—ERICA DE MANE

MAKE IT AHEAD
Prepare the tapenade a day in advance, if you like. Refrigerate, but bring back to room temperature before serving. The chicken can be brushed with the oil hours ahead, too. Refrigerate and then either return to room temperature or add one or two minutes to the grilling time.

QUAIL WRAPPED IN PROSCIUTTO

Instead of being trussed, each of these tiny birds is wrapped in a thin slice of prosciutto. In addition to making a delicious accompaniment, the ham keeps the lean birds moist during cooking. Cheese Polenta, page 200, is the perfect accompaniment.

WINE RECOMMENDATION
The earthy, uncomplicated but delicate flavor of the quail allows a subtly aromatic, medium-bodied wine to show its stuff. Look for a pinot noir, which can add a note of smoky perfume.

MAKE IT AHEAD
Get the quail all ready to go hours before cooking, if you like. Refrigerate, covered, and bring to room temperature before cooking (about an hour should do it).

SERVES 8

16 quail
1¼ teaspoons salt
½ teaspoon fresh-ground black pepper
16 fresh sage leaves, or 1 teaspoon dried
16 thin slices prosciutto (about ½ pound)

1. Heat the oven to 450°. Season the quail inside and out with the salt and pepper. Set a sage leaf, if using, on top of each of the quail and then wrap each bird with a slice of the prosciutto. Or if using dried sage, rub the inside of each quail with a pinch of sage before wrapping it with the prosciutto.

2. Put the prosciutto-wrapped quail on two baking sheets and cook until just done, about 15 minutes. The meat should still be a bit pink.

ROASTED CURED CHICKEN

Look no further for a roast chicken recipe that will give you moist meat and crisp golden-brown skin. The trick is in the brining. This brief curing process makes the meat slightly denser, juicy and well-seasoned throughout.

WINE RECOMMENDATION
A medium-bodied wine with plenty of juice and fruit will shine here. You can span the color spectrum—from a chardonnay to a fine rosé to a pinot noir to a St. Joseph from the Rhône.

SERVES 8

- 3 quarts water
- 1½ cups coarse salt
- 1½ cups dark-brown sugar
- 10 juniper berries
- 10 allspice berries
- 1 teaspoon peppercorns
- 2 bay leaves
- 3 chickens (about 3 pounds each)
- 6 tablespoons cooking oil

1. In a large pot, combine the water, salt, sugar, juniper berries, allspice berries, peppercorns and bay leaves. Bring to a boil, stirring so the salt and sugar dissolve. Cool to room temperature.

2. Put the chickens in a large bowl or pot. If you don't have a big enough container to hold the chickens and brine, use two or three separate ones. Pour the brine over the chickens, refrigerate and leave to cure at least 2 hours. Turn once or twice.

3. Heat the oven to 450°. Remove the chickens from the brine. Rinse them with water and pat dry with paper towels. Tuck their wings behind their backs and tie their legs together. Set on a rack in a large roasting pan and rub with the oil.

4. Roast the chickens, basting occasionally, for 30 minutes. Reduce the oven temperature to 350° and continue roasting the chickens until done, about 30 minutes longer. Because the chickens are cured, the meat will be pink even when it is thoroughly cooked. Transfer the birds to a cutting board and leave to rest in a warm spot for about 15 minutes. Carve the birds and serve.

MAKE IT AHEAD
You can make the brine a few days before using it to cure the chickens, if you like; cool and refrigerate it. The chickens must be put in the cure two hours before roasting and can sit in the brine up to twelve hours.

BRINING BIRDS

We came across the brining technique used in this recipe when testing Chef Michael Chiarello's Pastina with Brined Turkey and Wild Mushrooms for our *Pasta* cookbook. We liked the distinct cured flavor and moist texture so much that we decided to try it with chicken, too. We left one chicken to soak only two hours and a second one overnight. Both were deliciously moist. The chicken that soaked overnight was more thoroughly cured and therefore pinker, even when it was cooked through. It could almost be mistaken for ham. Take your choice of time depending on the effect you want. You might experiment with other birds as well, such as Cornish hens or capon.

THE BEST CHICKENS

You get what you pay for when it comes to chicken. Premium brands, such as Bell and Evans or Zacky, taste remarkably better than the standard supermarket bird. Kosher chickens are excellent, too. Try this test: Buy two single chicken breasts, one a premium and one a standard brand. Bring them to room temperature, season with salt, bake or broil until just done and then let sit for five minutes. Now taste. We're willing to bet you'll decide to pay the price for extra quality.

TO TRUSS OR NOT TO TRUSS

In traditional trussing, twine goes every which way. You practically need a map to guide you through the process. There is a certain satisfaction in learning the technique. But we've found that in most cases, just twisting the wings behind the back and tying the legs together makes the bird perfectly presentable in seconds.

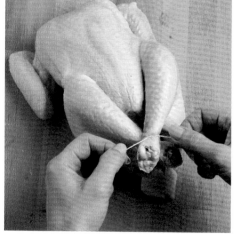

CHICKEN AND SHRIMP PAELLA

Spanish paella, its saffron-yellow rice studded with chicken, shrimp, spicy chorizo sausage, mussels and green beans, is a beautiful sight on the table. The dish looks festive presented in a traditional paella pan—a low, flat metal pan with handles—but a large, shallow baking dish will work as well.

WINE RECOMMENDATION
This is a perhaps surprisingly wine-versatile combination, welcoming choices from a crisp sauvignon/fumé blanc to a fine-quality rosé to a young *Crianza* (lightly wood-aged) red Rioja. Homemade sangria (page 116) would also be delicious, depending on the atmosphere you want to create.

SERVES 8

- 2 tablespoons olive oil
- ¼ pound chorizo or other dried, hot sausage, cut into ¼-inch slices
- 8 chicken thighs
- 3 onions, chopped
- 4 cloves garlic, minced
- 1 7-ounce jar pimientos, drained and chopped
- 1 28-ounce can (about 3½ cups) tomatoes, drained and chopped
- ½ cup dry sherry
- 4 teaspoons salt
- 5 cups water
- 2¾ cups rice
- ½ cup chopped flat-leaf parsley, plus more for garnish
- 4 teaspoons saffron
- ½ pound green beans, cut into 1½-inch lengths
- ¾ pound medium shrimp
- ½ pound small mussels, scrubbed and debearded
- 2 lemons, cut into wedges (optional)

1. In a large pot, heat the oil over moderately high heat. Add the chorizo and cook, stirring frequently, until browned, about 5 minutes. Remove and set aside. Add the chicken to the pot and brown well on both sides, about 8 minutes in all. Remove. Pour off all but 2 tablespoons of the fat. Reduce the heat to moderately low.

2. Add the onions and half the garlic and cook, stirring occasionally, until the onions are translucent, about 5 minutes. Add the pimientos, tomatoes, sherry and 1 teaspoon of the salt and cook, stirring occasionally, until the mixture is very thick, about 8 minutes.

3. Add the chicken and bring to a simmer. Cover, reduce the heat and simmer for 5 minutes. Add the water, rice, parsley, saffron and the remaining 3 teaspoons salt. Bring to a boil over moderately high heat, stirring occasionally. Reduce the heat and simmer, stirring frequently, for 12 minutes.

4. Meanwhile, bring a medium pot of salted water to a boil. Add the beans and cook until almost done, about 5 minutes. Drain the beans, rinse with cold water and drain thoroughly.

5. Heat the oven to 450°. Pour the rice and chicken into a 14½-inch paella pan or a large, shallow baking dish. Arrange the chicken and shrimp on the rice. Discard any mussels that have broken shells or that do not clamp shut when tapped. Press the mussels about ½ inch into the rice and bake the paella on the lowest rack in the oven for 8 minutes. Top with the green beans. Continue baking until the mussels open, the beans are hot and the rice, chicken and shrimp are just done, about 2 minutes longer. Sprinkle with parsley and serve with the lemon wedges.

MAKE IT AHEAD
You can make this dish, up to the point where you add the rice and water, several hours ahead. You can also cook the beans ahead. Wrap the chicken mixture, once it has cooled, and the beans separately and refrigerate them. Thirty minutes before serving, heat the chicken mixture and continue with the recipe.

WHICH RICE TO USE

The medium-grain rice grown in Valencia, Spain, is the one traditionally used in paella. The cooked grains of this rice, like those of Italian arborio, are especially moist and tend to cling together more than those of long-grain rice. Valencia rice is available in some specialty-food stores, or you can use the easier-to-find Italian arborio. For domestic rice that's similar, try California-grown, medium-grain rice, sold under various brand names. Nishiki, one of the best, is widely available in Asian markets. We've also had excellent results with Arkansas-grown, medium-grain rice, such as Goya brand, sold in supermarkets.

CHICKEN BIRYANI

Chicken cooked with an aromatic spice mixture and layered with buttermilk-flavored rice produces a wonderful biryani, a classic of Indian cuisine. It's a great dish to prepare ahead and is especially quick since the chicken doesn't need browning.

WINE RECOMMENDATION
This dish will bring up the aromatic fruit and mild creaminess of a fine riesling.

SERVES 8

1/3	cup cooking oil
2	tablespoons butter
1	onion, minced
2	cloves garlic, minced
1	tablespoon grated fresh ginger
2	teaspoons ground cumin
1/2	teaspoon ground cinnamon
1/2	teaspoon ground cloves
1/2	teaspoon ground cardamom
1/2	teaspoon chili powder
1/4	teaspoon turmeric
1 1/2	cups buttermilk
1	teaspoon sugar
3 3/4	teaspoons salt
2	chickens (3 pounds each), quartered
3	cups long-grain rice
4 1/2	cups water
2	limes, cut into wedges (optional)

1. In a large, deep frying pan, heat the oil and butter over moderately low heat. Add the onion, garlic and ginger and cook, stirring occasionally, until the onion is translucent, about 5 minutes. Add the cumin, cinnamon, cloves, cardamom, chili powder and turmeric and cook, stirring, for 1 minute longer. Stir in 1/2 cup of the buttermilk, the sugar and 2 3/4 teaspoons of the salt.

2. Add the chicken to the frying pan in a single layer. Bring to a simmer over moderate heat. Reduce the heat and continue simmering, covered, until the chicken is just done, about 25 minutes.

3. Meanwhile, in a large pot, combine the remaining 1 cup buttermilk and 1 teaspoon salt, the rice and water. Bring to a boil over moderately high heat. Reduce the heat to low and simmer, covered, until the rice is just done, about 20 minutes.

4. Heat the oven to 350°. In a large, deep baking dish, arrange 4 pieces of the chicken in a single layer. Cover with half of the rice and half of the spice mixture left over from cooking the chicken. Add the remaining chicken pieces and top with the remaining rice and spice mixture. Cover with a lid or aluminum foil and bake until heated through, about 10 minutes. Serve with the lime wedges.

MAKE IT AHEAD
You can layer the chicken and rice in the baking dish up to six hours ahead. Keep at room temperature for up to two hours; then reheat in a 350° oven until heated through, about twenty-five minutes. Refrigerate the biryani if you want to keep it longer than two hours. Either bring to room temperature by removing it from the refrigerator an hour before baking or add about ten minutes to the baking time.

FESTIVE BIRYANI

Biryani—layered meat, rice, exotic spices and herbs—is considered one of the more elaborate and festive Indian dishes and is usually reserved for special occasions. Different regions of India offer their own variations, generally based on marinated lamb or chicken. A mixture of spices, such as cardamom, cumin, turmeric, ginger, clove and cinnamon, flavors the dish, and yogurt and mint are often added. Basmati, the fragrant Indian rice, is the standard base, and garnishes such as pistachios, raisins, coconut or the most special of all, an edible silver leaf called *vark*, complete the dish luxuriously. The ingredients are steamed together in a tightly covered casserole, sometimes sealed with dough to hold in the perfumed vapor, until both meat and rice are cooked. Here we've simplified the intricate traditional biryani, still maintaining the exotic flavors. This version is made with regular long-grain white rice, but if you're going all out, fragrant basmati rice can only improve the dish.

Roast Capon with Leeks, Apples and Pine Nuts

Serving a large roasted bird is a practical way to entertain a group. In this recipe, juicy capon is matched with apples and leeks for a perfect autumn dinner. The brandy and herb butter that's spread under the skin keeps the breast moist and adds flavor.

WINE RECOMMENDATION
A flavorful, but not too heavy, wine such as a Beaujolais will work well with this hearty dish. If you're serving it after mid-November, a Beaujolais Nouveau would be fun for the full autumn-harvest effect.

SERVES 8

¼ cup pine nuts

8 tablespoons butter, at room temperature

4 leeks, white and light-green parts only, split lengthwise, cut crosswise into slices and washed well

4 ribs celery, sliced

2 Granny Smith apples, peeled, cored and cut into ½-inch pieces

4 tablespoons applejack or Calvados

1½ tablespoons fresh thyme leaves, or 1½ teaspoons dried

2 teaspoons salt

Fresh-ground black pepper

1 capon (about 8 pounds)

2 teaspoons cornstarch

1½ cups Chicken Stock, page 276, or canned low-sodium chicken broth

1. In a large frying pan, toast the pine nuts over moderately low heat, stirring frequently, until golden brown, about 4 minutes. Or toast in a 350° oven for 6 minutes. Put the pine nuts in a large bowl.

2. Melt 2 tablespoons of the butter in the frying pan over moderately low heat. Add the leeks and celery and cook, stirring occasionally, until soft, about 10 minutes. Add to the bowl.

3. In the same pan, melt 1 tablespoon of the butter over moderately high heat. Add the apples. Cook, stirring occasionally, until soft and light brown, about 5 minutes. Add to the bowl with 1½ tablespoons of the applejack, 1 tablespoon of the fresh thyme (or 1 teaspoon dried), 1 teaspoon of the salt and ¼ teaspoon pepper.

4. Put the remaining 5 tablespoons butter in a small bowl. Work in the remaining 2½ tablespoons applejack and ½ tablespoon fresh thyme (or ½ teaspoon dried), ¼ teaspoon of the salt and a pinch of pepper. ➤

5. Heat the oven to 425°. Set the capon on a work surface. Stuff the bird with the leek-and-apple mixture. With your fingers, loosen the skin from the breast, being careful to avoid tearing. Still using your fingers, spread half of the flavored butter on the breast under the skin. Rub the remaining butter over the legs and thighs. Twist the wings behind the bird to hold the neck skin. Tie the legs together (see photo, page 123). Sprinkle the capon with ½ teaspoon of the salt and ¼ teaspoon pepper.

6. Put the capon on a rack in a roasting pan. Roast for 40 minutes. Baste with the pan juices and reduce the oven temperature to 350°. Continue roasting, basting every 30 minutes, until just done (170°), about 1½ hours longer. Transfer the bird to a carving board and leave to rest in a warm spot for about 15 minutes.

7. In a small bowl, mix the cornstarch with 2 tablespoons of the stock. Pour off the fat from the roasting pan and set the pan over moderate heat. Add the remaining stock to the pan. Bring the stock to a boil, scraping the bottom of the pan to dislodge any brown bits. Simmer for 5 minutes. Stir the cornstarch mixture and add it to the pan. Simmer, stirring, until thickened, about 3 minutes longer. Add the remaining ¼ teaspoon salt and a pinch of pepper.

8. Remove the string from the bird. Spoon the stuffing into a bowl and carve the capon. Serve with the stuffing and sauce.

—KATHERINE ALFORD

MAKE IT AHEAD

Prepare the stuffing and flavored butter several days in advance, if that's most convenient, but don't stuff the capon until shortly before you put it in the oven. Roasted birds are best served relatively quickly, while the skin is still crisp and the meat moist. But since the capon must go into the oven about two-and-a-half hours before you plan to serve it, you'll have the work done well before your guests arrive.

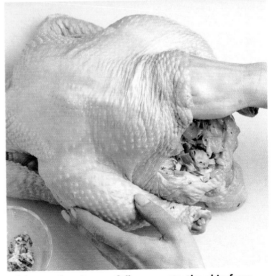

With your hands, carefully separate the skin from the meat. Then spread butter over the breast.

DUCK-AND-SHRIMP GUMBO

Thin slices of rare duck breast update this well known Louisiana soup. Served with rice, it's a meal in itself.

 **WINE RECOMMENDATION**
Down on the bayou, gumbo is strictly beer-drinking fare, but a hearty, uncomplicated red such as a zinfandel, Côtes du Rhône or barbera can withstand the onslaught of spices and is more appropriate to this sophisticated version.

SERVES 8

⅓ cup cooking oil, more if needed

½ pound andouille or other spicy smoked sausage, casing removed, halved lengthwise and cut crosswise into ¼-inch slices

3 duck breasts (about 6 ounces each), skin removed

½ cup flour

2 onions, chopped fine

2 ribs celery with leaves, ribs chopped fine, leaves chopped

1 red bell pepper, chopped fine

1 green bell pepper, chopped fine

3 cloves garlic, minced

1 28-ounce can (about 3½ cups) tomatoes with their juice, chopped

1½ quarts Chicken Stock, page 276, or canned low-sodium chicken broth

1½ teaspoons dried thyme

1 bay leaf

2 teaspoons salt

⅛ teaspoon cayenne

3 cups water

1½ cups rice

¼ cup chopped fresh or frozen okra

1 pound medium shrimp, shelled

¼ to ½ teaspoon Tabasco sauce

¼ teaspoon fresh-ground black pepper

4 tablespoons chopped fresh parsley

2 scallions including green tops, minced

1. In a large pot, heat the oil over moderately high heat. Add the andouille. Cook until the sausage is browned, about 4 minutes. With a slotted spoon, remove the sausage. Add the duck breasts to the pot. Brown on both sides, about 8 minutes in all. Remove and set aside.

2. Reduce the heat to moderate and let the fat cool slightly. Stir in the flour. If the sausage hasn't rendered enough fat, the mixture may be crumbly; add a little oil. Cook, stirring frequently, until the roux turns brown. Stir the mixture constantly until dark brown, about 10 minutes.

3. Add the onions, celery ribs, bell peppers and garlic and cook, stirring, 1 minute. Stir in the tomatoes with their juice, the stock, thyme, bay leaf, 1½ teaspoons of the salt and the cayenne. Cook, partially covered, stirring occasionally, until the vegetables are very tender, about 40 minutes. ➤

4. Meanwhile, bring the water to a boil with the remaining ½ teaspoon salt. Add the rice. Reduce the heat, cover and simmer until the rice is tender and all the water is absorbed, about 25 minutes.

5. Cut the duck breasts into thin diagonal slices. Add the sausage and okra to the soup and cook, covered, 10 minutes. Add the shrimp and cook 2 minutes. Add the duck and cook just until the shrimp are done, about 1 minute longer. Discard the bay leaf. Stir in the Tabasco sauce, black pepper, 2 tablespoons of the parsley, the celery leaves and scallions.

6. Stir the remaining 2 tablespoons parsley into the rice. Pack ⅓ cup of the rice into a measuring cup or small ramekin. Unmold in the center of a soup plate and repeat with the remaining rice. Ladle the gumbo around the rice.

MAKE IT AHEAD
Complete the soup through step three a few days ahead, if you like. Wrap the sausage and duck separately and refrigerate them and the soup. Wait to buy the shrimp until the day of or at most the day before serving.

VARIATION

CHICKEN-AND-SHRIMP GUMBO

Brown 2 pounds of chicken thighs in batches in place of the duck breasts. Remove them and make the roux as directed. Return the chicken to the pot with the vegetables and cook in the soup until just done, about 35 minutes. Remove. When cool enough to handle, remove the meat from the skin and bones and cut into bite-size pieces. Add the chicken to the soup with the shrimp and cook until the shrimp is just done, about 2 minutes.

ROAST VEAL WITH SAGE

This Italian-style veal roast is rubbed inside and out with fresh sage mixed with a generous quantity of black pepper. We also like this flavorful roast served at room temperature, especially when the weather begins to turn warm.

WINE RECOMMENDATION
It would be difficult to go wrong with any well-made, medium-bodied red. Particularly good would be a merlot-based wine like a St.-Emilion from Bordeaux.

SERVES 8

- 3 tablespoons butter
- 6 tablespoons chopped fresh sage, or 2 tablespoons dried
- 2 teaspoons fresh-ground black pepper
- 1 5-pound boneless veal shoulder roast, rolled and tied
- 1 teaspoon salt
- 1 tablespoon olive oil

1. Heat the oven to 450°. In a small saucepan, melt the butter over moderate heat. Stir in the fresh sage, if using, and the pepper and cook, stirring, just until the sage wilts, about 1 minute. Remove from the heat and let cool. If using dried sage, stir the sage and pepper into the melted butter and remove from the heat.

2. Untie the veal roast. Rub about a third of the sage mixture over the inside of the roast and sprinkle with ¼ teaspoon of the salt. Retie the roast, rub all over with the remaining sage mixture and sprinkle with the remaining ¾ teaspoon salt.

3. Heat the oil in a roasting pan in the oven for 5 to 10 minutes. Add the veal to the pan, fat-side up, and roast for 15 minutes. Turn the meat over and roast for another 15 minutes. Turn the meat again and roast until done, about 20 minutes longer. Transfer the roast to a carving board and leave to rest in a warm spot for about 15 minutes before slicing.

—BOB CHAMBERS

MAKE IT AHEAD
You can prepare the sage mixture and ready the veal for roasting hours ahead. Cover and refrigerate. Either bring the veal to room temperature before roasting or add a few extra minutes to the cooking time.

LOIN OF VEAL WITH THYME CREAM

This dish uses the traditional method of browning the meat on top of the stove first and then roasting it in the oven along with vegetables in a covered pan. The meat is beautifully golden on the outside and deliciously moist inside. Loin is one of the most luxurious cuts for roasting. Substitute boneless round, rump or shoulder, if you like. A touch of cream and thyme are added to the cooking juices for a sublime sauce.

WINE RECOMMENDATION
This is a wine-versatile dish that will bring out the finer qualities of everything from a creamy chardonnay to an oak-matured Rioja *Reserva*.

SERVES 8

    5   tablespoons butter
    2   tablespoons cooking oil
    1   5-pound boneless veal loin roast, tied
    2   carrots, chopped
    2   onions, chopped
    2   fennel bulbs, chopped
    8   parsley sprigs
    2   teaspoons dried thyme
    1   bay leaf
  ¼   teaspoon salt
  ½   teaspoon fresh-ground black pepper
    3   strips bacon
  ½   cup heavy cream
    1   tablespoon dry vermouth or dry white wine
1½   teaspoons chopped fresh thyme, or ½ teaspoon dried

1. Heat the oven to 325°. In a large, heavy, ovenproof pot, melt 2 tablespoons of the butter with the oil over moderately high heat. Add the veal roast and brown well on all sides, 10 to 15 minutes. Remove the veal. Pour off the butter and oil and wipe out any blackened bits with paper towels. Melt the remaining 3 tablespoons butter in the pot over moderate heat. Add the vegetables, parsley, the 2 teaspoons dried thyme and the bay leaf and cook, covered, until the vegetables have begun to soften, about 5 minutes.

2. Sprinkle the veal with the salt and ¼ teaspoon of the pepper. Top with the bacon. Put the veal in the pot with the vegetables and cover. Roast in the oven, basting occasionally, until done, about 1½ hours. Transfer the veal to a carving board and leave to rest in a warm spot for about 15 minutes.

3. Pour off most of the fat from the pot. Strain the cooking liquid into a medium saucepan and press the vegetables to get all the liquid. Add the remaining ¼ teaspoon pepper, the cream, vermouth and the ½ teaspoon dried thyme, if using, and

bring to a boil over moderately high heat. Boil until reduced to 1 cup, about 5 minutes. Strain and stir in the fresh thyme, if using.

4. Remove the bacon and strings from the veal roast and slice it. Serve with the thyme sauce.

MAKE IT AHEAD

You can keep the roast warm for about half an hour after it comes out of the oven. Once it's cooked, remove it from the pan and cover it loosely with aluminum foil. You can go ahead and prepare the sauce, too, and then reheat it over moderately low heat just before serving.

LOIN OF VEAL WITH MARJORAM CREAM

For an equally delicious alternative, use marjoram in place of the thyme. It has a stronger flavor than thyme, so add only 1½ teaspoons of dried when cooking the roast and 1 teaspoon fresh or ¼ teaspoon dried to the sauce.

■ ■ ■

LOIN OF VEAL WITH MUSTARD AND THYME CREAM

For an easy and attractive alternative, add 1 tablespoon of grainy mustard to the finished sauce.

■ ■ ■

LOIN OF VEAL WITH THYME JUS

Omit the cream and boil the sauce down to ¾ cup instead of 1 cup.

VEAL CHOPS WITH MUSHROOMS AND ROASTED GARLIC

Garlic cloves are roasted in olive oil until buttery soft. The garlic-flavored oil is then used to brown the mushrooms and the veal chops. It's easy to press the mellow garlic out of its skin with the side of a knife so that you can eat it with the chops. They're shown here with Herbed Mashed Potatoes, page 194.

WINE RECOMMENDATION
Though these veal chops are cooked with a white wine, the earthy flavors will be wonderful with a smoky, perfumed pinot noir or a fine Beaujolais.

SERVES 8

40	cloves garlic (about 2 heads), unpeeled
$1/2$	cup olive oil
1	pound mushrooms, cut into quarters
1	teaspoon salt
8	veal chops (about 1 inch thick)
$1/2$	teaspoon fresh-ground black pepper
$1/2$	cup dry white wine
1	cup Chicken Stock, page 276, or canned low-sodium chicken broth

1. Heat the oven to 325°. In a small baking dish, combine the garlic cloves and oil. Cover with a lid or aluminum foil and roast the garlic in the oven until the cloves are soft, about 40 minutes. Remove the garlic with a slotted spoon and put in a medium bowl. Reserve the oil. Raise the oven temperature to 450°.

2. In a large frying pan, heat 2 tablespoons of the garlic oil over moderate heat. Add the mushrooms and $1/2$ teaspoon of the salt and cook, stirring occasionally, until brown, about 8 minutes. Add to the garlic.

3. Season the veal with the remaining $1/2$ teaspoon salt and $1/4$ teaspoon of the pepper. In the frying pan, heat 2 more tablespoons of the garlic oil over moderately high heat. Add four of the chops and brown well on both sides, about 5 minutes in all. Remove and put in a large roasting pan. Brown the remaining chops in the same way, adding oil if needed, and add to the roasting pan.

4. Pour the wine and stock into the frying pan and bring to a boil, scraping the bottom of the pan to dislodge any brown bits. Simmer 5 minutes. Add the mushrooms and garlic and simmer 5 minutes longer. Stir in the remaining $1/4$ teaspoon pepper.

5. Just before serving, cook the veal in the oven until just done (it should still be slightly pink in the center), about 12 minutes. Reheat the sauce if necessary. Serve the chops with the mushrooms, garlic and sauce spooned over them. ➤

MAKE IT AHEAD

Roast the garlic a few days ahead, if you like. Leave it in the oil and store in the refrigerator. You can brown the mushrooms and veal chops and prepare the sauce several hours before serving. Put the chops in the roasting pan and keep them covered in the refrigerator. Either take them out an hour before cooking so that they return to room temperature or add a minute or two to the cooking time.

OSSOBUCO WITH BALSAMIC VINEGAR AND ROSEMARY

This uncomplicated preparation yields a full-flavored, rustic dish. In Italy a special utensil is provided each guest to extract the succulent marrow from the center of the bone. You can improvise with a narrow knife or thin spoon—a butter knife or demitasse spoon, for instance.

 WINE RECOMMENDATION
Many medium- to full-bodied Italian reds would be delicious, but this Northern Italian specialty has a regional affinity for the generously flavored reds of Piemonte. Look for a Barolo or Barbaresco for a special dinner or, for something less pricey, a barbera or dolcetto.

SERVES 8

- 8 veal shanks (2 inches thick)
- ¾ cup flour
- 2¼ teaspoons salt
- ½ teaspoon fresh-ground black pepper
- 2 tablespoons butter, more if needed
- 4 onions, chopped
- 4 carrots, chopped
- 2 ribs celery, chopped
- 8 cloves garlic, minced
- 4 teaspoons chopped fresh rosemary
- ½ cup balsamic vinegar
- 1 quart Chicken Stock, page 276, or canned low-sodium chicken broth
- 1 28-ounce can (about 3½ cups) tomatoes with their juice, chopped
- ¼ cup chopped flat-leaf parsley

1. Tie a piece of kitchen string around the circumference of each veal shank. Combine the flour with ¼ teaspoon of the salt and ¼ teaspoon of the pepper. Dredge the veal shanks in the flour and shake off the excess.

2. In a large ovenproof pot, melt the butter over moderately high heat. Add four of the shanks, brown well on both sides, about 10 minutes in all, and remove. Brown the remaining shanks, adding more butter if needed. Remove.

3. Reduce the heat to moderate. Add the onions, carrots, celery, garlic and rosemary to the pot and cook, stirring, until the vegetables are soft, about 10 minutes. Add the vinegar and cook until it has almost completely evaporated, about 4 minutes. Stir in the stock, the tomatoes with their juice and the remaining 2 teaspoons salt.

4. Heat the oven to 325°. Return the veal shanks to the pot and bring to a simmer on top of the stove. Cover and braise in the oven for 1 hour. Check the shanks occasionally; they should be simmering, not boiling vigorously. If necessary, reduce the

oven temperature to 300°. Uncover the shanks. Carefully turn each one. Continue cooking, uncovered, until the meat is very tender, about 1 hour longer.

5. Remove the veal shanks from the pot. You should have about 6 cups of flavorful sauce. If necessary, boil the sauce to reduce it and intensify the flavor. Add the remaining ¼ teaspoon pepper. Remove the string from each of the shanks before serving. Stir the parsley into the sauce and spoon it over the shanks.

MAKE IT AHEAD
If anything, ossobuco is better made ahead. Let it come to room temperature and then reheat in a 325° oven for about half an hour. Add the chopped parsley just before serving.

THE BONE WITH A HOLE

Ossobuco means "bone with a hole," specifically the shank bone of a calf. The dish ossobuco is made from one- to two-inch-thick pieces of veal shank. When buying ossobuco, ask your butcher to cut it from the meatier hind leg. And if you're buying the whole shank, take the ends of the bone, too; they make an excellent addition to stock. Many connoisseurs feel the whole point to ossobuco is the rich, flavorful marrow. Be sure to dig it out and give it a try.

WASABI-MARINATED STRIP STEAKS

In Japanese restaurants wasabi is blended with water to make the hot, spicy paste served as a condiment with sushi. Here we've added it to our marinade to flavor the steaks somewhat more subtly. Powdered wasabi is sold in small tins or jars in many supermarkets and in Asian markets, and it keeps practically forever.

WINE RECOMMENDATION
The assertive flavors of the marinade call for a wine with good acidity and relatively simple character, such as a young Chianti or dolcetto from Italy.

SERVES 8

¼ cup rice-wine vinegar

2 tablespoons soy sauce

1 teaspoon Asian sesame oil

2 cloves garlic, minced

1½ teaspoons grated fresh ginger

1 tablespoon powdered wasabi

3 pounds strip steaks (about 3), about 1 inch thick

½ teaspoon salt

1. In a small bowl, combine the vinegar, soy sauce, oil, garlic and ginger. Add the wasabi and stir until it dissolves.

2. Put the steaks in a shallow glass baking dish or stainless-steel pan, add the marinade and turn to coat. Cover and refrigerate for at least 4 hours, turning occasionally.

3. Light the grill or heat the broiler. Remove the steaks from the marinade and sprinkle with the salt. Grill or broil the steaks for 4 minutes. Turn the meat and cook to your taste, about 3 minutes longer for medium-rare. Transfer the steaks to a carving board and leave to rest in a warm spot for about 10 minutes. Cut the steaks into thin diagonal slices and serve.

MAKE IT AHEAD
The steaks can marinate for up to eight hours, but don't leave them in the marinade for much longer than that or their texture will turn from tender-but-firm to mushy.

Pictured are two slices of steak cut straight down (left) and two cut on the diagonal (right). As you can see, the size is almost doubled when the steak is cut on a sharp diagonal. This principle applies to cutting any meat, poultry or fish, either raw or cooked.

SIRLOIN WITH CHIMICHURRI SAUCE

A favorite Brazilian accompaniment to grilled meats, piquant bright-green Chimichurri Sauce makes a lively addition to broiled sirloin. The steak is shown here with Pommes Anna, page 197.

WINE RECOMMENDATION
A velvety, richer-styled California or Oregon pinot noir or a good-quality French Beaujolais will contrast beautifully with the recipe's spiciness.

SERVES 8

4 pounds sirloin steaks (about 2), 1½ inches thick

2 tablespoons olive oil

½ teaspoon salt

½ teaspoon fresh-ground black pepper

2 tablespoons butter

Chimichurri Sauce, right

1. Heat the broiler. Brush both sides of the steaks with the oil, sprinkle with the salt and pepper and dot with the butter.

2. Broil the steaks for 4 minutes. Turn the meat and cook to your taste, about 4 minutes longer for medium-rare. Transfer the steaks to a carving board and leave to rest in a warm spot for about 10 minutes. Cut into thin diagonal slices (see photo, page 141) and serve with the sauce.

MAKE IT AHEAD
The Chimichurri Sauce can be made a day in advance and will be even more piquant. While steaks should be broiled at the last minute, you can oil and season them and dot with butter an hour before broiling. Let them sit in the pan at room temperature.

CHIMICHURRI SAUCE

MAKES ABOUT 1⅓ CUPS

1 cup chopped flat-leaf parsley

2 shallots, chopped

2 cloves garlic, chopped

2 tablespoons chopped fresh thyme, or 2 teaspoons dried

3 small dried red chiles, seeded and chopped, or ¾ teaspoon dried red-pepper flakes

¾ cup water

½ cup red-wine vinegar

6 tablespoons olive oil

½ teaspoon salt

⅛ teaspoon fresh-ground black pepper

In a food processor or blender, puree the parsley, shallots, garlic, thyme and chiles with the water, vinegar, oil, salt and pepper.

STANDING RIB ROAST WITH CHILE-PEPPER SPICE RUB

Nothing quite tops a standing rib roast for extravagant entertaining, and yet it's not difficult to cook. Here's an updated version, hot and spicy with garlic, cumin, coriander, cloves and cayenne. Ask the butcher to trim the fat on the roast to about one-eighth inch and to remove the chine bone so that the meat is easy to carve.

WINE RECOMMENDATION
This complexly spiced roast calls for a boldly flavored but uncomplicated red. A zinfandel, Australian shiraz or Washington merlot fills the bill.

SERVES 8

1	onion, minced
4	cloves garlic, minced
4	teaspoons paprika
4	teaspoons dried oregano
2	teaspoons dry mustard
2	teaspoons ground cumin
2	teaspoons ground coriander
2	teaspoons cayenne
2	teaspoons salt
2	teaspoons fresh-ground black pepper
1/2	teaspoon ground cloves
1	4-rib standing rib roast (about 8½ pounds), trimmed and chine bone removed

1. Puree the onion and garlic with the paprika, oregano, mustard, cumin, coriander, cayenne, salt, black pepper and cloves in a food processor or blender. Put the roast on a rack in a roasting pan and spread about half of the puree on all sides of the roast. Turn the roast fat-side up and let stand at room temperature for 2 hours.

2. Heat the oven to 400°. Roast the meat for 30 minutes. Reduce the oven temperature to 350° and cook 1 hour and 15 minutes longer. Use a spoon to spread the remaining paste over the meat; this assures that even if the fat on top has shrunk away from the meat, the entire roast will be covered with a flavorful spice crust. Continue roasting until cooked to your taste, about 20 minutes longer for medium-rare (140°). Transfer the roast to a carving board and leave to rest in a warm spot for about 15 minutes. Carve into ½-inch slices and serve at once.

—STEPHANIE LYNESS

MAKE IT AHEAD
You can make the spice rub up to a day ahead. The roast needs at least two hours of marinating (at room temperature) and can be coated and refrigerated for up to six hours.

CARVING A RIB ROAST

Set the roast, fat-side up, on a cutting board. Cut the first boneless slice, about one-half inch thick, down to the bone. Then cut horizontally against the bone (as shown) to release it. Cut the next slice including the first bone. Continue slicing in the same way to get four slices with the bone and four without. Or, cut the meat off the bones in one piece and then slice it.

TESTING FOR DONENESS

While experienced chefs can simply prod a large roast with a finger and know whether it's rare, medium or well-done, most cooks are better off with an instant-read thermometer to test for internal temperature. It's what we use and have found to be more accurate than the leave-in thermometers. To use an instant-read thermometer, insert it a couple of inches into the meat, without touching bone or fat, and leave for about thirty seconds before reading. Generally speaking, count on 125° for rare, 140° for medium-rare, 150° for medium, 155° for medium-well and 170° for well-done.

BRAISED OXTAILS WITH RED WINE AND PORTOBELLO MUSHROOMS

Despite the name, this bony cut of meat comes from the tail of beef or veal. It's usually cut by the butcher into one-and-a-half- to two-inch lengths, and it makes a wonderfully full-flavored stew. There is one drawback: The meat can be fatty. So be sure to trim the oxtails before cooking and to skim the sauce thoroughly.

WINE RECOMMENDATION
You can let your red-wine desires run free here—nearly any medium- to full-bodied red will taste great. Among the excellent choices would be a cabernet sauvignon, Chianti Riserva or Châteauneuf-du-Pape. If the budget allows, cooking with these wines will cement the match.

SERVES 8

- 8 pounds oxtails, trimmed of excess fat
- 1 pound baby carrots, or regular carrots cut into 2½-inch lengths
- 2 ribs celery, cut into 1-inch diagonal slices
- 24 small white onions, about 1 inch in diameter, peeled
- 1 14-ounce can (about 1¾ cups) tomatoes with their juice
- 6 sprigs plus 3 tablespoons chopped flat-leaf parsley
- 1 teaspoon peppercorns
- 1 bay leaf
- 2 bottles red wine (750 ml each)
- 1 cup flour
- 2 teaspoons salt
- ⅛ teaspoon fresh-ground black pepper
- 6 tablespoons cooking oil, more if needed
- 1½ pounds portobello mushrooms, cut into ½-inch slices
- 3 cups water, more if needed
- 1 tablespoon chopped fresh thyme, or 1 teaspoon dried
- 1 tablespoon chopped fresh sage, or 1 teaspoon dried
- 1 tablespoon chopped fresh oregano, or 1 teaspoon dried

1. In a large glass or stainless-steel bowl, combine the oxtails, carrots, celery, onions, tomatoes with their juice, parsley sprigs, peppercorns, bay leaf and wine. Cover and marinate overnight in the refrigerator. The next day, drain the meat and vegetables, reserving the marinade along with the tomatoes. Dry the oxtails, carrots, celery and onions very well with paper towels.

2. Heat the oven to 350°. Combine the flour with ½ teaspoon of the salt and the ground pepper. Dredge the oxtails in the flour and shake off the excess. In a large frying pan, heat 3 tablespoons of the oil over moderately high heat. Add as many oxtails as will fit in the pan without crowding and brown well on all sides, about

10 minutes. Transfer to a large roasting pan. Brown the remaining oxtails, adding more oil if needed, and transfer to the roasting pan.

3. In the frying pan, heat another tablespoon of the oil over moderate heat. Add the carrots, celery and onions and cook, stirring occasionally, until the vegetables are golden, about 5 minutes. Remove. Heat the remaining 2 tablespoons oil in the pan. Add the mushrooms and cook, stirring occasionally, until tender, about 5 minutes. Add the mushrooms to the other cooked vegetables.

4. Pour the reserved marinade, including the tomatoes, over the oxtails. Add as much of the water as needed to just cover the meat. Add 1 tablespoon of the chopped parsley, the thyme, sage, oregano and the remaining 1½ teaspoons salt. Cover with aluminum foil and bake 2½ hours. Add the vegetables and continue cooking the oxtails, uncovered, until very tender, about 1 hour longer.

5. Remove the oxtails and vegetables. Discard the bay leaf, peppercorns and parsley sprigs. Skim the excess fat from the sauce. Pour the sauce over the oxtails and top with the remaining 2 tablespoons parsley.

—Stephanie Lyness

MAKE IT AHEAD
This rich, rustic winter stew only gets better as it sits. It makes sense to prepare it completely at least a day, and several days if you like, before serving.

Chipotle-Chile Beef Stew with Butternut Squash

A chipotle-chile puree lends a distinctive hot and smoky taste to this flavorful stew. The sweetness of the squash and red bell peppers provides a pleasant contrast to the chiles.

WINE RECOMMENDATION
The smokiness and heat of this stew call for a fruity, soft red wine such as a Beaujolais, Australian shiraz or French Bandol.

SERVES 8

4½ cups water

3 dried chipotle chiles

5 onions, 1 cut into quarters, 4 chopped

4 cloves garlic

1 14-ounce can (about 1¾ cups) tomatoes, drained

2 teaspoons dried oregano

1 teaspoon dried thyme

3 tablespoons red-wine vinegar

2¾ teaspoons salt

¾ cup flour

⅛ teaspoon fresh-ground black pepper

5 pounds beef chuck, cut into 1½-inch cubes

3 tablespoons cooking oil, more if needed

1 large butternut squash (about 3 pounds), peeled, seeded and cut into 1-inch pieces

2 red bell peppers, cut into thin strips about 1½ inches long

2 limes, cut into wedges (optional)

1. Bring ½ cup of the water to a boil. Put the chiles in a bowl and pour the boiling water over them. Let the chiles soak until softened, about 20 minutes. Reserve the soaking liquid. Stem and seed the chiles. In a blender, puree the chiles, quartered onion, garlic, tomatoes, oregano and thyme with the vinegar and 2½ teaspoons of the salt.

2. Combine the flour with the remaining ¼ teaspoon salt and the pepper. Dredge the beef in the flour. Shake off the excess. Reserve 3 tablespoons of the dredging flour.

3. In a large pot, heat the oil over moderately high heat. Add about a third of the meat. Brown well on all sides, about 8 minutes, and remove. Brown the remaining beef in two more batches, adding more oil if needed. Remove.

4. Reduce the heat to moderately low. Add the chopped onions and cook, stirring occasionally, until soft, about 5 minutes. Add the reserved flour and cook, stirring, for 1 to 2 minutes. Raise the heat to moderately high. Add the chile puree and cook, scraping the bottom of the pot, for 3 minutes longer. ➤

5. Return the beef to the pot with any accumulated juice. Add the reserved chile-soaking liquid and the remaining 4 cups water and bring to a simmer over moderately high heat. Reduce the heat and cook at a bare simmer, partially covered, for 1 hour and 20 minutes. Add the squash and bell peppers and cook, partially covered, until the meat and vegetables are tender, about 25 minutes longer. Serve with lime wedges, if you like.

MAKE IT AHEAD
As with most stews, this one improves on keeping. You can make it several days in advance and simply reheat gently before serving.

COOKING OILS

Choose a reasonably priced all-purpose cooking oil for your kitchen cupboard. Any nut, seed or vegetable oil with a high smoking point is fine. Peanut, sunflower, safflower and corn oil can all be heated to 400° before they begin to smoke and to develop an unpleasant taste. Each oil has a different flavor, and you'll find your own favorite. Safflower is the only one with almost no flavor.

BEEF TENDERLOIN WITH PEPPERCORN AND MUSTARD-SEED CRUST

A roasted beef tenderloin is always an impressive sight, but nothing could be simpler to prepare and serve. This one is coated with a wonderfully pungent mixture of crushed black peppercorns, coriander seeds and mustard seeds, and is served with an easy sour-cream sauce that features two kinds of mustard. We like this beef best hot or warm, but it's good at room temperature, too.

WINE RECOMMENDATION

Paging zinfandel—the true, tooth-coating red zinfandel, as nature intended it—or a similarly robust Rhône wine such as Gigondas.

SERVES 8

- 1 cup sour cream
- 1 tablespoon peppercorns
- 1 tablespoon coriander seeds
- 1 tablespoon mustard seeds
- 2 teaspoons salt
- 3 pounds beef tenderloin
- 1 teaspoon cooking oil
- 1 tablespoon Dijon mustard
- 1 tablespoon grainy mustard
- ¼ teaspoon fresh-ground black pepper

1. Line a strainer with a piece of cheesecloth, a coffee filter or a paper towel. Put the sour cream in the strainer and set the strainer over a bowl. Let the sour cream drain for at least 1 hour.

2. Heat the oven to 425°. Oil a roasting pan. Grind the peppercorns and the coriander and mustard seeds in a spice or coffee grinder or in a mortar with a pestle. They should have a coarse consistency. Add the salt.

3. Rub the beef with the oil and then with the spice mixture. Put the tenderloin in a roasting pan and cook until done to your taste, about 25 minutes for medium-rare (140°). Transfer the meat to a carving board and leave to rest in a warm spot for about 10 minutes before slicing.

4. Meanwhile, transfer the sour cream to a bowl. Stir in both mustards and the pepper. Serve with the beef.

MAKE IT AHEAD

You can let the sour cream drain overnight in the refrigerator. Prepare the sauce up to a day in advance and refrigerate it; bring to room temperature before serving.

ROAST LOIN OF PORK
WITH GREEN-OLIVE FILLING

Here the green-olive tapenade from the grilled chicken breasts, page 119, is transformed into a stuffing for roast pork. You can ask your butcher to cut the pork loins for stuffing, or you can do it yourself (see step one below). In either case, the stuffing makes an attractive design in the sliced pork.

WINE RECOMMENDATION
The bold, rustic flavors of this dish call for a medium-bodied red with character and a contrasting fruitiness, like a *Crianza* Spanish Rioja.

SERVES 8

4   pounds boneless pork loin

1   cup good-quality green olives, pitted and chopped

2   cloves garlic

3   anchovy fillets, or ¾ teaspoon anchovy paste

½   cup flat-leaf parsley leaves

1   tablespoon lemon juice
    Fresh-ground black pepper

3   tablespoons olive oil

6   tablespoons dry bread crumbs

½   teaspoon salt, more if needed

1   cup dry white wine

1   cup Chicken Stock, page 276, or canned low-sodium chicken broth

1. Cut the pork loin crosswise into 2 equal pieces. With a sharp knife, start 1 inch from one of the ends and cut into the loin to make a pouch for stuffing. Without cutting quite through to the other side of the loin, continue until you're an inch away from the other end. Repeat for the second piece of pork loin.

2. In a food processor, combine the olives, garlic, anchovies, parsley, lemon juice, ⅛ teaspoon pepper and 1 tablespoon of the oil. Work the mixture to a coarse paste. Add the bread crumbs and pulse the mixture a few times. Taste for seasoning. The olives and anchovies are salty, so additional salt may not be needed.

3. Fill the pockets with the olive stuffing. Tie string at 2-inch intervals around each loin so the stuffing does not come out during cooking. Season the outside of the loins with the salt and ¼ teaspoon pepper.

4. Heat the oven to 325°. In a large, ovenproof pot, heat the remaining 2 tablespoons oil over moderately high heat. Add the loins and brown well on all sides, about 10 minutes. Add the wine and stock and bring to a boil. Transfer to the oven and cook 30 minutes. Cover and continue to cook the pork until done, basting it

occasionally, about 1 hour longer. Transfer the pork loins to a carving board and leave to rest in a warm spot for about 15 minutes.

5. Cut the meat into slices and serve with the pan juices.

—ERICA DE MANE

MAKE IT AHEAD
You can stuff, roll and tie the pork early on the day of the dinner party. If the meat has been refrigerated, add a few extra minutes to the cooking time.

Tie the pork loins, overlapping the meat somewhat to keep the stuffing in during cooking.

SUMMER FARE

If you love this roast hot out of the oven, don't bump it out of your repertoire when the weather turns steamy. You'll be surprised how delicious it is cooled to room temperature. Make it ahead, if you like. It's even easier to slice neatly when it's cold. Arrange nicely on a platter, cover with plastic wrap and leave long enough so that it's no longer ice cold. If the meat seems a bit dry, drizzle with Classic or Lemon Pepper Vinaigrette, page 274.

FRESH HAM WITH BALSAMIC-CARAMELIZED ONIONS

Fresh ham, also called leg of pork, makes a delicious roast. It is most often sold with the bone in, so you may have to order boneless ham from your butcher. Without the bone, the meat cooks in under two hours and carving is a breeze.

WINE RECOMMENDATION
The straightforward flavors of this preparation will allow the exotic juiciness of pinot noir (including red French Burgundy) to shine.

SERVES 8

3½ to 4 pounds boneless fresh ham (leg of pork), rolled and tied

2 teaspoons salt

Fresh-ground black pepper

2 tablespoons butter

2 pounds onions (about 6), cut into thin slices

¼ cup balsamic vinegar

3 tablespoons water, more if needed

¾ cup Chicken Stock, page 276, or canned low-sodium chicken broth

1. Heat the oven to 425°. Sprinkle the ham with ½ teaspoon of the salt and ¼ teaspoon pepper. Set it on a rack in a roasting pan and roast in the oven for 20 minutes. Reduce the oven temperature to 325° and continue roasting the ham until it is cooked to medium-well (155°), about 1 hour and 20 minutes.

2. Meanwhile, in a large stainless-steel frying pan, melt the butter over low heat. Add the onions, 1 teaspoon of the salt and ¼ teaspoon pepper. Cover and cook, stirring occasionally, until the onions are very soft, about 20 minutes. Add the vinegar and water and cook, uncovered, stirring occasionally, until the onions are golden brown, about 15 minutes longer. If the onions begin to stick, add a few more tablespoons water. Remove from the heat and set aside.

3. Transfer the ham to a carving board and leave to rest in a warm spot for about 15 minutes. Skim all of the fat from the roasting pan. Set the pan over moderately low heat and add the stock, the remaining ½ teaspoon salt and ⅛ teaspoon pepper. Bring to a simmer, scraping the bottom of the pan to dislodge any brown bits.

4. Reheat the onions. Cut the ham into thin slices and arrange on a platter. Moisten with the *jus* and serve with the onions.

MAKE IT AHEAD
The onions can be prepared early in the day. Reheat just before serving. Loosely covered with foil, the cooked ham will stay warm for at least thirty minutes.

WINE-BRAISED HAM WITH SPICED PEACH CHUTNEY

Oven-braised in white wine with aromatic vegetables, this ham makes a welcome change from ordinary baked ham. It can be served hot, warm or at room temperature. The gingery chutney nicely offsets the saltiness of the meat.

WINE RECOMMENDATION
Since you're cooking with white wine, the textbook choice would be to drink white wine as well, and a mildly sweet riesling or chenin blanc will complement the contrasting flavors. On the other hand, so will a drier-style, fruity rosé, which also adds a burst of color to the presentation.

SERVES 8

- 2 carrots, chopped
- 2 onions, chopped
- 1 rib celery, chopped
- 1 leek, white and light-green part only, split lengthwise, chopped and washed well
- 10 parsley sprigs
- 10 peppercorns
- ½ teaspoon dried thyme
- 1 bay leaf
- 1 6-pound smoked picnic ham (shoulder)
- 1 bottle dry white wine (750 ml)

  Spiced Peach Chutney, opposite page

1. Heat the oven to 325°. In a large, ovenproof pot, combine the carrots, onions, celery, leek, parsley, peppercorns, thyme and bay leaf. Set the ham on top of the vegetables and add the wine. Bring to a simmer over moderately high heat.

2. Cover the pot, transfer to the oven and cook, basting the ham occasionally, until done, about 2 hours and 15 minutes. Transfer the ham to a carving board and leave to rest in a warm spot for about 15 minutes before slicing. Serve warm or at room temperature, with the chutney.

MAKE IT AHEAD
Cut up the vegetables and get the ham all set to pop in the oven hours before cooking it, if you like. Loosely covered with foil, the cooked ham will stay warm for at least thirty minutes. If you plan to serve it at room temperature, you can braise the ham two or even three days ahead, let cool and refrigerate. Remove from the refrigerator at least one hour before serving. You can make the chutney ahead, too. It will keep, covered and refrigerated, for at least a week.

SPICED PEACH CHUTNEY

Three types of ginger add real zing to this easy chutney. It's delicious with roast chicken and most other poultry, as well as with fresh and cured pork.

MAKES 2 CUPS

- 4 peaches, peeled, pitted and chopped, or one 12-ounce bag unsweetened frozen peaches, partially thawed and chopped
- 1 onion, chopped fine
- 2 tablespoons minced crystallized ginger
- 1 tablespoon minced fresh ginger
- 1 tablespoon brown sugar
- ½ teaspoon ground ginger
- ¼ teaspoon salt
- ¼ cup cider vinegar
- 2 tablespoons orange juice

In a large stainless-steel saucepan, combine all the ingredients. Bring to a simmer over moderate heat. Reduce the heat and simmer, stirring occasionally, until the peaches are soft but some pieces remain intact, 15 to 20 minutes. Remove the chutney from the heat and let cool.

PEELING PEACHES

The skins will often slip easily from perfectly ripe peaches. If yours are tougher customers, blanch them in a large saucepan of boiling water for twenty to thirty seconds. Drain and cool in cold water. Using your fingers or a small knife, pull off the skins.

HAM—CURED OR FRESH

With all the varieties out there, no wonder the term *ham* is confusing. Literally, it means simply the ham, or leg, of the pig. What we generally think of as ham is cured. The cure changes the flavor and texture of the meat and gives it a rosy-red color. Dry-cured hams are those such as prosciutto that are cured with salt and then air-dried rather than smoked. They are meant to be eaten raw. The most common hams sold today are cured with either salt or a salt-and-water brine and are smoked as well. To confuse matters, any cut that is prepared in this way, not just the leg, is now called ham. Fresh ham is quite different from the others in that it is the *uncured* leg, neither salted nor smoked. It tastes similar to other cuts of pork and makes a wonderful roast (see Fresh Ham with Balsamic-Caramelized Onions, page 155).

PORK TENDERLOIN
WITH POMEGRANATE SAUCE

Prepare this dish with fresh pomegranates when they're in season, during autumn and early winter. Or you can buy pomegranate juice at Middle Eastern markets and some health-food stores any time of year.

WINE RECOMMENDATION
Riesling and gewürztraminer are both classic accompaniments to pork in German and Alsatian kitchens, and those wines, with a classic crisp acidity balanced by a touch of sweetness, stand up beautifully to mildly sweet, sour and spicy sauces.

SERVES 8

1   orange
1   teaspoon grated lemon zest
½   teaspoon fennel seeds
½   teaspoon cumin seeds
½   teaspoon peppercorns
2   shallots, cut into thin slices
2   cloves garlic, chopped
2   tablespoons olive oil
3   pounds pork tenderloins
1¼ teaspoons salt
¼   teaspoon fresh-ground black pepper
4   tablespoons butter
1   small onion, chopped fine
1   cup pomegranate juice, from about 3 pomegranates
¼   cup dried currants

2   cups Chicken Stock, page 276, or canned low-sodium chicken broth
½   cup pomegranate seeds (optional)

1. Grate the zest from the orange and squeeze the juice. You should have about ½ cup of orange juice. In a large, shallow glass dish or stainless-steel pan, combine the orange zest and juice, the lemon zest, fennel seeds, cumin seeds, peppercorns, shallots, garlic and olive oil. Add the pork and turn to coat. Cover and leave to marinate at least 12 hours in the refrigerator.

2. Heat the oven to 450°. Remove the pork from the marinade and dry with paper towels. Season the pork with ½ teaspoon of the salt and ⅛ teaspoon of the pepper. In a large frying pan, heat 2 tablespoons of the butter over moderately high heat. Add the pork and brown well on all sides, about 5 minutes. Transfer to a roasting pan.

3. Add the onion to the frying pan and cook over moderately low heat, stirring occasionally, until very soft, about 8 minutes. Add the pomegranate juice and currants and bring to a boil, scraping the bottom of the pan to dislodge any brown bits. Add the stock, the remaining ¾

teaspoon salt and the remaining ⅛ teaspoon pepper. Bring back to a boil and cook until reduced to about 1¼ cups, about 15 minutes longer.

4. Just before serving, cook the pork tenderloins in the oven until done to medium, about 15 minutes. Transfer the pork to a carving board and leave to rest in a warm spot for about 10 minutes.

5. Meanwhile, cut the remaining 2 tablespoons butter into 6 pieces. Bring the sauce back to a simmer. Over the lowest possible heat, whisk in the butter in three batches, adding each batch when the previous one is incorporated. The butter should not melt completely but just soften to form a creamy sauce. Cut the pork diagonally into 24 thick slices (see photo, page 141). Arrange 3 slices on each plate and spoon the sauce around the meat. Sprinkle with the pomegranate seeds and serve.

—STEPHEN KALT
SPARTINA

MAKE IT AHEAD
Begin marinating the pork a day ahead, if you like. Brown the meat and prepare the sauce a few hours in advance. Then just before serving, cook the pork and finish the sauce.

PINK PORK IS SAFE

For years Americans were advised to cook pork until well-done in order to prevent trichinosis, an illness caused by parasites in the meat. With today's higher meat standards, the illness is uncommon (on average, under a hundred reported cases a year in the whole country). In any case, we now know that an internal temperature of 150° kills the parasites. At 150° even our currently available lean pork retains some juiciness. So cook your pork to medium, still ever so slightly pink, and enjoy the difference.

JUICING POMEGRANATES

We have to admit that extracting juice from pomegranates can be a messy business. Some people suggest first rolling the fruit on a hard surface to rupture all the pulp inside and then poking a hole in the skin and pouring the juice out. Sounds easy, but often the skin breaks prematurely, sending seeds hurtling all over you and your kitchen. The best method we've found is to cut the pomegranate in half and to squeeze it on a juicer or with a reamer, as you would an orange. Either way, the seeds scatter a bit. Put the pulp and leftover seeds in a sieve and press them with a ladle to get all the juice.

POLENTA LASAGNE

Parmesan-flavored polenta layered with Italian sausage, tomato sauce and plenty of mozzarella cheese is a combination of two Italian favorites. The result is both delicious and comforting.

WINE RECOMMENDATION
A not-too-fancy Italian red is the perfect choice with this hearty, rustic dish. Try a Vino Nobile di Montepulciano, a young Chianti or a dolcetto.

SERVES 8

2¼ quarts plus ⅓ cup water

1 tablespoon plus ½ teaspoon salt

2¼ cups coarse or medium cornmeal

6 tablespoons olive oil

1¾ cups grated Parmesan cheese

1½ pounds mild Italian sausage

1 onion, chopped

1 35-ounce can (about 4 cups) crushed tomatoes

1 teaspoon sugar

⅛ teaspoon fresh-ground black pepper

1½ pounds whole-milk mozzarella, cut into ¼-inch slices

1. In a large pot, bring 2¼ quarts of the water and 1 tablespoon of the salt to a boil. Add the cornmeal in a slow stream, whisking constantly. Whisk in 4 tablespoons of the oil. Reduce the heat to moderate and simmer, stirring frequently with a wooden spoon, until the polenta is very thick and pulls away from the sides of the pan, about 20 minutes. Stir in ½ cup of the Parmesan.

Spread the polenta evenly in a 10-by-14-inch baking dish or roasting pan and refrigerate until set, about 30 minutes.

2. Remove the sausage meat from its casing. In a large pot, heat the remaining 2 tablespoons oil over moderately low heat. Add the onion and cook, stirring occasionally, until translucent, about 5 minutes. Add the tomatoes, the remaining ½ teaspoon salt and the sugar and bring to a boil. Reduce the heat and simmer partially covered, stirring occasionally, until very thick, about 45 minutes. Add the pepper.

3. Meanwhile, in a large frying pan, brown the sausage over moderately high heat, stirring occasionally, about 5 minutes. Drain off the excess fat. Stir in 1¼ cups of the tomato sauce. Add the remaining ⅓ cup water to the remaining tomato sauce.

4. Heat the oven to 375°. Unmold the polenta onto a work surface and cut it into quarters to make slicing it into layers easier. Cut each quarter horizontally into two even layers. Spread 1 cup of the tomato sauce on the bottom of the baking dish or roasting pan. Put one of the polenta layers back into the dish or pan, covering the tomato sauce. Top with a third of the mozzarella. Spread the sausage mixture over the

cheese in an even layer. Top with about half of the remaining Parmesan and then another third of the mozzarella. Cover with the remaining layer of polenta and spread with the remaining tomato sauce. Top with the remaining Parmesan and mozzarella.

5. Bake the lasagne until brown and bubbling, about 35 minutes. Cover with aluminum foil and let rest in a warm spot for about 20 minutes. Cut into squares and serve.

MAKE IT AHEAD
You can prepare the lasagne, right up to the point of baking, a day in advance. Cover it with plastic wrap and refrigerate. Either take the lasagne out of the refrigerator about one hour before serving, so that it has time to come to room temperature before baking, or add a few minutes to the baking time.

BROWNING SAUSAGE

Unlike ground beef, which separates easily during browning, sausage meat tends to clump together. To help prevent sticking, mash the sausage meat with a fork as you cook it.

GARLIC-RUBBED RACK OF LAMB

We tried rubbing lamb racks with various flavorings before roasting but in the end decided that the old standby, garlic, tasted the best of all. Be sure to ask the butcher to remove the chine bone so that after cooking, you'll have no problem cutting the racks into individual chops.

WINE RECOMMENDATION
Lamb and red wine are two of the traditional products from the fields of Bordeaux, and a familiar combination at the region's tables. The Bordelais are onto something here.

SERVES 8

6   cloves garlic, minced

1   teaspoon salt

1/4   teaspoon fresh-ground black pepper

4   racks of lamb, trimmed

1/2   cup dry white wine

1   cup Veal or Beef Stock, page 277, or canned low-sodium beef broth

1. Heat the oven to 450°. Rub the garlic, salt and pepper all over each of the racks of lamb.

2. Set the racks, fat-side down, in a large roasting pan and roast in the oven 15 minutes. Turn the racks, reduce the heat to 400° and roast until cooked to your taste, about 10 minutes longer for medium-rare (140°). Transfer the racks to a carving board and leave to rest in a warm spot for about 10 minutes.

3. Meanwhile, skim off most of the fat from the roasting pan. Set the pan over moderate heat, add the wine and stock and bring to a boil, scraping the bottom of the pan to dislodge any brown bits. Simmer for 5 minutes.

4. Cut the racks between the ribs into individual chops. Put 3 chops on each plate and spoon some of the *jus* over the meat.

MAKE IT AHEAD
Because this recipe is so simple, there's almost nothing to do in advance. You can rub the lamb with the seasonings and put the racks in the pan a few hours ahead, if you like.

BRAISED LAMB SHANKS WITH CARAMELIZED ONIONS AND MINT

Lamb shanks are flavorful cuts of meat that make their own sauce during braising. Caramelized onions enrich the finished dish, and the refreshing taste of mint complements the deeper flavors.

WINE RECOMMENDATION
A full-bodied, tannic, spicy petite sirah from California is perfect for this pungent, rustic lamb preparation.

SERVES 8

- ¾ cup flour
- 2¼ teaspoons salt
-     Fresh-ground black pepper
- 8   lamb shanks (about ¾ pound each)
- 2   tablespoons cooking oil, more if needed
- 4   tablespoons butter
- 8   medium onions, 2 chopped, 6 cut into thin slices
- 3   ribs celery, chopped
- 2   carrots, chopped
- 2   cloves garlic, minced
- 2   cups dry white wine
- 1   quart Beef Stock, page 277, or canned low-sodium beef broth
- 2   cups plus 2 tablespoons water
- 1   teaspoon dried marjoram
- 2   tablespoons chopped fresh mint

1. Heat the oven to 325°. Combine the flour with ¼ teaspoon of the salt and ⅛ teaspoon pepper. Dredge the lamb shanks in the flour and shake off the excess. In a large, ovenproof pot, heat the oil with 2 tablespoons of the butter over moderately high heat. Add four of the lamb shanks, brown well on all sides, about 10 minutes in all, and remove. Brown the remaining shanks, adding more oil if needed. Remove the shanks and reduce the heat to moderately low.

2. Add the chopped onions, the celery, carrots and garlic and cook, stirring occasionally, until soft, about 5 minutes. Add the wine and simmer 2 minutes, scraping the bottom of the pan to dislodge any brown bits. Return the shanks to the pot. Add the stock, 2 cups of the water, the remaining 2 teaspoons salt and the marjoram. Bring to a simmer. Cover and cook in the oven 45 minutes. Turn the shanks and continue cooking, uncovered, until the meat is very tender, about 1 hour longer.

3. Meanwhile, heat the remaining 2 tablespoons butter in a large frying pan over low heat. Add the sliced onions, cover and cook, stirring frequently, until the onions are very soft, about 20 minutes. Uncover, raise the heat to moderate and cook, stirring, until the onions are golden brown, about 15 minutes longer. Add the remaining

2 tablespoons water and scrape the bottom of the pan to dislodge any brown bits. Set the caramelized onions aside.

4. Remove the shanks and strain the sauce, pressing about half of the vegetables though the strainer into the sauce to thicken it slightly. You should have about 4 cups. If necessary, boil the sauce down to reduce the volume. Add the caramelized onions, mint and ¼ teaspoon pepper and reheat. Pour the sauce over the lamb shanks and serve.

MAKE IT AHEAD

Lamb shanks are one of those lovely dishes that are short on work time and long on flavor. They just get better when made in advance. You can braise the lamb and finish the sauce days ahead. Let them come to room temperature and then reheat them together in a 325° oven for about half an hour, or somewhat longer if straight from the refrigerator. Add the chopped fresh mint just before serving.

Rather than trying to slice a rolling object, cut your onions in half lengthwise first, place them flat on a work surface and cut crosswise.

Boneless Leg of Lamb with Pommery Mustard, Garlic and Rosemary

Here's a great way to serve a leg of lamb without the difficulty of carving around the bone. Studding the lamb with garlic and spreading it with Pommery mustard and rosemary makes a beautiful roast that's full of flavor.

WINE RECOMMENDATION
The ripe berry flavors of a young New World cabernet sauvignon will provide a piquant contrast both to the roasted meat and to the mustard savor.

SERVES 8

1 boneless leg of lamb (about 5 pounds), rolled and tied

4 cloves garlic, cut in half lengthwise

2 tablespoons cooking oil

1/2 cup Pommery mustard or other grainy mustard

2 tablespoons chopped fresh rosemary

1 1/2 teaspoons grated lemon zest

1/4 teaspoon dry mustard

1/4 teaspoon salt

1/4 teaspoon fresh-ground black pepper

1. With a small knife, cut eight shallow incisions in the lamb and push a piece of garlic into each. Rub the roast with the oil.

2. In a small bowl, combine the Pommery mustard, rosemary, lemon zest, dry mustard, salt and pepper. Coat the lamb with the mustard mixture. Put the lamb on a rack in a roasting pan and let sit at room temperature for at least 1 hour.

3. Heat the oven to 425°. Put the lamb in the oven and roast for 20 minutes. Reduce the temperature to 325° and continue roasting until the meat is cooked to your taste, about 1 hour and 10 minutes for medium-rare (140°). Transfer the roast to a carving board and leave to rest in a warm spot for about 15 minutes before slicing.

—Michael Rich

MAKE IT AHEAD
You can prepare the roast by inserting the garlic and coating with the mustard up to four hours in advance. Keep the lamb refrigerated. One hour before roasting, remove the lamb from the refrigerator to bring it to room temperature. Not only is preparing the roast ahead practical, it boosts the flavors of garlic, mustard and rosemary in the meat.

WHAT IS POMMERY MUSTARD?

The full name of the mustard we call for in this recipe is Moutarde de Meaux Pommery, which is a delicious coarse-grained mustard from France. It's somewhat milder than smooth Dijon mustard and has a hint of sweetness. You can certainly use other good brands of grainy mustard, though they may vary slightly in flavor, some sweeter or hotter or more pungent.

SUMMER THRILL

Lamb is an elegant alternative to the usual barbecue fare, and its delicate flavor and natural tenderness make it ideal for grilling. Instead of the boneless leg of lamb in this recipe, use two bone-in lamb butts, about three-and-a-half pounds each. (The butt is the meaty top part of the leg.) Indirect heat works best for large cuts such as this one; so push the coals off to one side of the fire grate once they're covered with light-grey ash, set the cooking grill in place and put the lamb on the side opposite the fire. Cook, covered, for about an hour. Begin checking for doneness after about forty-five minutes. For that special smoky taste, add hickory wood chips to the fire halfway through the cooking time.

MOROCCAN LAMB WITH VEGETABLE COUSCOUS

A savory marinade seasons this tender cut of lamb. If weather permits outside cooking, or you have a stove-top grill, we suggest grilling the meat, which gives a flavorful crusty exterior. Of course broiling works just fine, too.

WINE RECOMMENDATION
Look for a rich red wine like those Morocco itself produces (or a Château Musar from Lebanon). More readily available are choices like Côtes du Rhône, zinfandel or Australian shiraz.

SERVES 8

½ cup cooking oil

1½ tablespoons grated onion

2 tablespoons lemon juice

2 cloves garlic, minced

2½ teaspoons ground coriander

1½ teaspoons ground cumin

1½ teaspoons salt

½ teaspoon fresh-ground black pepper

Large pinch cayenne

3½ to 4 pounds butterflied leg of lamb

Vegetable Couscous, page 189

1. In a large, shallow glass dish or stainless-steel pan, combine the oil, onion, lemon juice, garlic, coriander, cumin, salt, black pepper and cayenne. Add the lamb and rub the mixture all over the meat. Cover and let marinate in the refrigerator 1½ to 4 hours.

2. Light the grill or heat the broiler. Grill or broil the lamb for 5 minutes. Turn the meat and cook until done to your taste, about 5 minutes longer for medium-rare (140°). Some pieces of meat are thicker than others; so you may need to adjust the cooking time accordingly.

3. Transfer the lamb to a carving board and leave to rest in a warm spot for about 10 minutes. Cut the meat into thin diagonal slices (see photo, page 141) and serve with the Vegetable Couscous.

MAKE IT AHEAD
The lamb must be marinated at least one-and-a-half hours before cooking and can linger in the marinade for up to four hours. When you're ready to serve, the cooking takes only about eight minutes.

VENISON STEW
WITH PARSNIPS AND ROSEMARY

This tasty, stylish stew, with sweet parsnips and dried cranberries, is a hunter's dream. If you don't even know any hunters, we encourage you to try this recipe anyway. The meat is available from most butchers in autumn.

WINE RECOMMENDATION
This is a chance to bring out a true winter-weight red such as a Côte Rôtie from the Rhône, a Barolo from Italy or a fine cabernet sauvignon from almost anywhere.

SERVES 8

1	cup flour
2¼	teaspoons salt
	Fresh-ground black pepper
4	pounds boneless venison shoulder, cut into 1-inch cubes
3	tablespoons cooking oil, more if needed
3	tablespoons butter
2	onions, chopped
3	ribs celery, chopped
1½	teaspoons chopped fresh rosemary, or ½ teaspoon dried
2	bay leaves
2	cloves
2	cups red wine
1	quart Veal or Beef Stock, page 277, or canned low-sodium beef broth
5	parsnips, peeled and cut into 1½-by-½-inch sticks
24	small mushrooms
⅓	cup dried cranberries

1. Combine the flour with ¼ teaspoon of the salt and ⅛ teaspoon pepper. Dredge the venison in the flour. Shake off the excess.

2. In a large pot, heat the oil and butter over moderately high heat. Add a third of the meat. Brown well on all sides, about 8 minutes. Remove. Brown the remaining meat in two more batches, adding more oil if needed. Remove.

3. Add the onions, celery, rosemary, bay leaves and cloves. Cook until the onions are translucent, about 5 minutes.

4. Return the meat to the pot with any accumulated juice. Add the wine, stock, the remaining 2 teaspoons salt and ¼ teaspoon pepper. Bring to a simmer over moderately high heat. Reduce the heat and simmer, covered, until the venison is almost tender, about 1½ hours.

5. Add the parsnips and cook for 20 minutes. Add the mushrooms and dried cranberries. Simmer until the meat and vegetables are tender, about 10 minutes longer. If the stew seems too thick, add some stock or water.

—ERICA DE MANE

MAKE IT AHEAD
You can prepare the stew through step four several days ahead but don't peel or cut the parsnips too far in advance. Reheat the stew and finish the recipe as directed.

LOW-FAT VENISON

Because full-flavored venison has little fat, the meat is perilously easy to overcook to the dry stage. Depending on the cut, venison should be either cooked briefly to medium-rare or very slowly braised or stewed. Be especially careful not to let this stew boil, which would assure you of dry meat. Keep it at a bare simmer; the liquid should move just slightly and only a few bubbles break the surface.

PARSNIPS ANYONE?

Too many people pass up parsnips. That can only be because too few cooks have tasted the vegetable's sweet, nutty flavor. A parsnip isn't at all like a turnip, which we admit can take some getting used to. Parsnips look like stocky, albino carrots. We predict love at first bite. For the best flavor, though, they shouldn't be wider than about two inches at the stem end.

WILD-MUSHROOM AND GOAT-CHEESE LASAGNE

With its earthy wild mushrooms, butternut squash and goat cheese, this lasagne is a sophisticated twist on an old entertaining favorite. By rights it doesn't belong in this book, but it tastes so good that we couldn't resist including it. Don't be discouraged by the long preparation time. It can all be done in advance so that you can relax with your guests and enjoy this sumptuous vegetarian dinner.

WINE RECOMMENDATION
This is prime territory for pinot noir, a wine that will match this combination with fruitiness and a touch of smoky, oaky earthiness.

SERVES 8

½ ounce dried porcini mushrooms

½ cup boiling water

1 butternut squash (about 2 pounds), peeled, seeded and cut into ¼-inch slices

3 tablespoons olive oil

2½ teaspoons salt

1½ pounds mixed wild mushrooms, such as shiitake, cremini and portobello

1 pound white mushrooms

4 shallots, sliced

Fresh-ground black pepper

⅓ cup cognac or other brandy

1½ pounds mild goat cheese, such as Montrachet, at room temperature

1¾ cups heavy cream

2 eggs

2 cloves garlic, minced

2 tablespoons chopped flat-leaf parsley

1 head escarole (about 1½ pounds), leaves cut into 2-inch pieces

1 pound dried lasagne noodles

1. Put the dried mushrooms in a small bowl and pour the boiling water over them. Soak until softened, about 20 minutes. Remove the mushrooms and strain their liquid into a bowl through a sieve lined with a paper towel. Rinse the mushrooms well to remove any remaining grit and chop them.

2. Heat the oven to 375°. Put the squash slices on a baking sheet, brush with 1 tablespoon of the oil and sprinkle with ¼ teaspoon of the salt. Cover with aluminum foil and bake until the squash is tender, about 25 minutes. Set aside.

3. If using shiitakes or portobellos, remove the stems. Slice all of the mushrooms. In a large frying pan or pot, heat the remaining 2 tablespoons oil over moderately low heat. Add the shallots. Cook, stirring

172

occasionally, until translucent, about 5 minutes. Increase the heat to moderately high. Add the chopped porcini and sliced fresh mushrooms, $1\frac{1}{2}$ teaspoons of the salt and $\frac{1}{4}$ teaspoon pepper. Cook until soft, about 8 minutes. Add the porcini liquid and cognac. Cook, stirring occasionally, until almost dry, about 10 minutes.

4. With an electric mixer, blend the goat cheese, $\frac{3}{4}$ cup of the cream, the eggs, garlic, parsley, $\frac{1}{2}$ teaspoon of the salt and $\frac{1}{8}$ teaspoon pepper. Transfer $\frac{3}{4}$ cup of the mixture to another bowl and stir in the remaining 1 cup cream. Reserve this thinner mixture to top the lasagne.

5. In a large pot of boiling, salted water, cook the escarole 2 minutes. Remove with a slotted spoon. Rinse with cold water and drain thoroughly. Squeeze a handful at a time to remove as much water as possible. Chop the escarole and season with the remaining $\frac{1}{4}$ teaspoon salt. Cook the lasagne in the same pot until almost tender but still slightly underdone, about 10 minutes. Drain. Rinse with cold water and dry on paper towels.

6. To assemble the lasagne, lightly brush a 10-by-14-inch baking dish or roasting pan with oil. Lay several strips of pasta, slightly overlapping, in the pan. Spread a third of the goat-cheese mixture on the noodles and top with a third of the mushrooms, squash and escarole. Add two more layers of pasta, goat cheese and vegetables. Finish with a final layer of pasta. Pour the reserved cream mixture over the lasagne.

7. Cover with foil and bake 1 hour. Uncover and continue baking the lasagne until bubbling and hot in the center, about 30 minutes longer. Let rest in a warm spot 15 minutes before cutting.

—Katherine Alford

MAKE IT AHEAD

The lasagne can be assembled a full day in advance, but don't pour the reserved cream mixture over the lasagne until just before baking. Simply let the lasagne come to room temperature, top with the reserved sauce and bake it before serving. If you don't have time to let the lasagne warm up before baking, add a few minutes to the cooking time.

SIDE DISHES

ROASTED MEDITERRANEAN VEGETABLES

Roasting brings out the best in vegetables, caramelizing them to a sweet golden brown. An additional secret here is adding a little feta cheese and fresh herbs to the vegetables in the final stages of cooking.

SERVES 8

1 large red onion, cut into 1-inch pieces

2 heads garlic, cloves separated and peeled

2 fennel bulbs, each cut into 8 wedges

2 red bell peppers, cut into 1½-inch squares

1 eggplant, cut into 1½-inch cubes

1½ pounds small new potatoes, cut into halves, or larger ones, cut into chunks

¾ pound baby carrots

½ pound green beans, cut into 1½-inch pieces

½ cup olive oil

2½ teaspoons salt

¼ teaspoon fresh-ground black pepper

3 tablespoons chopped mixed fresh herbs, such as marjoram, thyme and rosemary, or 1 tablespoon dried herbs

½ cup dry vermouth or dry white wine

¼ pound feta cheese, crumbled

3 tablespoons chopped fresh basil or flat-leaf parsley

1. Put one oven rack in the upper third of the oven and another in the lower third. Heat the oven to 500°.

2. In a large bowl, combine the vegetables and oil. Sprinkle the vegetables with the salt, pepper and dried herbs, if using, and mix well. Divide the vegetables between two large roasting pans and spread each batch in an even layer. Sprinkle with the vermouth.

3. Roast the vegetables in the oven for 15 minutes. Stir them and then switch the pans from one rack to the other. Roast another 15 minutes. Divide the cheese and the fresh herbs, if using, between the two pans and mix well. Rotate the pans again and continue roasting until the vegetables are well browned, 15 to 20 minutes longer. Serve topped with the basil or parsley.

—JIM FLINT

MAKE IT AHEAD
You can prepare all of the vegetables for cooking, except the potatoes, and toss them with the oil hours ahead. When ready to roast, cut the potatoes and add them to the rest of the vegetables. You can complete the roasted vegetables up to half an hour in advance and keep them in a 150° oven. ➤

KEEPING FRESH HERBS GREEN

Some fresh herbs, such as basil and oregano, turn brown soon after they are chopped. When using these herbs, it's best to chop them with a stainless- rather than carbon-steel knife and to do so just before adding them to the dish. Or you can chop the herbs in advance and immediately stir them into a little oil.

THE TOUGH HERB

With Mediterranean-style grilling and roasting all the rage, it's easy to get carried away and start sprinkling rose- mary everywhere. We love it, too; just make sure, though, that you chop both the fresh and the dried herb into fine bits. Even with lengthy cooking, spiky rosemary leaves remain hard and unpleasant to eat if left whole or in large pieces.

RED, YELLOW AND PURPLE POTATOES

If you want to make Roasted Mediter- ranean Vegetables, previous page, es- pecially colorful, mix the potatoes. You can use half a pound of small red new potatoes, half a pound of Yukon Gold and half a pound of small purple new potatoes.

SPICY GREEN BEANS WITH GARLIC AND GINGER

This quick stir-fry can be made with broccoli, sugar snap peas or snow peas as well as with green beans.

SERVES 8

2   pounds green beans

3   tablespoons cooking oil

2   cloves garlic, minced

1   teaspoon grated fresh ginger

1   scallion including green top, chopped

⅛ to ¼ teaspoon dried red-pepper flakes

½   teaspoon salt

2   tablespoons soy sauce

2   tablespoons chopped cilantro

1.   In a large pot of boiling, salted water, cook the beans until tender, about 10 minutes. Drain, rinse with cold water and drain again thoroughly.

2.   In a wok or large frying pan, heat the oil over moderately high heat. Add the garlic and cook, stirring, until fragrant, about 30 seconds. Add the ginger, scallion and red-pepper flakes and cook, stirring, about 15 seconds longer.

3.   Raise the heat to high, add the beans and salt and cook, stirring constantly, until heated through, 1 to 2 minutes. Add the soy sauce and cilantro and cook, stirring

frequently, until the soy sauce is reduced to a glaze, about 1 minute longer.

—STEPHANIE LYNESS

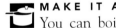

MAKE IT AHEAD
You can boil the beans a day ahead and keep them wrapped in the refrigerator, but don't actually stir-fry until just before serving.

GREAT GINGER

Grate ginger on the small holes of a standard grater and discard the fibrous part of the root that stays in your hand. Grated ginger gives more flavor than minced.

ROASTED ASPARAGUS WITH BROWN BUTTER

Roasting asparagus is easier than boiling or steaming and also makes the tender, succulent spears more flavorful than the other methods. Here, fragrant, slightly nutty-tasting brown butter lends even more depth of flavor.

SERVES 8

3 tablespoons butter

3 pounds asparagus

1 tablespoon olive oil

¾ teaspoon salt

½ teaspoon fresh-ground black pepper

1. Heat the oven to 450°. In a small saucepan, melt the butter over moderate heat and cook until golden brown, about 2 minutes. Remove from the heat and cover to keep warm.

2. Snap off the tough ends of the asparagus and discard them. On a large baking sheet, toss the asparagus with the oil, salt and pepper. Spread the asparagus out on the baking sheet and roast until just tender, 5 to 7 minutes for thin spears, 8 to 10 minutes for medium or 10 to 12 for thick spears.

3. Transfer the asparagus to a platter or individual plates and pour the brown butter over the spears.

MAKE IT AHEAD
The brown butter can be made ahead and reheated. The asparagus, though, looks and tastes better when served immediately rather than cooked and then warmed over. You can toss the spears in the oil, salt and pepper, spread them on the baking sheet hours ahead and wait until the last minute to roast them. Or you can serve the roasted asparagus at room temperature with extra olive oil rather than the brown butter.

BROCCOLI RABE WITH OVEN-DRIED TOMATOES AND PINE NUTS

Hours of slow drying give even pale, tasteless winter tomatoes a sweet, concentrated flavor that complements the somewhat bitter taste of the broccoli rabe. The tomatoes work well with broccoli, green beans and cauliflower, too, as does the whole recipe. Broccoli rabe, the old Italian favorite, used to be something of a specialty item in America, but you can find it in most supermarkets now. When fresh, it's bright green and has tender stems. Old broccoli rabe can be tough.

SERVES 8

8 plum tomatoes, cored and cut in half lengthwise, or 16 sun-dried tomato halves

1¾ teaspoons salt

3 tablespoons pine nuts

2½ pounds broccoli rabe, trimmed and cut into 1½-inch pieces

⅓ cup olive oil

3 cloves garlic, minced

2½ teaspoons chopped fresh rosemary, or ¾ teaspoon dried

2 teaspoons lemon juice

⅛ teaspoon fresh-ground black pepper

1. Put the plum tomatoes, if using, cut-side up on a baking sheet and sprinkle with 1 teaspoon of the salt. Let stand 1 hour.

2. Heat the oven to 200°. Dry the tomatoes in the oven until shriveled but still juicy (they shouldn't be hard and dry), about 6 hours. Let them cool and then cut them crosswise into thin slices. Or, if using sun-dried tomatoes, cut each half into thin slices.

3. In a small frying pan, toast the pine nuts over moderately low heat, stirring frequently, until golden brown, about 4 minutes. Or toast in a 350° oven for 6 minutes.

4. In a large pot of boiling, salted water, cook the broccoli rabe until tender, about 4 minutes. Drain. Heat the oil in the same pot over moderate heat. Add the garlic and rosemary and sauté, stirring, for 30 seconds. Add the broccoli rabe and the remaining ¾ teaspoon salt and cook, stirring, until hot. Stir in the tomatoes. Remove from the heat and add the pine nuts, lemon juice and pepper.

—STEPHANIE LYNESS

MAKE IT AHEAD
You might want to dry double the number of tomatoes while you're at it since they keep so well. Packed in a jar, covered with olive oil and refrigerated, they'll last at least a couple of weeks. The pine nuts can be toasted well ahead, too. And you can boil the broccoli rabe a day before serving.

SAUTEED CUCUMBERS WITH PROSCIUTTO AND CREAM

Though popular in France, cooked cucumbers are a novelty to most Americans. They are delicious simply sautéed in butter and even better when given a Northern Italian twist with prosciutto and cream.

SERVES 8

4½ pounds cucumbers (about 7), peeled, seeded and cut crosswise into ¼-inch slices

1½ tablespoons white-wine vinegar

¾ teaspoon sugar

1 teaspoon salt

6 tablespoons butter

¾ cup heavy cream

3 ounces thin-sliced prosciutto, cut into thin strips

¼ cup chopped flat-leaf parsley

¼ teaspoon fresh-ground black pepper

1. In a large bowl, combine the cucumbers, vinegar, sugar and ⅛ teaspoon of the salt. Let sit for 20 minutes, then drain. (The vinegar and salt draw out excess water).

2. In a large frying pan, melt the butter over moderately high heat. Add the cucumbers and the remaining salt and cook, stirring frequently, until the cucumbers are tender but not brown, about 8 minutes. Add the cream and cook, stirring, until the cream has thickened into a sauce, about 4 minutes. Remove the pan from the heat and stir in the prosciutto, parsley and pepper.

—ERICA DE MANE

MAKE IT AHEAD
You can sauté the cucumbers hours in advance. Shortly before serving, add the cream and cook to reheat the cucumbers and thicken the cream. Then stir in the remaining ingredients.

CUCUMBER RAITA

Indian raitas are immensely varied, but cucumber is a favorite ingredient. This refreshing yogurt condiment complements grilled lamb or beef and most poultry, as well as Salmon Tandoori, page 100.

SERVES 8

1	cup plain yogurt
1	cucumber, peeled, seeded and diced
1	clove garlic, minced
1	tablespoon chopped fresh mint
1½	teaspoons chopped flat-leaf parsley
¼	teaspoon salt

1. Put the yogurt in a strainer lined with cheesecloth, a coffee filter or a paper towel and set it over a bowl. Let drain for 1 hour.

2. Transfer the yogurt to a bowl and stir in the cucumber, garlic, mint, parsley and salt. Refrigerate until ready to serve.

MAKE IT AHEAD
You can drain the yogurt a few days ahead, if you like, and stir in the remaining ingredients early on the day you plan to serve the raita.

SAUTEED GREENS WITH PEPPERS AND LIME

Two hearty greens, each with its own unique taste and texture, are sweetened with onion and bell pepper and spiked with hot pepper and lime. Three pounds of greens will seem like a lot, but they wilt to less than one-quarter of their raw volume. Don't omit a thorough washing, or the leaves may be gritty.

SERVES 8

1½ pounds kale, stems removed, leaves washed well and cut into 1½-inch pieces

¼ cup cooking oil

1 onion, chopped

1 red bell pepper, cut into thin slices

1½ pounds Swiss chard, leaves and top 2 inches of stems washed well and cut into 1½-inch pieces

1¼ teaspoons salt

¼ teaspoon dried red-pepper flakes

2 tablespoons chopped cilantro

2 teaspoons lime juice

1. In a large pot of boiling, salted water, cook the kale until just tender, about 5 minutes. Drain.

2. Heat the oil in the same pot over moderate heat. Add the onion and bell pepper and cook, stirring occasionally, until the onion is golden brown, about 7 minutes. Stir in the kale. Add the Swiss chard, salt and red-pepper flakes. Cook, stirring occasionally, until the Swiss chard wilts, about 1 minute. Cover and cook, stirring occasionally, until all the greens are tender, about 10 minutes longer. Remove the pot from the heat and stir in the cilantro and lime juice.

—STEPHANIE LYNESS

MAKE IT AHEAD
The greens can be made a few days ahead and reheated, but don't add the cilantro and lime juice until shortly before serving.

SOUTHWESTERN SUCCOTASH

Succotash was never like this. Our version is an enticing partner to a wide variety of dishes. Even when the succotash is made with frozen corn and lima beans, the flavor is intriguing. Each bite makes you want another one.

SERVES 8

3 tablespoons butter

1 onion, chopped

2 cloves garlic, minced

1 jalapeño pepper, seeded and minced

½ teaspoon ground coriander

½ teaspoon anise seeds, chopped coarse

¼ teaspoon ground cumin

3 cups fresh (cut from about 5 ears) or frozen corn kernels

2 10-ounce packages frozen lima beans, thawed

1¾ teaspoons salt

¾ cup water

⅓ cup chopped cilantro

2 to 3 tablespoons lime juice (from about 2 limes)

¼ teaspoon fresh-ground black pepper

1. In a large frying pan, melt the butter over moderately low heat. Add the onion, garlic and jalapeño. Stir in the coriander, anise seeds and cumin and cook, stirring occasionally, until the onion is translucent, about 5 minutes.

2. Raise the heat to moderate. Add the corn, lima beans, salt and water. Cook, stirring occasionally, until the corn is just done, 5 to 7 minutes. Remove the pot from the heat and stir in the cilantro, lime juice and black pepper.

—KATHERINE ALFORD

MAKE IT AHEAD
Cook the onion mixture hours ahead if it's convenient. That will leave about five minutes of cooking before you serve.

PLAYING WITH FIRE

Jalapeños are not quite so hot as other Mexican chiles, but never underestimate their power. Chop them fine enough to avoid biting into a large piece and always wash your hands after working with jalapeños to eliminate the danger of transferring their fiery oils to a tender part of your body. Eyes are particularly vulnerable. Respect the heat of these addictive peppers, and you'll never get burned.

FRESH-CORN PUDDING

Packed with both grated and whole kernels of corn, this savory pudding should be reserved for the summer months when fresh corn is at its best. Bake the pudding in an attractive dish if you have one so that you can take it right from the oven to the table.

SERVES 8

6	ears corn
4	scallions including green tops, chopped
1¼	cups half-and-half
3	eggs, beaten to mix
2	tablespoons butter, melted
½	teaspoon chopped fresh thyme, or ¼ teaspoon dried
1	teaspoon salt
⅛	teaspoon fresh-ground black pepper
2	ounces Gruyère cheese, grated (about ½ cup)

MAKE IT AHEAD
You can prepare all the ingredients and stir them together a few hours ahead. If the mixture separates, give it a stir before pouring it into the baking dish, topping with cheese and baking.

1. Heat the oven to 375°. Butter a 2-quart gratin or shallow baking dish. With the coarse side of a grater, grate the corn from three of the cobs. Using a sharp knife, cut the corn kernels from the remaining three cobs. Put all of the corn in a large bowl.

2. Stir in the scallions, half-and-half, eggs, butter, thyme, salt and pepper. Pour the mixture into the gratin dish and sprinkle with the cheese. Bake the pudding in the oven until the center is just set, about 25 minutes.

CORN COUSCOUS

Fresh corn and couscous are an uncommon match, but we find they complement each other perfectly. The corn gives sweetness and the couscous provides its buttery flavor and pleasant, soft graininess. Use frozen corn, if you like; here it's not a compromise. Serve this amazingly quick side dish with almost any meat or fish, as well as with Black-Pepper Seared Tuna, page 101.

SERVES 8

- 3 cups fresh (cut from about 5 ears) or frozen corn kernels
- 1 quart water
- 2¾ teaspoons salt
- 2⅔ cups couscous
- 4 tablespoons butter, cut into pieces
- ¼ cup milk
- ⅛ teaspoon fresh-ground black pepper

1. In a food processor or blender, puree the corn kernels. In a large pot, combine the corn, water and salt and bring to a boil. Reduce the heat and simmer 1 minute.

2. Stir in the couscous and bring back to a simmer. Cover. Remove the pot from the heat and let stand for 5 minutes. Stir in the butter, milk and pepper. Serve warm or at room temperature.

MAKE IT AHEAD You can puree the corn and measure out the remaining ingredients several hours ahead. That way it should take you only about fifteen minutes to cook the corn couscous before serving. You can also complete the dish up to eight hours ahead and keep it, tightly covered, in the refrigerator. Shortly before serving, heat the corn couscous, covered, over low heat or in a 325° oven for about twenty minutes, stirring occasionally. Don't stir too much; reheated couscous can get gummy. If you do make the dish in advance, add an extra one-quarter cup or so of milk to keep it moist. Or simply remove it from the refrigerator about an hour ahead and serve it at room temperature.

VEGETABLE COUSCOUS

Now available in most supermarkets, couscous requires only a few minutes to prepare. Simply add it to boiling water, cover and leave until the water is absorbed and the couscous is fluffy. Here, flavors from North Africa blend into a spicy vegetable sauce to top the couscous. This dish makes an ideal accompaniment for the Moroccan Lamb, page 169.

SERVES 8

- 2 cups water
- 2¼ teaspoons salt
- 1⅓ cups couscous
- 2 tablespoons cooking oil
- 3 onions, chopped
- 1 red bell pepper, cut into thin slices about 2 inches long
- 4 cloves garlic, minced
- 2¼ teaspoons ground coriander
- 1½ teaspoons ground cumin
- ¾ teaspoon turmeric
- ⅛ teaspoon ground cloves
- ⅛ teaspoon cinnamon
- ¼ teaspoon cayenne
- 2⅓ cups Chicken Stock, page 276, or canned low-sodium chicken broth
- ¾ cup canned tomatoes with their juice, chopped
- 3 tablespoons dried currants or raisins

1. In a medium saucepan, bring the water to a boil. Add ¼ teaspoon of the salt and the couscous. Cover. Remove the pot from the heat and let the couscous stand for 5 minutes. Set aside in a warm place.

2. In a medium frying pan, heat the oil over moderately low heat. Add the onions and bell pepper and cook, stirring occasionally, until the onion is translucent, about 5 minutes. Increase the heat to moderate. Add the garlic, coriander, cumin, turmeric, cloves, cinnamon, the remaining 2 teaspoons salt and the cayenne and cook, stirring, 2 minutes longer.

3. Stir in the stock and tomatoes and cook, uncovered, until the vegetables are very soft, about 10 minutes. Add the currants and cook 3 minutes longer. Top the couscous with the vegetable mixture.

MAKE IT AHEAD
The vegetable mixture can be prepared several days ahead. Reheat it and make the couscous shortly before serving.

ACORN-SQUASH RINGS

These attractive slices of acorn squash are baked and served with the skin, which softens as it cooks and can be removed easily as the squash is eaten. It's shown here with Roast Loin of Pork with Green-Olive Filling, page 152.

SERVES 8

3 acorn squash (about 4½ pounds), cut crosswise into ½-inch slices

6 tablespoons butter

½ teaspoon salt

¼ teaspoon cayenne

1. Heat the oven to 400°. Butter two large baking sheets. Using a small knife or a teaspoon, remove the seeds from the squash slices. Put the slices in a single layer on the baking sheets.

2. In a small pot, melt the butter with the salt and cayenne. Brush the squash with half of the butter mixture and bake until soft, 15 to 20 minutes. Using a wide metal spatula, turn the squash. Brush with the remaining butter mixture and bake until the squash is tender and golden brown, about 10 minutes longer.

—RICK SPINELL
SPINELL'S LITCHFIELD FOOD COMPANY

EASY SLICING

You'll find a serrated knife is the best utensil for cutting through the hard squash. The slices look prettiest as rings, but you can also cut the squash in half from stem to blossom end, put each half flat on the cutting surface and cut crosswise. This is easier than slicing the whole squash.

MAKE IT AHEAD
You can bake the squash slices up to four hours ahead. Leave them on the baking sheets. Let cool and then cover them with plastic wrap. Fifteen minutes before serving, heat them in a 350° oven until hot through.

WILD RICE WITH CURRANTS AND SAUTEED APPLES

The addition of currants and apples gives this classic side dish an unexpected texture and sweetness. A flavorful match for many holiday dishes, it's a particularly appropriate addition to an autumn dinner table.

SERVES 8

1½ cups wild rice

1½ cups Chicken Stock, page 276, or canned low-sodium chicken broth

2 cups water

1 teaspoon salt

1½ tablespoons butter

1 onion, chopped

2 teaspoons chopped fresh thyme, or ¾ teaspoon dried

1 tart apple, such as Granny Smith

⅓ cup dried currants

1. Rinse the rice in several changes of cold water and drain. In a medium pot, combine the rice, stock, water and salt. Bring to a boil over moderate heat. Cover, reduce the heat to moderately low and cook at a gentle boil until the rice is tender. The cooking time can vary from 35 to 60 minutes. If necessary, drain the rice.

2. In a medium frying pan, heat 1 tablespoon of the butter over moderately low heat. Add the onion and thyme and cook, stirring occasionally, until the onion is translucent, about 5 minutes. Remove.

3. Peel, core and slice the apple (see photo, page 247). Cut the slices in half. Melt the remaining ½ tablespoon butter in the frying pan over moderate heat. Sauté the apple, stirring occasionally, until it is soft and lightly browned, about 10 minutes.

4. Stir the onion, apple and currants into the cooked rice and reheat if necessary.

MAKE IT AHEAD
Wild rice reheats much better than white. You can make this dish a day ahead, if you like, so that the flavors have time to blend. Reheat the rice on top of the stove over low heat or in a double boiler.

New Potatoes with Herb Oil

Use the smallest red or white new potatoes you can find for this dish. We like the look of the little "two-bite" ones, and because you don't cut them, exposing raw potato, they don't stick to the baking sheet. If you can only get larger ones, halve or quarter them according to size.

SERVES 8

½ cup fresh basil or parsley leaves

6 tablespoons olive oil

3 pounds small red or white new potatoes (approximately 1½ inches in diameter), or larger boiling potatoes

1½ teaspoons coarse salt

1. Heat the oven to 425°. Oil a large baking sheet. In a blender, puree the basil with the oil.

2. In a large bowl, toss the potatoes with ¼ cup of the herb oil and the salt. Spread the potatoes on the baking sheet and roast, turning once or twice, until tender, about 25 minutes. Toss the potatoes with the remaining herb oil and serve.

MAKE IT AHEAD You can prepare the herb oil a few hours in advance, or longer than that if you don't mind the basil or parsley losing its bright-green color.

HERBED MASHED POTATOES

There's nothing like mashed potatoes made with real cream. But if you prefer, you can use milk or half-and-half instead. Don't forget, though, that in this recipe we've already replaced nearly half of the usual milk or cream with potato-cooking water.

SERVES 8

4 pounds baking potatoes (about 8), cut into quarters

1 cup heavy cream

¼ pound butter

2¼ teaspoons salt

¼ teaspoon fresh-ground black pepper

¼ cup mixed chopped fresh herbs, such as basil, parsley, tarragon, chives, chervil and/or thyme

1. Put the potatoes in a large saucepan of salted water. Bring to a boil and simmer until tender, about 20 minutes. Reserve ¾ cup of the water and drain the potatoes.

2. Work the potatoes through a ricer, food mill or sieve back into the saucepan. Discard the skins. Add the reserved potato-cooking water, the cream, butter, salt and pepper and beat with a wooden spoon over moderate heat until hot. Stir in the herbs.

MAKE IT AHEAD
Believe it or not, mashed potatoes can be made a day ahead and still taste good. Reserve half the cream and the herbs to add when reheating the potatoes. If they seem too thick, add a few tablespoons warm water.

VARIATIONS

BACON MASHED POTATOES

Chop four strips of bacon, fry until crisp and drain on paper towels. Add to the potatoes with the other ingredients. Omit the mixed herbs.

■ ■ ■

GARLIC AND ROSEMARY MASHED POTATOES

Cook and mash 8 peeled garlic cloves along with the potatoes. Use 4 tablespoons butter and 4 tablespoons olive oil rather than all butter. Heat the butter and oil over moderately low heat. Add 1 tablespoon chopped fresh rosemary and cook for 1 minute. Add the mixture to the potatoes with the other ingredients. Omit the mixed herbs.

PARMESAN POTATO WEDGES

These golden-brown wedges are so addictive that you may find yourself making them for a snack. Use flavorful Yukon Golds if you can find them.

SERVES 8

8   medium Yukon Gold potatoes (about 5 ounces each) or 2½ pounds baking potatoes, cut lengthwise into quarters

2   tablespoons olive oil

1½   teaspoons salt

½   teaspoon fresh-ground black pepper

½   cup grated Parmesan cheese

1. Heat the oven to 425°. Generously oil a large baking sheet. In a large bowl, toss the potatoes with the 2 tablespoons oil, the salt and pepper. Spread the potatoes, cut-side down, on the baking sheet and bake, turning once or twice, until golden brown and tender, 20 to 22 minutes.

2. Transfer the potatoes to a large bowl, add the cheese and toss to coat. Spread the potatoes on the baking sheet and return to the oven until the cheese begins to melt, 1 to 2 minutes.

MAKE IT AHEAD
If you want to cut up the potatoes before your guests arrive, put them in a bowl of cold water. They'll last for hours without turning brown. Pat dry with paper towels before baking.

POTATO AND LEEK GRATIN

The traditional combination of potatoes and leeks really shines in this gratin that's as yummy as it is simple.

SERVES 8

- 2 tablespoons butter, at room temperature
- 3 leeks, white and light-green parts only, split lengthwise, cut into thin slices and washed well
- 3 pounds baking potatoes (about 6), peeled and cut into thin slices
- 3 teaspoons salt
- ¼ teaspoon fresh-ground black pepper
- 2 cups heavy cream
- ¼ pound Gruyère cheese, grated (about 1 cup)

1. Heat the oven to 300°. Grease a 2-quart gratin or shallow baking dish with the butter. Spread half of the leeks in the dish and top with half of the potatoes. Sprinkle with 1½ teaspoons of the salt and ⅛ teaspoon of the pepper. Layer the remaining leeks in the dish and top with the remaining potatoes. Sprinkle with the remaining 1½ teaspoons salt and ⅛ teaspoon pepper.

2. Pour the cream over the potatoes and sprinkle the cheese on top in an even layer. Bake the gratin until the potatoes and leeks are tender and the top is golden brown, about 1½ hours. If the top has not browned sufficiently, heat the broiler and broil for 1 to 2 minutes.

MAKE IT AHEAD
You can put the gratin together about twenty minutes before baking. If you assemble it farther ahead, the potatoes will start to turn brown, though they'll still taste good. After cooking, you can cover the gratin loosely with aluminum foil and keep it warm for at least twenty minutes.

POMMES ANNA

One of the classic French potato creations, Pommes Anna is a side dish that steals the spotlight with its elegant simplicity. Although this dish requires some last-minute attention, your guests will be rewarded with an impressive golden-brown potato cake (see photo, page 143).

SERVES 8

3   pounds baking potatoes (about 6), peeled and cut into very thin slices

2   teaspoons salt

¼   teaspoon fresh-ground black pepper

¼   pound butter, melted

1. Rinse the potato slices in cold water. Don't leave them in the water very long, or they will curl. Pat the potato slices dry with paper towels.

2. In a large bowl, toss the potatoes with the salt and pepper. Brush a 10-inch nonstick frying pan with some of the butter, making sure to coat both the bottom and the sides of the pan. Arrange some of the potato slices in overlapping, concentric circles, completely covering the bottom of the pan. Line the sides of the pan with two layers of slices, sliding the edges under the bottom layer to form a "potato bowl." Drizzle some of the butter over the potatoes. Continue layering the potatoes, more haphazardly after the first couple of layers, drizzling some of the butter over every few layers.

3. Over moderate heat, cook the potatoes until lightly browned on the bottom, about 5 minutes. Cover, reduce the heat to very low and continue cooking until the potatoes are translucent on top and a toothpick slides in and out easily, 20 to 25 minutes. Turn the frying pan every 5 minutes for even browning and jerk the pan vigorously every now and then to be sure the potatoes aren't sticking.

4. Uncover the pan, turn the heat up to moderate and cook 1 minute. Reduce the heat to low and cook until the bottom and sides are golden brown and crisp, about 20 minutes. Using a long metal spatula, check the bottom frequently to be sure it doesn't burn. Remove the pan from the heat and let the potatoes sit for about 3 minutes. Invert a serving plate over the potatoes and flip the pan over to unmold. If any potatoes stick to the pan, just pick them up and replace them on top of the potato cake. Cut into wedges and serve.

MAKE IT AHEAD
Complete the recipe through step three before your guests arrive. You can leave the potatoes partially covered and at room temperature for two or three hours until twenty-five minutes before you're ready to serve the main course. Then finish cooking.

ORZO WITH PESTO AND LEMON

Pesto and lemon make a wonderful flavor combination that turns orzo into a perfect side dish for chicken or fish. It's good with meat, too. Homemade and ready-prepared pesto both work well, though you might use a bit more of the store-bought since the flavor isn't so intense as that of fresh.

SERVES 8

- 1 pound orzo
- 1 cup Pesto alla Genovese, page 275
- 2 tablespoons lemon juice
- 4 teaspoons grated lemon zest (from about 2 lemons)
- ½ teaspoon salt

1. In a large pot of boiling, salted water, cook the orzo until just done, about 12 minutes. Drain.

2. In a large bowl, stir together the orzo, pesto, lemon juice, lemon zest and salt.

MAKE IT AHEAD
You can prepare the pesto for this dish and combine it with the lemon zest and salt several hours in advance. Press plastic wrap directly onto the pesto mixture so that no air gets to it. Then when you're ready to serve, you need only boil the pasta and toss with the pesto and lemon juice.

BAKED POLENTA WITH WILD-MUSHROOM TOPPING

Polenta's light corn flavor adapts easily to a variety of accompaniments, and it can be as rustic or as elegant as you desire. Here it's topped with an aromatic combination of wild mushrooms, garlic and fresh sage.

SERVES 8

1½ quarts water

3 teaspoons salt

2 cups coarse or medium cornmeal

5½ tablespoons butter or olive oil

¾ cup grated Parmesan cheese

1 pound mixed wild mushrooms, such as shiitake, cremini and portobello

1 shallot, minced

2 cloves garlic, minced

2 teaspoons chopped fresh sage, or ¾ teaspoon dried

¼ teaspoon fresh-ground black pepper

1. Heat the oven to 350°. Oil an 8-by-12-inch baking dish. In a medium saucepan, bring the water and 2 teaspoons of the salt to a boil. Add the cornmeal in a slow stream, whisking constantly. Reduce the heat to moderate. Simmer, stirring frequently with a wooden spoon, until the polenta is very thick and pulls away from the sides of the pan, about 20 minutes. Stir in 4½ tablespoons of the butter and ½ cup of the Parmesan. Spread the polenta in the prepared dish.

2. If using shiitakes or portobellos, remove the stems. Slice all the mushrooms. In a large frying pan, melt the remaining 1 tablespoon butter over moderately low heat. Add the shallot and cook, stirring, until translucent, about 3 minutes. Add the garlic and cook, stirring, until fragrant, about 30 seconds. Add the mushrooms, sage and remaining teaspoon salt and cook, stirring occasionally, until the mushrooms are brown, about 5 minutes. Add the pepper. Pour the mixture over the polenta and sprinkle with the remaining cheese. Bake until lightly browned, about 10 minutes.

MAKE IT AHEAD
The polenta can be entirely assembled and refrigerated up to two days ahead. If it's cold rather than room temperature, bake it a few extra minutes.

VARIATION

CHEESE POLENTA

When served right from the pot, polenta has a soft and creamy texture. Just add the butter and Parmesan as described in step one and serve at once. For a more assertive flavor, add a few ounces of Gorgonzola instead of the Parmesan.

WARM EGGPLANT SALAD

Asian accents make this eggplant dish a pleasant surprise. It's especially good for perking up plain grilled chicken, fish or pork.

SERVES 8

3¼ pounds eggplant (about 2), cut into 1½-inch cubes

3 tablespoons cooking oil

1 teaspoon salt

2 scallions including green tops, chopped

¼ cup warm water

3 tablespoons rice-wine vinegar or white-wine vinegar

1½ tablespoons soy sauce

¼ teaspoon Asian sesame oil

¼ teaspoon fresh-ground black pepper

2 tablespoons chopped fresh basil

2 tablespoons chopped cilantro

1. Heat the oven to 400°. Oil two baking sheets. In a large bowl, toss the eggplant with the 3 tablespoons cooking oil and the salt. Spread the eggplant on the baking sheets. Bake in the oven, stirring occasionally, until the eggplant is soft and brown, about 35 minutes. It may stick to the baking sheets during cooking; be sure to loosen the cubes with a wooden spoon or spatula so that they don't burn. Transfer the eggplant to a large bowl and let cool slightly.

2. Stir in the scallions, water, vinegar, soy sauce, sesame oil and pepper. Just before serving, stir in the basil and cilantro. Serve the salad warm or at room temperature.

MAKE IT AHEAD
You can complete step one several days before serving. Then reheat the eggplant in a 350° oven and stir in the remaining ingredients. Or complete the recipe a day or two ahead and serve it at room temperature, adding the basil and cilantro at the last minute.

VARIATION

ITALIAN EGGPLANT SALAD

We've matched the roasted eggplant with Asian ingredients here, but if Italian is more your style, omit the cilantro, replace the scallions with some sautéed garlic, and add an additional ¼ teaspoon salt. Use 2 tablespoons of balsamic vinegar and 3 of olive oil in place of the rice-wine vinegar, soy sauce and sesame oil.

SAUTEED JAPANESE EGGPLANT WITH SOY, MIRIN AND SESAME-OIL SAUCE

We love this unique and delicious way of cooking the small, narrow Japanese eggplant. The vegetable is sliced and fanned out, browned with a little oil and served topped with a simple Asian sauce. The dish is also good just drizzled with plain soy sauce.

SERVES 8

½   cup soy sauce

½   cup mirin (sweet Japanese cooking wine)*

1   teaspoon Asian sesame oil

8   small Japanese eggplant (about 1¾ pounds in all), stems removed

¼   cup cooking oil

*Available at Asian markets

1. In a small bowl, combine the soy sauce, mirin and sesame oil.

2. Heat the oven to 200°. Beginning 1 inch from the top, cut each eggplant lengthwise into ¼-inch slices. Press the eggplant gently to fan out the slices. Brush the slices on both sides with the cooking oil.

3. In a large nonstick frying pan over moderate heat, cook three or four of the eggplant until browned on the bottom, about 6 minutes. Turn and cook until the eggplant are browned and tender, about 6 minutes longer. Put them on a large baking sheet and keep warm in the oven. Cook the remaining eggplant in the same way. Drizzle the eggplant with a little of the sauce and serve with the remaining sauce.

—ALVIO RENZINI

MAKE IT AHEAD

You can make the eggplant and sauce several hours in advance. Cook the eggplant and put them all on a baking sheet. Keep at room temperature. Fifteen minutes before serving, heat in a 350° oven for about ten minutes.

To make eggplant fans, cut lengthwise and push gently to spread the slices. The same technique is used for the Poached Pears in Cassis, page 249.

ROASTED BEETS
WITH BASIL AND PINE NUTS

This is a stylish, Mediterranean-flavored dish that nevertheless isn't too unusual even for a traditional holiday dinner. You can substitute chopped almonds or walnuts if you don't have pine nuts.

SERVES 8

2 pounds beets

⅓ cup pine nuts

2 tablespoons olive oil

¼ cup chopped fresh basil

½ teaspoon salt

⅛ teaspoon fresh-ground black pepper

1. Heat the oven to 375°. Wrap the beets tightly in aluminum foil and bake until they are tender when pierced with the tip of a knife, about 1½ hours. When the beets are cool enough to handle, peel and cut them into ½-inch dice.

2. In a small frying pan, toast the pine nuts over moderately low heat, stirring frequently, until golden brown, about 4 minutes. Or toast the nuts in a 350° oven for 6 minutes.

3. In a large frying pan, heat the oil over moderate heat. Add the beets and cook until hot, about 5 minutes. Stir in the basil, salt and pepper. Transfer the beets to a serving bowl and sprinkle with the pine nuts.

—ERICA DE MANE

MAKE IT AHEAD
The beets can be cooked, peeled and diced up to two days ahead. You can toast the pine nuts well in advance, too, and keep them in an airtight container. Shortly before serving, reheat the beets in the olive oil and add the basil, salt and pepper. The pine nuts are added at the last minute so that they don't get soggy.

MEXICAN BLACK-BEAN SALAD

Black beans mixed with red onion, tomatoes, jalapeños, lime juice and cilantro make a lively and colorful salad that goes well with grilled meat or fish any time of year, but especially in the warmer months.

SERVES 8

- 1 pound (about 2 cups) dried black beans
- 3½ teaspoons salt
- 1 red onion, cut into ¼-inch dice
- 2 tomatoes, seeded and cut into ¼-inch dice
- 2 jalapeño peppers, seeded and minced
- ½ cup V8 juice or tomato juice
- ¼ cup lime juice (from about 2 limes)
- ¼ cup lemon juice
- ¼ cup chopped cilantro
- ¼ cup chopped flat-leaf parsley
- ¼ teaspoon fresh-ground black pepper

1. Soak the beans overnight in enough cold water to cover by at least 2 inches. Or bring the beans to a boil, cover, remove from the heat and let sit for 1 hour. Drain.

2. Put the beans in a large pot with enough fresh water to cover by at least 2 inches. Bring to a boil, reduce the heat and simmer, partially covered, for 1 hour. Add 1½ teaspoons of the salt and continue cooking until the beans are tender, about 15 minutes longer. Remove from the heat, drain and let cool slightly.

3. In a large bowl, combine the onion, tomatoes, jalapeños, V8 juice, lime juice, lemon juice, cilantro, parsley, the remaining 2 teaspoons salt and the black pepper. Stir in the beans. Chill for at least 2 hours and preferably 4 hours.

MAKE IT AHEAD Prepare the salad anywhere from two hours to a day ahead. It actually improves on standing because the flavors blend, but after a day the onion flavor gets too strong.

Cipollini in Marsala Glaze

Simmering these small, flat, onion-like bulbs in Marsala and then cooking the liquid down to a rich, brown glaze brings out their delicious sweetness. Cipollini are increasingly available in specialty markets and are worth looking for.

SERVES 8

4 tablespoons butter

2 pounds cipollini (about 24), peeled

1 teaspoon sugar

3 cloves

1 cup dry Marsala

½ teaspoon salt

1. In a large frying pan, melt the butter over moderate heat. Add the cipollini, sugar and cloves and cook, stirring occasionally, until the cipollini are browned, about 8 minutes. Add the Marsala and salt, reduce the heat and simmer, covered, for 15 minutes. Turn the cipollini over and cook, covered, until tender but not falling apart, about 10 minutes longer.

2. Uncover the pan and raise the heat to moderately high. Cook the cipollini and liquid, shaking the pan occasionally, until the liquid is reduced to a thick glaze, about 3 minutes. Discard the cloves and serve.

—Erica De Mane

MAKE IT AHEAD You can make the cipollini a day ahead. Reheat gently on top of the stove.

Quick Peeling of Cipollini

Don't waste time peeling cipollini the way you would large onions, which would take forever. First blanch them in boiling water for about ten seconds. Drain, rinse with cold water and drain again. Cut off the root. The peel should slip off easily. You can also simply soak the cipollini in warm water for about half an hour to get much the same loosening effect.

INDIAN-SPICED RED LENTILS

Don't be dismayed when the little red (really orange) lentils fall apart and turn yellow during cooking. They always do. The excellent flavor of the carefully spiced, but not hot, lentils makes up for any aesthetic loss.

SERVES 8

4	tablespoons cooking oil
1	rib celery, chopped fine
1	onion, chopped fine
1½	cups red lentils
3	cups water
1	teaspoon salt
1	teaspoon ground coriander
½	teaspoon ground cumin
1½	teaspoons grated fresh ginger
2	tablespoons chopped cilantro

1. In a medium pot, heat 1 tablespoon of the oil over moderately low heat. Add the celery and half of the onion and cook, stirring occasionally, until translucent, about 5 minutes. Add the lentils, water and salt and cook, uncovered, until the lentils are tender, about 25 minutes.

2. Heat the remaining 3 tablespoons oil in a small frying pan over moderate heat. Add the remaining chopped onion and cook, stirring occasionally, until brown, about 5 minutes. Add the coriander, cumin and ginger and cook for 1 minute. Add this onion mixture to the lentils. Just before serving, stir in the cilantro.

MAKE IT AHEAD
The lentils can be cooked several days ahead and reheated before serving. For the best flavor, wait until no more than a few hours ahead to sauté and add the onions and spices.

FRENCH-LENTIL SALAD

Vertes du Puy lentils are the small green ones from France. They're ideal for salads because they keep their shape during cooking. Most specialty-food shops carry these lentils, but if you can't find them, try the more common brown variety, which cook more quickly and may fall apart a bit when tossed.

SERVES 8

- 6 tablespoons olive oil
- 1 yellow onion, chopped fine
- 1 carrot, chopped fine
- 1 clove garlic, minced
- 1 quart water
- 1 pound (about 2 cups) Vertes du Puy or brown lentils
- ¼ teaspoon dried thyme
- 1 bay leaf
- 1½ teaspoons salt
- 3 tablespoons red-wine vinegar
- 2 teaspoons Dijon mustard
- ¼ teaspoon fresh-ground black pepper
- 2 tablespoons minced red onion
- 2 tablespoons chopped fresh parsley

1. In a medium saucepan, heat 1 tablespoon of the oil over moderately low heat. Add the yellow onion, the carrot and garlic and cook, stirring occasionally, until the onion is translucent, about 5 minutes.

2. Add the water and bring to a boil. Stir in the lentils, thyme, bay leaf and 1 teaspoon of the salt. Cook, partially covered, stirring occasionally, until the lentils are tender, about 45 minutes. Discard the bay leaf.

3. In a large bowl, whisk together the vinegar, mustard, the remaining ½ teaspoon salt and the pepper. Add the remaining 5 tablespoons oil slowly, whisking. Add the lentils to this vinaigrette and stir in the red onion and parsley. Serve warm or at room temperature.

—GRACE PARISI

MAKE IT AHEAD The entire salad will keep well for a couple of days. After that, the raw onion becomes acrid and the parsley limp and discolored. You can cook and dress the lentils several days ahead, though, and add the raw onion and parsley later.

Clockwise from back left: Aged mimolette, Bleu d'Auvergne and assorted chèvres

THE CHEESE COURSE

ANYONE WHO'S BEEN TO EUROPE is probably familiar with the cheese course. Both in formal restaurants and in casual home settings, bringing out some cheese after the main course is pretty much the norm. In this country, though, the idea of eating cheese after dinner is only now emerging from the culinary shadows.

The cheese course adds a touch of simple, succulent elegance to a meal. A small slice of a nice creamy goat cheese from the Loire, a bit of hard-to-find English farmhouse cheddar or a lovely golden piece of Parmigiano-Reggiano really rounds off a meal just perfectly. Perhaps because it is still somewhat unexpected here, a cheese course can transform an already enjoyable dinner into something special—without a bit of extra cooking.

There are no laws that legislate obscure complexities into the life of a cheese course. It can be as elegant as an array of cheeses served on a centuries-old silver platter or as familiar as a wedge of good local cheddar set out on a wooden cutting board with a basket of bread.

CHOOSING CHEESE

The oft-used term "dessert cheese" has led many honest people into a well-intentioned, but misdirected, limiting of their cheese choices to those that are mild, creamy, almost sweet—like cheesecake without the sugar. This inevitably brings them to triple crèmes—those exceptionally rich, fat-added cream cheeses from France. Triple crèmes like Explorateur, Brillat-

A DOZEN GREAT CHEESES

CAMEMBERT
A good French Camembert from Normandy is hard to find in this country, but if you come across one, it will make an excellent ending to a fine meal. A properly ripened Camembert should be soft, supple to the touch and, when you cut it, creamy throughout. (If it's cakey and firm in the center, it's too young and of little use to you. Conversely, if it's shrunken and hardening around the edges, it's too old, and also short on appeal.) Good Camembert should have a full flavor that hints of mushrooms and fresh cream. Serve it with apples and pears.

FRENCH MOUNTAIN COMTE
Comté is the cheese of the Jura Mountains in eastern France. A well-made piece of Comté can be an exceptional ending to a meal. Look for a piece that's been cut from a full eighty-pound wheel, one that has been aged for a good ten or more months. Unfortunately, most of what is brought to North America is far younger and of little character. Taste before you buy. A good Comté should be well balanced, never "bitey," with a buttery hazelnut flavor that grows on the tongue and slowly expands to fill your entire mouth with its silky-smooth, savory, sensual flavors. On its home turf, Comté is traditionally served after the meal, accompanied by toasted walnuts and a glass of the delicious local dessert wine Vin Jaune.

PONT L'EVEQUE
Although it is given little recognition on this side of the Atlantic, Pont l'Evêque is the second great cheese of Normandy. Like its better-known partner Camembert, Pont l'Evêque is the kind of cheese the French adore after dinner. It has a complex woodsy flavor and soft and supple texture.

TO SERVE AFTER DINNER

REBLOCHON

An after-the-meal classic, Reblochon is a six-inch-wide, semi-soft disk of delicious cheese from the mountains of the Haute Savoie in southeastern France. Its hallmarks are a nice, fruity nose and a smooth, savory, buttery flavor as it melts in your mouth.

ROQUEFORT

Good Roquefort isn't salty. It isn't sharp. Instead, it's beautifully balanced, a blue-cheese blessing on your tongue. Grapes and toasted walnuts are good table companions. Spread on a slice of French bread, a good Roquefort is hard to beat.

SELLES-SUR-CHER

A well-made French goat cheese is a perfect addition to almost any cheese course, and Selles-sur-Cher is one of the best. A traditional cheese of the Berry region, it's creamy on the tongue but flavorful enough to hold its own after dinner. Serve it with slices of ripe pear, if you like.

FARMHOUSE CHEDDAR

There are only a few English farms left making traditional farmhouse cheddar, but their cheeses *are* available here. They have a golden color, a warm, close, nearly flaky texture and a nutty, penetrating flavor. Toasted Brazil nuts are a nice accompaniment, as are apples.

STILTON

The great British blue cheese is a classic after dinner. A good Stilton should be creamy, the texture of soft butter, with greenish veins set off against a pale cream-colored paste. Spread it on crackers (try it with English Bath Oliver Biscuits) and serve it with a glass of aged port. Stilton matches up nicely with ripe pears, crisp apples or red or black grapes.

PARMIGIANO-REGGIANO

Parmigiano may be the absolute, all-time, number-one cheese to eat after dinner. If you've never tasted real Parmigiano-Reggiano, it's difficult to imagine that Parmesan cheese could be the perfect ending to a great meal. Get those green cardboard containers from the supermarket out of sight and out of mind. What we're talking about here comes from graceful, sixty-pound wheels of well-aged, handmade cheese from the hills of Parma, not from smokestack factories and high-production packing lines. Break bits of Parmigiano off a bigger chunk while you sit and share a good story after dinner. It's got a lovely, nutty flavor, subtly sweet, combined with a succulent savoriness. Take note on your tongue of the tiny crystals that form in the cheese. Well-made Parmigiano-Reggiano is a cheese you could eat at the end of meal after meal. Every evening you'll discover new intricacies and insights into its flavor.

TALEGGIO

Northern Italy's great contribution to the cheese course, good Taleggio is cave-aged to develop a deep, creamy, tongue-tickling flavor.

AGED GOUDA

Firm aged Goudas have incredible flavor that hints of butterscotch, fresh cream and well-aged cognac. We're talking about cheeses aged at least two years. If you can find one that's three years old, better still. When you catch one on display, buy it up. It will keep well for months.

SWISS SBRINZ

If you like Parmigiano-Reggiano, you'll want to try Swiss Sbrinz. Similarly aged, it has a dense, granular texture and a richly buttery, elegant flavor that's delightful after dinner. It's a hit alongside a handful of toasted hazelnuts.

Savarin and St. André can be delicious after dinner. But they're hardly the only ticket to get into the cheese course.

Quite simply, choose cheeses you like. The only ones that don't work well after dinner are smoked or spiced cheeses; their flavors tend to be too intrusive when you're trying to make your way gently from savory to sweet.

We offer just three rules of thumb:

1. Choose cheeses whose flavors are compatible with those of the main course. When you're serving, let's say, a pungent garlic-and-saffron-scented bouillabaisse for dinner, you'll want to find cheeses that won't get lost in the aftermath of the main course, perhaps a well aged goat cheese, maybe a bit of beautiful blue Roquefort. On the other hand, if you're serving a delicate fresh trout, look for cheeses with softer, less assertive flavors—a nicely aged Comté, for example, or a mild, young goat cheese.

2. Follow the regional styles of the main dish. If you're serving the Milanese specialty ossobuco, look for the cheeses of northern Italy: Gorgonzola, Taleggio, maybe some Fontina Val d'Aosta. More often than not the cheeses of the region will be well suited to the local cooking. After a few hundred years together, one will have adapted to the other to create a mutually rewarding culinary relationship. If you're serving food from a culture that doesn't eat much cheese, it's probably a good idea to skip the cheese course. Most Asian cuisines would fall into this category.

3. Pick the best cheeses you can find. Buy small quantities but buy the best. A few slivers of a great cheese will satisfy in a way

A FEW CHEESE-BOARD IDEAS

ENGLISH SELECTION: English farmhouse cheddar, farmhouse Lancashire, Stilton, farmhouse Cheshire. (Note: Be sure to seek out true farmhouse versions of Cheshire, cheddar, Lancashire and other British cheeses. Their factory counterparts are usually severely lacking in flavor. Stilton is the lone exception, since it hasn't been made on the farm in decades.)

FRENCH: Comté, Roquefort, Selles-sur-Cher (or another nicely aged goat cheese), Pont l'Evêque, Camembert.

ITALIAN: Gorgonzola, Parmigiano-Reggiano, Taleggio, Fontina Val d'Aosta.

ALL-AMERICAN: Dry Jack, farmhouse cheddar, Maytag Blue, aged domestic goat cheese.

ASSORTED GOAT CHEESES: Four different goat cheeses with contrasting flavors, shapes and sizes.

ASSORTED MOUNTAIN CHEESES: Aged Comté, well-aged Gruyère, Fontina Val d'Aosta, Reblochon.

A BEVY OF BLUES: Gorgonzola, Roquefort, Stilton, Maytag Blue.

that mediocre cheese never will. Eat it slowly. Don't rush to judgment. Let the flavors settle on your tongue and melt their way around your mouth. This soft melt-in-the-mouth cheese moment is what makes eating cheese in the latter part of the meal such a potent pleasure.

Regardless of which cheeses you choose, always taste before you buy. You may know you like Stilton, but the difference from one Stilton to the next can be enormous. Any good merchant should give you the chance to sample before you spend.

How much cheese should you serve, and how many types?

You don't need much cheese for the cheese course, really. In most cases, a half-ounce to an ounce per person per cheese is more than enough. The point is to linger, to let the flavors lilt, not to fill up.

A single, simple, superb cheese will do just fine. Or you can serve up to five. More than that is overwhelming. By the time you get to your sixth or seventh cheese, your palate will be plodding, struggling to keep up with the complexities of the cheeses.

Mixing and matching: Which cheese goes with which?

When you decide to put together a selection of four or five cheeses, there are no hard and fast rules you have to abide by. Most important, find diversity in flavor. If you're looking to make a striking visual impression, take time to find cheeses that contrast in shape, color and size. A

A SPECIAL-OCCASION CHEESE COURSE

PARMIGIANO-REGGIANO AND TRADITIONAL BALSAMIC VINEGAR

This is a special take on the cheese course, an exceptional culinary treat for a very special occasion. You'll need a wedge of nicely aged Parmigiano-Reggiano and a tiny flask of traditional balsamic vinegar. Skip the readily available, perfectly edible balsamic sold at the supermarket and seek out real *aceto balsamico tradizionale*. Aged for at least a dozen years in a series of six or seven wooden barrels, traditional balsamic vinegar has a compelling, complex flavor with hints of berries and plums, a touch of oak and a whiff of vanilla. Try dipping small pieces of Parmigiano in the balsamico; the soft sweetness of the vinegar plays perfectly on the nutty, savory flavors of the cheese.

---

standard recipe for a good five-cheese board is an aged cheddar, a semi-soft cheese like Pont l'Evêque, a well-aged mountain Gruyère or Comté, a nice goat cheese and a blue cheese like Stilton or Roquefort. Eat them in that order—mildest to strongest, so that the flavors of the stronger cheeses don't overwhelm the subtleties of their milder comrades in curd.

Take note, too, that if you're serving a group of guests with a particular interest in learning about food and regional cuisine, you can create quite an interesting cheese course by playing with the diversity notion and putting out a platter of seemingly similar cheeses. Few of us get the opportunity to taste, say, four different "Swiss-type" cheeses at one sitting, but for the true cheese lover, it's an enlightening experience. Try an aged Gruyère, a French Comté, a Swiss Appenzell and a Swiss Emmental on one cheese tray, and you'll find that each has its own distinctive identity and character, which stands out strikingly next to its cousins. You can accomplish the same goal with four or five contrasting goat cheeses or three different farmhouse cheddars.

SERVING CHEESE

Bread, fruit, crackers—these are all fine accompaniments to cheese. Just a loaf of crusty bread is plenty. If you want to meld the cheese course and dessert into one end-of-the-meal merriment, fresh fruit are excellent additions: a handful of grapes, a couple of ripe figs, a tree-ripened peach. Toasted nuts, such as walnuts, hazelnuts or almonds, can be nice, too. Fruit and a nut bread might be the best of both worlds. Goat cheeses have a particular affinity for walnut breads.

🍇 SERVING WINE WITH CHEESE

Wine and cheese can be the peanut butter and jelly of higher gastronomy, a pair of culinary soul mates. The greatest challenge is the almost bewildering array of possible matches. Here are a few very general aids to navigation.

Continuing with the main-course red wine makes practical and gustatory sense given the right kinds of cheese. A young, tannic, full-bodied red will stand up to strong cheeses. If you're in the middle of a fine, older bottle, you'll want milder cheeses that won't compete with the nuanced maturity of the wine. Many full-flavored creamy or runny cheeses, like Brie or Camembert, can make a red wine taste bland (and a white wine taste like paste). By all means, eat these fine cheeses, but pause for a bit of bread before

the next sip, and don't expect wine magic.

Remember, too, that very ripe or very strong cheeses can present special challenges when it comes to matching them with wine. So if you're planning to serve something truly funky, be sure to taste the prospective wine and cheese together beforehand.

Blue cheeses have a tradition of their own, one that includes Stilton with port, and Roquefort or Gorgonzola with sweet, dessert-style wines like Sauternes. The idea here is to set up a contrast by serving a rich, sweet, full-flavored wine.

Chèvre may be the wine-friendliest of cheeses, at least in its milder, more youthful state. Creamy, younger chèvres can be lovely with white wines that combine body and acidity, such as sauvignon blanc

Bring the cheese to room temperature.

Get the cheese out on the counter well before you're ready to eat. Eating cheese at 35° is like eating potatoes without salt: You get the idea, but you'll never grasp the true greatness. Bringing cheese to the right temperature is always worth the few minutes of advance planning it takes.

You'll get the most flavor when you bring your cheeses to what is commonly, though often misleadingly, referred to as room temperature before you serve them. The term actually refers to a temperature

(including Sancerre) or white Rhône wines.

Certain tricks can help smooth the matching process. Apples or pears tone down pungent cheese flavors; most nuts will neutralize some of a youthful wine's tannin.

—RICHARD NALLEY

TASTE TEST

If you doubt the difference twenty-five or so degrees can make in the flavor of a cheese, try for yourself. Cut a slice from any good piece of cheese and let it sit on the counter for a few hours to get it into the right temperature range. Put the rest back in the refrigerator. When you're ready, take a taste of each. It's incredible how much more flavor will emerge from the piece you've allowed to warm to room temperature.

range of 50° to 70°, not to the precise temperature of the room you happen to be eating in.

How long does it take to bring a cheese to the right temperature? Well, on a cold winter's day in Aspen, it could take six hours. On a hot day in the Florida Keys, it might be no more than thirty minutes. Try it a few times, and you'll get the hang of it.

Let your cheese breathe.

If your cheeses are wrapped in plastic—as is much of the cheese sold in this country—you'll want to unwrap them at least an hour before serving so that they have a chance to breathe. Otherwise, they tend to taste a bit flat; the oxygen deprivation seems to diminish the character and quality of the cheese. Access to the open air makes cheese respond with the added life and luster you want.

—ARI WEINZWEIG

DESSERTS

WARM CHOCOLATE HAZELNUT POLENTA CAKES WITH WHITE-CHOCOLATE SAUCE

Dark, rich and moist yet surprisingly light and airy, this Italian-inspired dessert is a lovely balance of textures and flavors that will delight even the most discriminating chocolate aficionados. We especially like the flavor of hazelnuts, but if you have trouble finding them or want to save the time it takes to roast them, you can use three tablespoons of almond butter, sold in jars in health-food stores, or even peanut butter in place of the hazelnuts. If you do use peanut butter, cut the sugar by one tablespoon.

SERVES 8

- ¼ cup hazelnuts
- 5 tablespoons sugar
- 8 ounces semisweet chocolate, chopped
- 4 tablespoons unsalted butter
- 3 tablespoons coarse or medium cornmeal
- ½ cup milk
- ½ teaspoon vanilla extract
- 3 large eggs, at room temperature, separated
- 1 large egg white, at room temperature
  White-Chocolate Sauce, page 281
- 8 sprigs fresh mint (optional)

1. Heat the oven to 350°. Butter eight 5-ounce ramekins or 6-ounce custard cups. Put the hazelnuts on a baking sheet and bake in the oven until the skins crack and loosen and the nuts are golden brown, about 10 minutes. Wrap the hot hazelnuts in a kitchen towel and firmly rub them together to loosen most of the skin. Discard the skin. Puree the hot hazelnuts in a food processor with 1 tablespoon of the sugar until very smooth, about 3 minutes.

2. Melt the chocolate in a double boiler, stirring frequently, until smooth. Remove from the heat and stir in the hazelnut paste.

3. In a small saucepan, melt the butter over moderate heat. Add the cornmeal and cook, stirring, for 3 minutes. Add the milk and reduce the heat. Cook, stirring, until the polenta is thick, about 5 minutes. Stir in the vanilla. Add the hot polenta to the chocolate and stir until smooth. Cool slightly. Stir in the egg yolks.

4. Heat the oven to 375°. Bring water to a simmer for the water bath. In a large bowl, beat the egg whites until foamy. Continue beating the egg whites, adding the remaining 4 tablespoons sugar gradually, until they hold firm peaks when the beaters are

lifted. Fold a third of the egg whites into the chocolate mixture to lighten it. Fold in the remaining whites until just combined. Do not overmix.

5. Divide the batter among the prepared ramekins. Put the ramekins in a roasting pan and pour in enough of the simmering water to reach about halfway up the sides of the ramekins. Carefully transfer the roasting pan to the lower third of the oven and bake until a knife inserted into the center of one cake comes out clean, 16 to 18 minutes. To serve, unmold the warm cakes onto plates and pour the sauce around the edge. Top with the mint sprigs, if using, and serve at once.

—KEVIN CAULDWELL
SAN DOMENICO NY

MAKE IT AHEAD
The batter for these luscious little cakes can be made a day ahead. Put it in the ramekins, cover with plastic wrap and refrigerate. Add another four minutes to the baking time.

MELTING CHOCOLATE

Melt all chocolate using gentle heat to avoid scorching or lumping. Because the milk solids in white and milk chocolate are particularly sensitive to heat, they should be stirred almost constantly as they melt; dark chocolate need only be stirred frequently. The traditional way to melt chocolate gently is in a double boiler. Two other good methods are:

■ **In a microwave.** Put chopped chocolate in a microwave-safe container and microwave at medium until the chocolate turns shiny, about one-and-a-half to four minutes. Stir the chocolate until completely melted. Stir white and milk chocolate after one-and-a-half minutes. Do not overheat chocolate, especially white and milk chocolate, or it may become grainy.

■ **In the oven.** Heat the oven to 200°. Put chopped chocolate in a metal bowl. Stir frequently until shiny, about four minutes. Stir until smooth. We don't recommend this method for white or milk chocolate.

MOLTEN CHOCOLATE CAKES

Take a forkful of this delectable dessert and the warm, soft dark-chocolate center flows out. This specialty, now cropping up all over, already has quite a following at the restaurant Jo Jo in New York City, which serves over eighty of the cakes each night. For the total experience, add a small scoop of vanilla ice cream to each serving.

SERVES 8

8 ounces bittersweet chocolate, preferably Valrhona, chopped

15 tablespoons unsalted butter

4 large eggs, at room temperature

4 large egg yolks, at room temperature

½ cup sugar

7 tablespoons flour

1. Heat the oven to 325°. Butter and flour eight 5-ounce ramekins or 6-ounce custard cups. Set them on a baking sheet. Melt the chocolate with the butter in a double boiler, stirring occasionally, until smooth. Cool slightly.

2. In a large bowl, beat the eggs, egg yolks and sugar with an electric mixer on medium-high speed until pale yellow, about 10 minutes. Reduce the speed and add the flour gradually. Add the melted chocolate. Continue beating until glossy, about 5 minutes. Divide among the prepared ramekins.

3. Bake in the middle of the oven until the cakes are set around the edges but the centers move slightly when the ramekins are jiggled, about 12 minutes.

4. Run a small, sharp knife around the edge of each ramekin and turn the cakes out onto plates. Serve warm, with ice cream if you like.

—JEAN-GEORGES VONGERICHTEN
JO JO

MAKE IT AHEAD
You can refrigerate the filled ramekins for up to six hours. Bake the chilled batter for about eighteen minutes rather than twelve.

VALRHONA CHOCOLATE

Many chefs consider Valrhona chocolate from France to be the best there is. Its high proportion of cocoa butter is ideal for this dessert, which needs a luscious flowing texture. If you can't find it, use another bittersweet chocolate; add two tablespoons butter to make up for the lower cocoa-butter content. Or mail-order Valrhona from Maison Glass, 111 East 58th Street, New York, NY 10022 (1-800-UCALL-MG).

BITTER-CHOCOLATE MOUSSE WITH WHITE-CHOCOLATE SAUCE

Luscious, rich and chocolatey, this mousse is a simple yet sophisticated dessert that's bound to be a hit with chocolate lovers. The bitter-chocolate mousse and sweet white-chocolate sauce balance each other perfectly.

SERVES 8

2 large eggs

⅓ cup sugar

3 ounces semisweet chocolate, chopped

2½ ounces unsweetened chocolate, chopped

1⅓ cups heavy cream

6 tablespoons unsalted butter, at room temperature

White-Chocolate Sauce, page 281

1. In a large bowl, beat the eggs with the sugar. Set the bowl over a large sauce-pan containing an inch of hot but not simmering water (see photo, page 233). Using a hand-held mixer or a whisk, beat the egg mixture for 8 minutes. Remove the bowl from the heat and beat the mixture until completely cool, about 7 minutes.

2. Melt the chocolate in a double boiler, stirring frequently, until smooth. Keep warm.

3. In a large bowl, beat the cream just until it holds soft peaks when the beaters are lifted. Add the butter to the melted chocolate, whisking until smooth. Add the chocolate mixture to the egg mixture. Fold in the cream. Chill for at least 30 minutes.

4. To serve, spoon the bitter-chocolate mousse into bowls. Drizzle with the White-Chocolate Sauce.

MAKE IT AHEAD
You can prepare the mousse a day in advance, if you like, and the sauce several days ahead.

EVEN FANCIER

To really dress up this mousse, top it with large white-chocolate curls. They're easy if you have a good-size chunk of white chocolate (a four-ounce piece works well) and if it's at room temperature. Just shave off large curls, scraping the whole surface of the chocolate with a vegetable peeler. You can keep them in an airtight tin for a long time, but because they're so delicate, they must remain absolutely undisturbed. Once you feel confident that you can make them quickly, you may prefer to do them just before serving.

CHOCOLATE AND MINT-TEA POTS DE CREME

Rich, creamy chocolate with a delightful mint flavor, this is the ultimate pot de crème. Best of all, our no-bake version takes only minutes to prepare.

SERVES 8

 3 cups light cream

 3 mint-tea bags

12 ounces semisweet chocolate, chopped

 9 large egg yolks

   Whipped Cream, page 280

   Crystallized Mint Leaves, right
   (optional)

1. In a medium saucepan, bring the light cream to a simmer over moderately high heat, stirring occasionally. Remove the cream from the heat and add the mint-tea bags. Cover and let the tea infuse for 15 minutes. Remove the tea bags.

2. Add the chocolate to the cream and slowly bring just to a simmer, stirring frequently, over moderate heat. Remove from the heat and whisk until completely smooth.

3. In a large bowl, whisk the egg yolks to mix. Slowly pour the hot cream over the egg yolks, whisking. Strain.

4. Pour the chocolate custard into eight 5-ounce ramekins or 6-ounce custard cups and let cool. Chill in the refrigerator until set, at least 2 hours.

5. Serve the pots de crème topped with the whipped cream, and decorated with the mint leaves if you like.

MAKE IT AHEAD
The pots de crème can be made up to a day in advance, and the crystallized mint leaves are even better if made several hours ahead.

CRYSTALLIZED MINT LEAVES

Simple and pretty, crystallized mint is handy for decorating almost any kind of dessert.

MAKES 24 LEAVES

24 fresh mint leaves

 1 egg white, beaten to mix

1/4 cup sugar

With a pastry brush, coat both sides of the mint leaves with a thin layer of the egg white. Sprinkle with the sugar. Let dry on a baking sheet at room temperature for at least 1 hour.

Chocolate-and-Toffee Gateau with a Butter-Pecan Crust

Deliciously decadent with layers of crisp butter pecan, sticky toffee and smooth chocolate, all topped with whipped cream and chocolate curls—this dessert's a real show-stopper. It's perfect for special occasions, and while it may look and taste complicated, it's surprisingly easy; each element in the recipe is quick to put together. We like bittersweet chocolate because it contrasts pleasantly with the sweetness of the toffee and the pecan crust, but semisweet is also a good choice.

SERVES 8

1⅔ cups pecan pieces

¾ cup plus 6 tablespoons dark-brown sugar

9 tablespoons unsalted butter, 6 tablespoons melted and cooled

1 teaspoon vanilla extract

Pinch salt

3¾ cups heavy cream

12 ounces bittersweet or semisweet chocolate, 8 ounces chopped

1 tablespoon granulated sugar

1. Heat the oven to 350°. Butter the bottom of a 9-inch springform pan. Cover the bottom with a round of parchment paper and butter the paper.

2. In a food processor, process the pecans and 6 tablespoons of the brown sugar until coarsely ground. Add the melted butter, ½ teaspoon of the vanilla and the salt and pulse just to mix. Press the nut mixture evenly in the bottom of the prepared pan and set it on a baking sheet. Bake the pecan crust in the middle of the oven until the edges are just beginning to brown, about 10 minutes. Cool on a rack.

3. In a small saucepan, bring the remaining ¾ cup brown sugar, the remaining 3 tablespoons butter and ¾ cup of the cream to a boil over moderately high heat, stirring frequently. Continue boiling, stirring occasionally, until the toffee almost reaches the thread stage, about 5 minutes. A candy thermometer should register 225°. Stir in the remaining ½ teaspoon vanilla. Transfer to a bowl and let cool. Or refrigerate for about 15 minutes to cool quickly. Spread the toffee over the pecan crust. Chill until firm, at least 30 minutes.

4. In a medium saucepan, bring 2 cups of the cream to a boil over moderately high heat, stirring occasionally. Put the chopped chocolate into a medium bowl and pour the boiling cream over the chocolate. Let sit for 5 minutes and then whisk until smooth. Chill in the freezer until very cold and

somewhat thickened, 20 to 30 minutes. With an electric mixer on low speed, beat the chocolate cream until thick but still spreadable, about 1 minute. Do not over-beat or the chocolate will be grainy. Spread over the toffee layer. Cover with plastic wrap and chill for at least 2 hours.

5. In a medium bowl, beat the remaining 1 cup cream with the granulated sugar just until it holds firm peaks when the beaters are lifted. Spread the whipped cream over the chocolate.

6. Scrape a vegetable peeler along the remaining piece of chocolate to form small, delicate curls. Decorate the top of the cake with small mounds of the curls, using a mound to mark each slice. Chill the cake until ready to serve. Remove the sides of the springform pan. If necessary, smooth the sides of the cake.

For an easy cake decoration, scrape the surface of a piece of chocolate using short strokes with a vegetable peeler to form little chocolate curls. This technique works best when the chocolate is at room temperature. If it's cold, warm it in your hands.

MAKE IT AHEAD
You can make the cake through step three a day in advance. You can also get a head start by making some of the components even farther ahead. The chocolate cream will keep in the refrigerator for two days before beating, and it's actually better made well before assembling the dessert to ensure that it's as cold as possible. You can make the pecan crust two days ahead as well and keep it at room temperature. Several hours before serving, whip the cream, spread it on the cake and decorate with the chocolate curls.

MOCHA TRUFFLE CAKE WITH ESPRESSO SAUCE

Espresso figures prominently in this dense, chocolatey dessert; it's in the cake and sauce and even garnishes the top in the form of chocolate-covered coffee beans. If you don't have an espresso machine, you can use instant espresso powder to make the coffee.

SERVES 8

- 12 ounces semisweet chocolate, chopped
- 1½ cups granulated sugar
- ¾ cup very hot espresso or strong coffee
- ¾ pound unsalted butter, at room temperature
- 6 large eggs, at room temperature
- 1 tablespoon vanilla extract
- ¼ cup confectioners' sugar
  Whipped Cream, page 280
- ⅓ cup chocolate-covered coffee beans, chopped (optional)
  Espresso Sauce, page 283

1. Heat the oven to 350°. Butter the bottom and sides of a 9-inch springform pan. Cover the bottom of the pan with a round of parchment paper and butter the paper.

2. In a food processor, grind the chocolate with the granulated sugar. With the motor running, pour the hot espresso into the food processor. Process until the chocolate is completely melted, about 15 seconds. Scrape down the sides with a spatula. Add the butter and process until incorporated. Add the eggs and vanilla and process until the mixture is smooth and creamy, about 5 seconds. Pour the batter into the prepared pan and smooth the top.

3. Bake in the middle of the oven until the edges of the cake have puffed and the center is just set, about 55 minutes. Cool in the pan on a wire rack for 30 minutes. Cover and refrigerate for at least 3 hours. Remove the sides of the springform pan, then sift the confectioners' sugar over the cake. Slice and serve topped with the whipped cream, and the chocolate-covered coffee beans, if using, each slice surrounded by the Espresso Sauce.

MAKE IT AHEAD This is a great cake to prepare in advance; in fact, it's better the next day when the flavor is fully developed. It will keep for several days. The sauce, too, can be made days ahead.

Frozen Cappuccino Souffle

A frozen soufflé is a trompe l'oeil dessert. A foil collar taped around the soufflé dish supports the creamy dessert as it freezes. When you remove the foil, the dessert looks like a high-rising baked soufflé. Individual soufflés (see box below) are shown here.

SERVES 8

1¼ cups sugar

½ cup water

4 large eggs, at room temperature

4 large egg yolks, at room temperature

6 tablespoons coffee liqueur

3 cups heavy cream

2 teaspoons coarse-ground coffee beans

Unsweetened cocoa powder, for dusting

1. Cut a 30-inch-long piece of aluminum foil and fold it lengthwise in thirds. Wrap the foil around a 1½-quart soufflé dish to form a collar that extends at least 2 inches above the rim of the dish, and secure the foil with tape. Lightly brush the inside of the foil with flavorless cooking oil, such as safflower.

2. In a small, heavy saucepan, combine the sugar and water. Bring to a boil over moderately high heat and boil (brushing the inside of the saucepan occasionally with a pastry brush dipped in water, to dissolve any sugar crystals) until the syrup reaches the soft-ball stage, 5 to 8 minutes. A candy thermometer should register 238°.

3. Meanwhile, in a large bowl, using an electric mixer on medium speed, beat the eggs and egg yolks until pale yellow, about 10 minutes. Beat in the hot syrup in a thin stream. Add the liqueur and continue beating until the mixture is thick and completely cool, about 10 minutes.

4. In a large bowl, beat the cream until it holds firm peaks when the beaters are lifted. Fold the coffee beans and about a third of the cream into the egg mixture. Then fold in the remaining cream in two batches. Put the mixture into the prepared dish and smooth the top. Freeze until firm, 6 to 8 hours. Before serving, dust the top of the soufflé with cocoa. Remove the foil.

MAKE IT AHEAD
You can make the soufflé two or three days in advance. Once it's frozen, cover the top with plastic wrap to protect it.

Even Fancier

With just a little more work, you can make individual soufflés, using eight five-ounce ramekins. Everyone gets a miniature soufflé, and serving is easy.

HAZELNUT SEMIFREDDO WITH DARK-CHOCOLATE SAUCE

A slice of this smooth, near-frozen Italian favorite, intensely flavored with roasted hazelnuts and presented in a puddle of dark-chocolate sauce, is a rich yet refreshing end to any dinner. Look for hazelnuts in health-food stores if they're not available in your market.

SERVES 8

1½ cups hazelnuts

1 cup sugar

4 large eggs, separated

1½ cups heavy cream

Dark-Chocolate Sauce, page 282

1. Heat the oven to 350°. Put the hazelnuts on a baking sheet and bake in the oven until the skins crack and loosen and the nuts are golden brown, about 10 minutes. Wrap the hot hazelnuts in a kitchen towel and firmly rub them together to loosen most of the skin. Discard the skin. Puree the hot hazelnuts in a food processor with ½ cup of the sugar until very smooth, about 3 minutes. Cool to room temperature.

2. Line a 9-by-5-inch loaf pan with plastic wrap, using enough so that some hangs over the ends, and put it in the freezer. In a medium bowl, beat together the egg yolks and ¼ cup of the sugar. Set the bowl over a medium saucepan filled with 1 inch of hot but not simmering water (see photo, opposite page). Using a hand-held electric mixer or a whisk, beat the egg-yolk mixture for

5 minutes. Remove the bowl from the heat and beat the mixture until it is completely cool, about 7 minutes.

3. In a medium bowl, beat the cream just until it holds firm peaks when the beaters are lifted.

4. In a large bowl, beat the egg whites until foamy. Continue beating the egg whites, adding the remaining ¼ cup sugar gradually, until they hold firm peaks when the beaters are lifted.

5. Transfer the egg-yolk mixture to a large bowl. Fold in the hazelnut paste. The mixture will be very thick. Fold in half of the beaten egg whites to lighten it; then fold in the remaining whites until just combined. Fold in the whipped cream until just combined. Spoon the mixture into the prepared loaf pan, cover the pan with a piece of plastic wrap and freeze the semifreddo until hard, about 8 hours.

6. To serve, pull the hazelnut semifreddo out of the pan by the plastic wrap. Peel off the plastic wrap. Cut the semifreddo into eight slices. Spoon some of the

Dark-Chocolate Sauce onto each dessert plate, top the sauce with a slice of semifreddo and serve.

MAKE IT AHEAD
The semifreddo must be prepared at least eight hours in advance so that it has time to freeze, and it can be kept frozen for up to a week.

When you need to beat a delicate egg mixture over heat, set a bowl on top of a pot that has about one inch of hot but not simmering water in it. You will, in effect, be making a roomy double boiler. Match the size of the pot to the size of the bowl.

FOLDING TRICK

Try the usual folding method with a different implement. Although most directions specify a rubber spatula for folding one ingredient into another, chefs often use a whisk. We find the many wires of a whisk fold faster and more thoroughly.

SEMIFREDDO

A luscious cold and creamy Italian dessert, semifreddo has a firm yet fluffy texture all its own, different from that of ice cream or any other frozen dessert. The literal translation of *semifreddo* is "half frozen." It should start out thoroughly frozen. By the time you unmold, slice and serve it, the dessert will be just the right consistency.

Vanilla Semifreddo with Amaretti and Dark Chocolate

A slice of this Italian-style dessert combines smooth and creamy frozen mousse with crunchy layers of crumbled amaretti cookies, chocolate bits and chopped almonds. Serve it in a pool of Chocolate Sauce.

SERVES 8

¼ cup slivered almonds

8 amaretti cookies, crumbled

2 ounces semisweet chocolate, chopped

1 tablespoon cognac or other brandy

3 large eggs, separated

⅓ cup sugar

1 cup heavy cream

1 teaspoon vanilla extract

Chocolate Sauce, page 283

1. In a food processor, chop the almonds. Add the cookies and chocolate and pulse until the mixture is finely chopped. Transfer the amaretti mixture to a medium bowl. Add the cognac and stir to mix.

2. Line a 9-by-5-inch loaf pan with plastic wrap, using enough so some hangs over the ends, and put it in the freezer. In a medium bowl, beat together the egg yolks and half the sugar. Set the bowl over a medium saucepan filled with 1 inch of hot, not simmering, water (see photo, page 233). Using a hand-held electric mixer or a whisk, beat the egg-yolk mixture for 5 minutes. Remove the bowl from the heat and beat the mixture until it is completely cool, about 7 minutes.

3. In a medium bowl, beat the cream and vanilla just until the cream holds firm peaks when the beaters are lifted. In a large bowl, beat the egg whites until foamy. Continue beating the egg whites, adding the remaining sugar gradually, until they hold firm peaks when the beaters are lifted.

4. Fold the egg-yolk mixture, the cream and the egg whites together until just combined. Spoon a third of this cream mixture into the prepared pan and smooth the surface. Sprinkle with half of the amaretti mixture. Top with another third of the cream mixture. Sprinkle with the remaining amaretti mixture and top with the remaining cream mixture. Smooth the top. Cover with plastic wrap and freeze until hard, about 8 hours.

5. To serve, pull the semifreddo out of the pan by the plastic wrap. Peel off the plastic wrap. Cut the semifreddo into eight slices. Spoon some of the Chocolate Sauce onto each dessert plate, top the sauce with a slice of semifreddo and serve.

MAKE IT AHEAD
The ideal do-ahead dessert, semifreddo can be made up to a week in advance.

TIRAMISU

Translated as "pick-me-up" from the Italian, tiramisu is hard to resist, with its espresso-infused ladyfinger layer topped with a light and creamy mascarpone mousse and covered with cocoa.

SERVES 8

1½ cups hot espresso or very strong coffee

¾ cup sugar

2 7-ounce packages dried ladyfingers, preferably imported Italian savoiardi

6 large eggs, at room temperature, separated

1 pound mascarpone cheese

¼ cup unsweetened cocoa powder

1. Combine the espresso and ¼ cup of the sugar. Stir to dissolve the sugar and cool to room temperature. Line the bottom of a 9-by-13-inch baking dish with half of the ladyfingers, fitting them together tightly. Brush the ladyfingers with half of the espresso. Cover with a second layer of ladyfingers and brush with the remaining espresso.

2. In a medium bowl, beat together the egg yolks and 6 tablespoons of the sugar. Set the bowl over a medium saucepan filled with 1 inch of hot but not simmering water (see photo, page 233). Using a hand-held electric mixer or a whisk, beat the egg-yolk mixture for 5 minutes. Remove the bowl from the heat and beat the mixture until it is completely cool, about 7 minutes.

3. In a large bowl, whisk the mascarpone just until smooth. Add the egg-yolk mixture and whisk until just combined.

4. In a medium bowl, beat the egg whites until foamy. Continue beating the egg whites, adding the remaining 2 tablespoons sugar gradually, until they hold firm peaks when the beaters are lifted. Fold a third of the whites into the mascarpone mixture to lighten it. Fold in the remaining whites.

5. Spread the mousse on the ladyfingers and smooth the top. Chill for at least 6 hours. Not more than 30 minutes before serving, sift the cocoa over the top. Spoon into bowls or onto dessert plates.

MAKE IT AHEAD
Tiramisu needs to chill several hours, and you can certainly make it a day ahead.

SAVOIARDI SUBSTITUTE

If you can't find the dried Italian lady fingers called *savoiardi*, the fresh super-market variety will do. They won't ab-sorb so much espresso as the crisp ones; use three-quarters of a cup of coffee with two tablespoons sugar.

MIXED-BERRY COBBLER

Bursting with berries under a feathery-light topping, this refined cobbler is a celebration of the fruits of summer. Serve it warm topped with a scoop of vanilla ice cream or at room temperature accompanied by whipped cream.

SERVES 8

½ cup brown sugar, more if the berries are tart

4 pints mixed berries, such as strawberries (quartered), blueberries, raspberries and blackberries

2 tablespoons kirsch or rum

¼ pound unsalted butter, at room temperature

¾ cup granulated sugar

1 large egg, at room temperature

1½ cups cake flour

1½ teaspoons baking soda

1 teaspoon cream of tartar

½ teaspoon salt

½ cup buttermilk

1 quart vanilla ice cream, or Whipped Cream, page 280

1. Heat the oven to 375°. Butter two 9-inch glass pie plates and coat the bottom and sides with the brown sugar, leaving any excess on the bottom.

2. In a large bowl, combine the berries and kirsch and set aside to macerate.

3. Using an electric mixer, cream the butter with the granulated sugar until fluffy, about 5 minutes. Beat in the egg.

4. In a medium bowl, whisk the flour with the baking soda, cream of tartar and salt. Put the buttermilk in a small saucepan over low heat. Stir until just warm to the touch. Add the dry ingredients and the buttermilk to the butter mixture, alternating, in 3 batches, beginning with the dry ingredients and mixing until just combined.

5. Divide the berries between the two prepared dishes. Spoon the batter onto the fruit and spread in an even layer almost to the edge of the pie plates. Put the plates on a baking sheet and bake in the middle of the oven until the topping is well browned and the fruit is bubbling, about 30 minutes. Be sure the whole surface is a dark golden brown. Leave in the oven longer if necessary so the batter is thoroughly cooked. Remove to a rack to cool for 15 minutes. Serve warm or at room temperature, in wedges, with ice cream or whipped cream.

MAKE IT AHEAD
Although no one would turn this down on the second day, the cobbler is best on the day it's baked. You can either assemble it a few hours ahead of time and put it in the oven about an hour before serving, which will allow time for it to cool down a little, or bake it several hours ahead and serve it at room temperature. ➤

Even Fancier

For an especially attractive dessert, make the cobbler in individual dishes. Use eight shallow baking dishes, five inches in diameter, in place of the pie plates. Reduce the amount of berries to three-and-a-half pints so that the juice won't bubble over the edge. Spread the topping to approximately one inch away from the edges and bake at 400° for about twenty minutes.

Using All-Purpose Flour Instead of Cake Flour

Because cake flour contains less gluten than all-purpose flour, it helps to produce a light and fine-textured cake. If you don't have cake flour, though, you can often just use slightly less all-purpose flour. For this recipe, remove one tablespoon from the one-and-a-half cups.

Baking with Room-Temperature Ingredients

When butter and eggs are at room temperature, they can swell to a greater volume than when they're stone-cold. Cake batter and cookie and biscuit dough blend more smoothly when all the ingredients, including flour and milk, are at the same temperature. When a recipe calls for butter at room temperature, take the butter out of the refrigerator at least one hour before you plan to use it. Cut it into half-inch slices, put it in a bowl and leave to warm up. Or if you haven't planned far enough in advance, use the microwave oven to take the chill off the butter. Cut the butter into pieces, put it in a microwave-proof bowl and microwave at low, stirring every thirty seconds, for two minutes. Eggs will take about one hour to come to room temperature. Don't pop them in the microwave for a quick warm-up—eggs microwaved in their shell will explode. Instead, put the eggs in a bowl of warm water, and they'll be ready in five minutes. Be sure the water is not too hot or the eggs will begin to cook.

BLUEBERRY CROSTATA

Anyone who likes blueberries will find this Italian-style tart irresistible. A delicate almond crust spread with cooked blueberries provides the base for plenty of fresh berries, baked just long enough to get them juicy. The method for making the delicious pastry is especially quick: Simply stir the dry ingredients into the butter and eggs. Serve each slice at room temperature with a dollop of whipped cream, or warm with a small scoop of lemon sorbet.

SERVES 8

2　pints blueberries

5　tablespoons granulated sugar

6　tablespoons water

2　3-inch-long strips lemon zest

⅛　teaspoon cinnamon

2　tablespoons cornstarch

　　Almond Tart Shell, next page

¼　cup confectioners' sugar

　　Whipped Cream, page 280,
　　or 1 pint lemon sorbet

1. In a medium saucepan, combine 1 pint of the blueberries, the granulated sugar, 4 tablespoons of the water, the lemon zest and cinnamon. Bring to a boil over moderately high heat. Reduce the heat and simmer, partially covered, until the berries are very soft, about 10 minutes.

2. In a small bowl, stir the remaining 2 tablespoons water with the cornstarch until smooth. Add the cornstarch mixture to the pan and bring to a boil, stirring. Reduce the heat and simmer 1 minute, stirring. Strain into a bowl, pressing on the blueberries to get all the liquid. Let cool.

3. Heat the oven to 375°. Put the filling in the tart shell and spread it evenly. Spread the remaining pint of blueberries on top of the filling in an even layer. Sift the confectioner's sugar over the top of the tart. Bake until hot, about 20 minutes. Cool in the pan on a rack for 20 minutes. Serve the tart warm or at room temperature with the lemon sorbet or whipped cream.

■ MAKE IT AHEAD
You can make the cooked filling up to two days ahead. The dough for the tart shell can wait in the refrigerator for up to two days before you roll it out, and you can bake it a day before adding the fruit and baking for the final twenty minutes. ➤

ALMOND TART SHELL

MAKES ONE 9-INCH TART SHELL

- ⅓ cup slivered almonds
- 1½ cups flour
- ¼ teaspoon salt
- 8½ tablespoons unsalted butter, at room temperature
- 6 tablespoons sugar
- 1 large egg, at room temperature
- 1 large egg yolk, at room temperature

1. With a nut grater, or in a food processor or blender, grind the almonds to a powder. In a medium bowl, whisk together the almonds, flour and salt.

2. Using an electric mixer, cream the butter with the sugar until fluffy, about 5 minutes. Beat in the egg and egg yolk. Stir in the dry ingredients until well blended. Shape the dough into a flat disk and wrap tightly. Refrigerate until firm, at least 1 hour.

3. On a lightly floured work surface, roll the dough out to a ⅛-inch-thick round. Drape the dough into a 9-inch tart pan with a removable bottom and press the dough against the sides of the pan. Trim the pastry even with the rim of the pan. Refrigerate for 30 minutes.

4. Heat the oven to 375°. Prick the bottom of the shell every inch or so with a fork. Bake in the middle of the oven until golden brown, about 20 minutes. Cool and fill.

PEACH SHORTCAKE WITH CITRUS SUGAR

Rich shortcake piled high with fresh peaches makes a beautiful and delicious summer dish. You can also enjoy it in the winter with frozen peaches. Because you toss them with sugar, orange juice and mint, you can get away with less perfect peaches than you would need for a plainer version of shortcake.

SERVES 8

- 1 orange
- 1 lemon
- ⅔ cup plus 3 tablespoons sugar
- 2¾ cups flour
- 4 teaspoons baking powder
- ¼ teaspoon salt
- ¼ pound cold unsalted butter, cut into ¼-inch cubes
- 2¼ cups heavy cream, more if needed
- 1 egg, beaten to mix
- 12 peaches, or two 20-ounce bags unsweetened frozen peaches, thawed
- 2 tablespoons chopped fresh mint, plus 8 sprigs for garnish

1. Heat the oven to 375°. Grate the zest from the orange and lemon and combine with ⅓ cup of the sugar. Squeeze the juice from the orange and reserve. In a large bowl, whisk half of the citrus sugar, the flour, baking powder and salt to combine. Cut or rub in the butter until the mixture is the texture of coarse meal with a few pea-size pieces remaining. Stir in ¾ cup of the cream. If needed, add more cream, a tablespoon at a time, just until the mixture forms a dough when pressed together.

2. On a floured work surface, roll the dough ¾ inch thick. Using a 3-inch round cutter, stamp out eight circles. Brush the tops with the egg and sprinkle with the remaining citrus sugar. Put on an ungreased baking sheet and bake until golden brown, 15 to 20 minutes. Transfer to a rack to cool.

3. Peel and slice the peaches. In a glass or stainless-steel bowl, combine the peaches, orange juice, ⅓ cup of the sugar and the chopped mint. Set aside. In a large bowl, beat the remaining 1½ cups cream and 3 tablespoons sugar just until the cream holds firm peaks when the beaters are lifted.

4. Shortly before serving, split the shortcakes in half. Put the bottoms on dessert plates. Top with half the peaches and half the whipped cream. Cover with the shortcake tops. Spoon the remaining whipped cream on the shortcakes. Top each with 2 peach slices and a sprig of mint. Surround with the remaining peaches and their juice.

MAKE IT AHEAD
Prepare the shortcakes and peaches several hours ahead; keep at room temperature. The whipped cream can be made ahead, too, and refrigerated until serving. If it softens, simply whisk it a bit to thicken.

ITALIAN PLUM CAKE
WITH CINNAMON PLUM COMPOTE

This buttery cake loaded with fresh plums and accompanied by more plums in a simple compote makes the most of the late-summer fruit. Be sure to use large plums to get the sculptured effect on the top. The cake looks complicated though it's really an easy, homey one. Bring it to the table whole so that everyone can see how pretty it is before you cut it. Cinnamon or Ginger Ice Cream, page 264, or plain vanilla ice cream is delicious with the warm cake. Or serve whipped cream if the dessert is at room temperature.

SERVES 8

¼ pound unsalted butter, at room temperature

¾ cup sugar

2 large eggs, at room temperature

1 cup flour

1 teaspoon baking powder

  Pinch salt

4 large red and/or black plums (about 1 pound), pitted and cut into quarters

½ teaspoon cinnamon mixed with 1 tablespoon sugar

  Cinnamon or Ginger Ice Cream, page 264, or Whipped Cream, page 280

  Cinnamon Plum Compote, next page

1. Heat the oven to 350°. Butter and flour a 9-inch springform pan. Using an electric mixer, cream the butter with the sugar until fluffy, about 5 minutes. Beat in the eggs one at a time. In a medium bowl, whisk the flour with the baking powder and salt. Add the dry ingredients to the butter mixture and mix well with a wooden spoon.

2. Scrape the batter into the prepared pan and spread it evenly. Arrange the plums in two circles, skin-side up, on the batter (see photo, next page). Sprinkle with the cinnamon sugar.

3. Bake the cake in the middle of the oven until a toothpick inserted in the center of the cake comes out clean, about 1 hour. Cool in the pan on a rack for 30 minutes. Carefully remove the sides of the springform pan and allow the cake to cool another 10 to 15 minutes. Serve warm with the ice cream or at room temperature with the whipped cream, with the plum compote alongside.

MAKE IT AHEAD
The cake is best on the day it's made, but you can bake it hours before serving. Make the Cinnamon Plum Compote several days ahead, if you like. ➤

Cinnamon Plum Compote

MAKES 6 CUPS

- 1 cup red wine
- 1 cup water
- ⅓ cup sugar, more if the plums are tart
- ½ cinnamon stick
- 2 pounds red and/or black plums (about 8), halved and pitted
- ½ teaspoon lemon juice

1. In a medium stainless-steel saucepan, combine the wine, water, sugar and cinnamon stick and bring to a simmer over moderately high heat. Add the plums. Bring back to a simmer and cook, partially covered, until the plums are just tender, about 15 minutes. Pour into a glass or stainless-steel bowl and let cool.

2. Remove the cinnamon stick and add the lemon juice.

Arrange the plum quarters on the batter, skin-side up, in two circles. You don't need to press them in. The batter will rise around them.

APPLE ORANGE CRISP WITH PECAN TOPPING

A luxurious version of an all-American dessert, this old favorite couldn't be simpler or more delicious. Either Cinnamon or Ginger Ice Cream, page 264, or vanilla ice cream would be the perfect accompaniment.

SERVES 8

3 cups pecan halves or pieces

1⅔ cups dark-brown sugar

6 tablespoons granulated sugar

1½ cups flour

1 tablespoon cinnamon

1 tablespoon ground ginger

½ pound unsalted butter, at room temperature

2 teaspoons vanilla extract

8 pounds tart apples, such as Granny Smith (about 16), peeled, cored and cut into eighths

1 tablespoon grated orange zest

1. Heat the oven to 375°. Butter two 9-inch glass pie plates or baking dishes. In a food processor, chop the pecans fine. Transfer to a large bowl. In the food processor, put 1 cup of the brown sugar, the granulated sugar, flour, cinnamon, ginger, butter and vanilla. Pulse just until the mixture forms small crumbs. Add to the pecans and stir just until combined.

2. In a large bowl, combine the apples with the remaining ⅔ cup brown sugar and the orange zest. Put into the prepared pie plates. Sprinkle the crumb mixture over the top. Cover loosely with aluminum foil and bake in the middle of the oven for 35 minutes. Remove the foil and continue baking until the apples are tender and the topping has browned, about 20 minutes. Cool at least 15 minutes before serving. Serve in wedges, either warm or at room temperature.

MAKE IT AHEAD
You can make this dish hours ahead. Serve at room temperature or, if you prefer it warm, heat in a 250° oven for 15 minutes.

VARIATION

PEAR AND DRIED-CHERRY CRISP

For a delicious alternative, use pears in place of the apples and toss one-half cup of dried cherries with the pear, brown-sugar and orange-zest mixture. The cherries add a festive holiday touch to the dish, and their slight tartness is a pleasant foil to the brown-sugar topping.

HOT APPLE TART WITH THYME SYRUP

Fresh thyme and Golden Delicious apples make a perfect match in this exceptional tart. It cooks quickly because there's just a single layer of apple slices on a round of very thin pastry. Make the easy-to-roll dough in minutes with a food processor. Vanilla ice cream and thyme syrup add the finishing touch.

SERVES 8

Flaky Pastry Dough, opposite page

1⅓ cups sugar

1 cup water

1 tablespoon fresh thyme leaves, or 1 teaspoon dried

4 Golden Delicious apples (about 2 pounds)

2 tablespoons unsalted butter, cut into ¼-inch cubes

1 quart vanilla ice cream

1. Heat the oven to 425°. On a lightly floured work surface, roll half of the pastry dough into a ¹⁄₁₆-inch-thick round. Drape it over a 9-inch tart pan with a removable bottom. Roll the rolling pin across the top of the pan so the pastry falls to the bottom of the pan. Repeat with the remaining dough, using another 9-inch tart pan with a removable bottom. With a fork, prick the rounds every inch or so. Chill at least 30 minutes.

2. In a medium saucepan, combine the sugar, ⅔ cup of the water and the thyme and bring to a boil. Boil for 30 seconds. Pour the mixture into a bowl and let cool.

3. Just before assembling the tarts, peel the apples, cut them in half lengthwise and cut out the cores. Cut each half crosswise into ⅛-inch slices. Arrange the slices on the pastry in overlapping rows (see photo, opposite page).

4. Brush ¼ cup of the thyme syrup on each tart. Dot with the butter. Bake on the lowest rack in the oven until the apples are golden brown, about 25 minutes.

5. Remove the sides from the tart pans and cut each tart into quarters. Stir the remaining ⅓ cup water into the remaining thyme syrup. Top each slice of the tart with a scoop of ice cream, drizzle the remaining syrup over all and serve at once.

MAKE IT AHEAD
The dough should be made at least four hours ahead so that it's easy to work with, and it can be refrigerated for a day either before or after rolling. Keep it tightly wrapped in plastic. The best way to prepare the whole dessert ahead is to finish baking the tarts and transfer them from the tart pans to a baking sheet. Just before serving, heat them in a 400° oven until hot through, about eight minutes. Cut into quarters and serve.

Flaky Pastry Dough

MAKES ENOUGH DOUGH FOR TWO 9-INCH ROUNDS

1¾ cups flour

12 tablespoons cold unsalted butter, cut into ¼-inch cubes

½ teaspoon salt

3 tablespoons ice water

1. Put the flour, butter and salt in a food processor and pulse until the butter is in pieces the size of peas. Add the water and process just until the dough comes together.

2. Shape the dough into 2 flat disks and wrap tightly. Refrigerate for at least 4 hours.

For this tart, you want a disk rather than a shell of pastry. Drape the dough over the pan and roll the pin across the top. The pastry will fall to the bottom of the pan. It will extend up the sides a bit, as in the photo below, but will shrink down during baking.

The easiest way to slice an apple is to put each cored half on a work surface and cut down.

For a pretty effect, arrange the apple slices in overlapping rows on top of the dough.

POACHED PEARS IN CASSIS WITH KIR SORBET AND LEMON POUND CAKE

These pears get their intense flavor from crème de cassis, the French black-currant liqueur. The sorbet is based on a French aperitif called *kir*, a mixture of three parts dry white wine to one part crème de cassis.

SERVES 8

3¼ cups water

3¼ cups dry white wine

¾ cup sugar

3 3-inch-long strips lemon zest

1 vanilla bean, or 1½ teaspoons vanilla extract

4 large ripe but firm pears, peeled, cut in half lengthwise and cored

2 cups crème de cassis

8 sprigs fresh mint (optional)

Lemon Pound Cake, next page

1. In a medium stainless-steel saucepan, combine the water, wine, sugar, lemon zest and vanilla bean, if using. Bring to a simmer over moderately high heat. Reduce the heat to low and simmer, partially covered, for 5 minutes. Add the vanilla extract, if using.

2. Add the pears and bring back to a simmer over moderately high heat. Reduce the heat and simmer, partially covered, just until the pears are tender when pierced, 8 to 10 minutes. Transfer the pears to a medium bowl. Reserve the poaching liquid. Pour the crème de cassis over the pears, let cool completely and then chill for at least 1 hour. Drain off 1 cup of the cassis and reserve.

3. Strain the poaching liquid. Pour 2 cups of it and the 1 cup reserved cassis into an ice-cream maker and freeze according to the manufacturer's instructions. Put a 1-quart container in the freezer to chill. Transfer the sorbet to the chilled container. Store in the freezer until hard enough to scoop, about 30 minutes.

4. Cut the pear halves into fan shapes by slicing them lengthwise into ¼-inch slices, leaving 1 inch attached at the top (see photo, page 203). Fan them out on plates. Pour the remaining cassis over the pears and put a sprig of mint, if using, at the top of each pear. Serve with the sorbet and a slice of the pound cake.

MAKE IT AHEAD All the elements of this dessert can be finished two days ahead. The pears improve on sitting as they absorb more of the cassis flavor and color. The sorbet maintains a perfect texture because of its high alcohol content.

LEMON POUND CAKE

A lemon glaze poured over the hot cake makes this delicious pound cake moist and citrusy. It's a good addition to Poached Pears in Cassis, previous page, and also makes a great tea cake.

MAKES ONE 9-INCH LOAF

¼ pound unsalted butter, at room temperature

1⅓ cups sugar

2 large eggs, at room temperature

2 teaspoons grated lemon zest

1½ cups flour

1½ teaspoons baking powder

½ teaspoon salt

½ cup milk

⅓ cup lemon juice (from about 2 lemons)

1. Heat the oven to 350°. Butter a 9-by-5-inch loaf pan. Using an electric mixer, cream the butter with 1 cup of the sugar until fluffy, about 5 minutes. Beat in the eggs one at a time. Add the lemon zest.

2. In a medium bowl, whisk the flour with the baking powder and salt. Add the dry ingredients and the milk to the butter mixture, alternating, in 3 batches, beginning with the dry ingredients and mixing until just combined. Do not overmix. Scrape the batter into the prepared pan and smooth the top.

3. Bake the cake in the middle of the oven until a toothpick inserted in the center comes out clean, 45 to 50 minutes.

4. Combine the remaining ⅓ cup sugar with the lemon juice and pour over the top of the hot cake as soon as it comes out of the oven. Cool completely in the pan on a rack. Carefully remove the cake from the pan. Cut into slices and serve.

MAKE IT AHEAD
The cake can be made two days ahead; the lemon flavor will intensify. If you are keeping the cake for just a day, leave it out at room temperature uncovered. You'll have the best crust that way. If you're keeping it two days, though, wrap it in foil.

IS YOUR OVEN TEMPERATURE RIGHT?

The actual temperature in an oven, especially an older one, may not correspond with the dial setting. To be certain of the temperature, use an oven thermometer. The right temperature is especially important in baking, where even 25° can make a big difference.

Warm Lemon Mousse with Raspberries and Vanilla Ice Cream

Similar to a soufflé but less tricky to prepare, this tangy, warm lemon mousse is baked with raspberries and topped with a small scoop of mellow vanilla ice cream for a delectable contrast of temperature and flavor.

SERVES 8

⅔ cup lemon juice (from about 3 lemons)

2 teaspoons grated lemon zest

3 large eggs, at room temperature, separated

4 large egg yolks, at room temperature

4 tablespoons unsalted butter

1½ cups sugar

Pinch salt

1½ pints raspberries

1 pint vanilla ice cream

1. Heat the oven to 250°. Lightly butter eight 11-ounce ramekins or custard cups and set them on a baking sheet.

2. In a medium saucepan over moderate heat, cook the lemon juice, lemon zest, eggs, egg yolks, butter, ¾ cup of the sugar and the salt, whisking constantly, until very hot, 6 to 8 minutes. Do not boil. Pour the mixture into a large bowl and whisk until smooth.

3. In another large bowl, beat the egg whites until foamy. Continue beating, adding the remaining ¾ cup sugar gradually, until the whites hold firm peaks when the beaters are lifted. Fold the egg whites into the lemon mixture, just until blended.

4. Divide half of the mousse among the ramekins. Put 6 raspberries in each rame-kin. Top with the remaining mousse.

5. Bake in the middle of the oven until the mousse has risen and is just set around the edges but still soft in the center, about 20 minutes. Top with a small scoop of vanilla ice cream and several raspberries. Serve at once.

MAKE IT AHEAD
You can prepare the dessert through step four several hours ahead. Keep the ramekins, uncovered, in the refrigerator. Because they'll be cold when you put them in the oven, add about two minutes to the baking time.

BREAD PUDDING WITH DRIED CHERRIES AND BOURBON SAUCE

With a crisp surface of sugar-topped bread, this Southern pudding is a winner. While you can serve it plain, we recommend making the sauce, which turns an already delicious dessert into an extravagant finale.

SERVES 8

½ cup dried cherries

6 tablespoons bourbon

4 tablespoons unsalted butter, at room temperature

1 day-old French baguette (about 16 inches long), cut into ¼-inch slices

3 cups milk

1 cup heavy cream

6 large eggs

2 large egg yolks

¾ cup sugar

Pinch salt

1 teaspoon vanilla extract

½ teaspoon cinnamon mixed with 2 tablespoons sugar

Bourbon Sauce, opposite page

1. In a small pot, bring the cherries and bourbon to a simmer and cook over low heat until the cherries soften and the bourbon is absorbed, about 5 minutes. Let cool. Scatter the cherries over the bottom of a 3-quart shallow baking or gratin dish.

2. Butter one side of the bread slices, using all the butter. Overlap them, buttered-side up, in two layers on top of the cherries.

3. Heat the oven to 350°. Bring water to a simmer for the water bath. In a medium saucepan, bring the milk and cream just to a simmer. In a large bowl, whisk together the eggs, egg yolks, sugar, salt and vanilla. Pour the hot milk and cream over the egg mixture, whisking just until mixed. Strain this custard over the bread in the baking dish. Sprinkle with the cinnamon sugar.

4. Put the baking dish in a roasting pan and pour in enough of the simmering water to reach about halfway up the sides of the dish. Carefully transfer the roasting pan to the upper half of the oven and bake until the pudding is just set, about 35 minutes. Remove the pudding from the water bath and cool to warm or room temperature. Serve with the Bourbon Sauce.

MAKE IT AHEAD
Make the sauce two days ahead, if you like, and refrigerate. Remove it from the refrigerator about thirty minutes before serving. You can make the pudding up to four hours ahead and keep it at room temperature until ready to serve. Of course you can refrigerate it and keep it longer, but the top won't remain crisp.

BOURBON SAUCE

MAKES ABOUT 2 CUPS

5 large eggs
¼ pound unsalted butter
1 cup light-brown sugar
5 tablespoons bourbon

1. In a large bowl, whisk the eggs until combined. In a medium saucepan, melt the butter with the sugar over moderately low heat, stirring frequently, until warm. Add the bourbon and continue heating until hot but not simmering. Whisk the hot syrup into the eggs.

2. Pour the mixture back into the pan and heat, stirring constantly with a wooden spoon, until hot but not simmering, about 1 minute. Do not simmer or the sauce may curdle. Strain and cool. Skim any foam from the surface. Serve at room temperature.

BEST BREAD

The long, thin French baguette is traditional for bread pudding in New Orleans, the stronghold of American bread pudding, and the small slices look nice. But of course you can use any good-quality bread. When we call for day-old bread here, we assume that it has been wrapped well in foil or plastic. If left uncovered, baguettes can become rock hard and difficult to slice. If you want to make the bread pudding but don't have any day-old bread on hand, cut slices from a fresh baguette and put them on baking sheets to dry for about one hour. Alternatively, let the slices dry in a 200° oven for ten minutes, turning them once.

BAKING CUSTARD IN A WATER BATH

Since custard is a delicate mixture containing a high proportion of eggs, which curdle easily, it benefits from a moderately low, steady temperature during baking. The best way to ensure even heat is to cook it in a water bath, as described in this recipe. The water loses and gains heat much more slowly than the air in the oven, thereby cushioning the custard against sudden changes in temperature.

ALMOND CAKE WITH STRAWBERRIES IN BALSAMIC VINEGAR

You'll be amazed that this delicious cake contains little more than almonds, sugar and egg whites. It's moist and flavorful and is a perfect foil for the delectable combination of fresh strawberries and balsamic vinegar. The cake, a specialty of the exceptionally talented French chef and teacher Fernand Chambrette, is also good served plain as a tea cake.

SERVES 8

3 tablespoons unsalted butter, at room temperature

5 cups sliced almonds

1¾ cups plus 2 tablespoons confectioners' sugar

6 large egg whites, at room temperature

1 teaspoon vanilla extract

1 teaspoon grated lemon zest

Strawberries in Balsamic Vinegar, next page

1. Heat the oven to 350°. Coat the bottom and sides of a 9-by-2-inch cake pan evenly with all the butter. Add ¾ cup of the almonds. Rotate the pan to coat the bottom and sides. Turn the pan upside down and tap lightly to remove any nuts that do not cling.

2. In a food processor, grind the remaining 4¼ cups almonds and 1¾ cups of the sugar to a powder. Transfer the mixture to a medium bowl.

3. In a large bowl, beat the egg whites until foamy. Continue beating, adding the remaining 2 tablespoons sugar gradually, until the whites hold firm peaks when the beaters are lifted. Beat in the vanilla and lemon zest until just mixed.

4. Add the almond mixture to the egg whites half a cup at a time, folding gently just until combined. Do not overmix. The batter will be dense.

5. Put the batter into the prepared pan and smooth the top. Bake in the middle of the oven until the top is browned and the center springs back when touched lightly, 35 to 40 minutes. Remove from the oven and cool in the pan on a rack. Turn out onto a serving plate. Serve accompanied by the Strawberries in Balsamic Vinegar.

MAKE IT AHEAD
The cake is so moist that it keeps well for up to five days. You can prepare the berries and toss them with the sugar, water and vinegar four hours before serving. ➤

STRAWBERRIES IN BALSAMIC VINEGAR

MAKES 6 CUPS

4 pints strawberries, 1 pint hulled, 3 pints hulled and sliced

¼ cup sugar

2 tablespoons water

1 tablespoon balsamic vinegar

1. In a food processor or blender, puree the whole strawberries. Strain into a large bowl, pressing the pureed strawberries through the sieve.

2. Stir in the sugar, water and vinegar. Add the sliced strawberries and toss gently.

VARIATIONS

Instead of the Strawberries in Balsamic Vinegar, try one of these variations. Simply toss the ingredients together and macerate at least 20 minutes and up to 6 hours, stirring once or twice.

■ ■ ■

MIXED BERRIES IN RASPBERRY LIQUEUR

2½ pints mixed berries, such as strawberries (quartered), blueberries, raspberries and blackberries

¼ cup sugar

2 tablespoons raspberry liqueur or other berry liqueur

■ ■ ■

PINEAPPLE AND LITCHIS IN KIRSCH

This is best served thoroughly chilled.

2 pineapples, peeled, cored and cut into bite-size pieces

2 11-ounce cans litchis (about 24), drained, cut into halves

¼ cup sugar

2 tablespoons kirsch

■ ■ ■

MANGO IN RUM

5 mangoes, peeled and cut crosswise into slices

⅓ cup brown sugar

2 tablespoons lime juice

3 tablespoons rum

ESPRESSO-AND-RUM CREME CARAMEL

The French classic of smooth custard with its own built-in caramel sauce takes on a whole new dimension when flavored with espresso and rum.

SERVES 8

- 2 cups plus 1 tablespoon sugar
- 1 cup water
- 1 quart milk
- 2 tablespoons plus 1 teaspoon instant espresso powder
- 6 large eggs
- 4 large egg yolks
- ¼ cup dark rum

1. Heat the oven to 350°. In a medium, heavy saucepan, combine 1½ cups of the sugar with the water. Bring the mixture to a boil over moderately high heat and boil (brushing the inside of the saucepan occasionally with a pastry brush dipped in water, to dissolve any sugar crystals) until the sugar turns a rich, tea-like brown. Immediately remove from the heat. Very carefully, pour this caramelized sugar into eight 11-ounce ramekins or custard cups. Rotate the ramekins if necessary to spread the caramel evenly over the bottom of each. Set aside.

2. Bring water to a simmer for the water bath. In a medium saucepan over moderately high heat, bring the milk, the remaining ½ cup plus 1 tablespoon sugar and the espresso powder almost to a simmer, stirring occasionally, to dissolve the sugar and espresso powder.

3. In a large bowl, whisk together the eggs, egg yolks and rum until just combined. Pour the hot milk over the egg mixture, whisking. Strain the custard into a large measuring cup or pitcher and skim any foam from the surface.

4. Divide the custard among the prepared ramekins. Put them into a roasting pan. Pour enough of the simmering water into the roasting pan to reach about halfway up the sides of the ramekins. Carefully transfer the roasting pan to the lower third of the oven and bake until the custard is just set but still jiggles in the center when the ramekins are touched, about 30 minutes. Remove the ramekins from the water bath and let cool. Refrigerate until cold, at least 2 hours.

5. To serve, press around the edges of the custards to loosen them. Unmold onto serving plates.

MAKE IT AHEAD
Like many custards, crème caramel is every bit as good when made a day ahead. Keep the ramekins of custard in the refrigerator, covered with plastic wrap. If last-minute unmolding isn't convenient, you can unmold the custards onto dessert plates up to an hour in advance and keep them in the refrigerator.

GINGER CREME BRULEE

Smooth, ginger-spiced custard under crackling caramel, this luxurious dessert
is a delight of contrasting flavors and textures.

SERVES 8

1 quart light cream

2 teaspoons minced fresh ginger

1 vanilla bean, or 1½ teaspoons vanilla extract

¼ teaspoon grated lemon zest

Pinch salt

9 large egg yolks

⅔ cup granulated sugar

6 to 8 tablespoons light-brown sugar

1½ pints raspberries (optional)

1. Heat the oven to 300°. In a medium saucepan, bring the cream, ginger, the vanilla bean, if using, the lemon zest and salt almost to a simmer over moderate heat, stirring occasionally. Remove from the heat, cover and let infuse 10 minutes.

2. Bring water to a simmer for the water bath. In a large bowl, whisk the yolks and granulated sugar until well blended and just slightly thickened, about 1 minute. Bring the cream almost to a simmer. Pour it slowly into the yolk mixture, whisking gently. Add the vanilla extract, if using. Strain the custard into a large measuring cup or pitcher.

3. Put eight 6-ounce ramekins or small gratin dishes in a roasting pan. Pour the custard into the ramekins. Pour enough simmering water into the roasting pan to reach about halfway up the sides of the ramekins. Carefully transfer the roasting pan to the lower third of the oven and bake until the custard is just set but still jiggles in the center when the ramekins are touched, 35 to 40 minutes. Remove the ramekins from the water bath and let cool. Refrigerate uncovered until cold, at least 2 hours.

4. Heat the broiler. Sift 2 teaspoons of the brown sugar over the top of each custard in a thin layer. (If you are using gratin dishes, you'll need the larger quantity of sugar.) Set the ramekins on a baking sheet. Broil 3 to 4 inches from the heat until the sugar caramelizes, 30 seconds to 2 minutes; watch carefully. Let cool. Arrange the raspberries, if using, on top of the caramel, around the edge of each ramekin.

MAKE IT AHEAD

Baking the custard ahead is a good idea; it needs at least two hours to chill and will keep perfectly, covered with plastic wrap, for up to two days. Shortly before serving dinner, broil the topping and put the dessert in the refrigerator to cool. The farther ahead you caramelize the sugar, the greater the risk that it will soften, but it should last at least an hour.

BUBBLE-FREE CUSTARD

When combining the cream and yolks for custard, whisk gently. Vigorous whisking makes bubbles that are hard to get rid of, and you'll want a perfectly smooth surface for the caramel topping.

TAKING IT TO THE TOP

When a certain size ramekin or baking dish is specified in a recipe, you can check the volume by filling it up to the very top with water and then pouring the water into a measuring cup.

A TOPPING AS SMOOTH AS GLASS

The moisture in brown sugar makes it clump. To get an even coating, first spread the sugar on a baking sheet and let it dry at room temperature overnight. If you dry the sugar, you'll need only about a quarter cup.

SOME LIKE IT HOT

While crème brûlée is usually served cold, it's also delicious warm. Bake the custard, let it cool to warm and then go ahead and caramelize it.

COLD ORANGE ZABAGLIONE WITH RASPBERRIES

Light and refreshing, this zabaglione made with an orange-flavored dessert wine, such as Electra or Essencia, is an ideal complement to fresh raspberries. Of course you can always use the traditional sweet Marsala instead.

SERVES 8

- 7 large egg yolks
- ¾ cup sugar
- 1 cup orange-flavored dessert wine, such as Electra or Essencia, or sweet Marsala
- ½ teaspoon vanilla extract
- ½ teaspoon grated lemon zest
- 1 cup heavy cream
- 1 pint raspberries

MAKE IT AHEAD

The zabaglione can be made ahead and assembled with the fruit several hours before you plan to serve it. Eventually the emulsion separates, but it holds, remaining light and fluffy, for a surprisingly long time.

1. In a large bowl, beat together the yolks, sugar, wine, vanilla and zest. Set the bowl over a large saucepan filled with 1 inch of hot, not simmering, water (see photo, page 233). Using a hand-held electric mixer or a whisk, beat the egg-yolk mixture 5 minutes. Remove from the heat and beat until the mixture is completely cool and mounds when the beaters are lifted, about 7 minutes.

2. In a large bowl, beat the cream just until it holds firm peaks when the beaters are lifted. Fold in the egg mixture until just combined.

3. Divide the raspberries among 8 dessert goblets. Top with the zabaglione. Chill for at least 30 minutes.

PRUNE AND ARMAGNAC ICE CREAM

Unusual as the combination sounds, prunes and Armagnac have a real affinity for each other. In France, you frequently find them served either over or in ice cream. For a no-work dessert, just macerate the prunes in the Armagnac and ladle them over store-bought vanilla ice cream.

MAKES ABOUT 1³/₄ QUARTS

- ³/₄ pound (about 2 cups) pitted prunes
- ³/₄ cup Armagnac
- 3 cups milk
- 2 cups heavy cream
- 1 cup sugar
- 1 vanilla bean, split lengthwise, or 1¹/₂ teaspoons vanilla extract
- 10 large egg yolks

1. In a glass or stainless-steel bowl, combine the prunes and Armagnac and let sit at room temperature, covered with plastic wrap, for 24 hours. Drain the prunes, reserving the Armagnac. Cut the prunes into quarters.

2. In a large saucepan, combine the milk, cream and ¹/₂ cup of the sugar. Scrape the seeds from the vanilla bean, if using, and add the seeds and the bean to the milk mixture. Cook over moderate heat, stirring frequently with a wooden spoon, until the sugar dissolves and the mixture is hot, 6 to 8 minutes. Then remove from the heat, cover and let infuse for 10 minutes.

3. In a large bowl, whisk the egg yolks with the remaining ¹/₂ cup sugar until pale yellow, about 3 minutes. Bring the milk mixture to a simmer, uncovered, stirring frequently. Pour the hot milk into the yolks in a thin stream, whisking. Pour the mixture back into the pan and cook over moderately low heat, stirring constantly, until it is just thick enough to coat a spoon, 3 to 5 minutes. Do not let the custard boil or it may curdle. Strain into a bowl and let cool. Stir in the reserved Armagnac and the vanilla extract, if using. Cover and refrigerate until very cold, about 4 hours.

4. Pour the cold custard into an ice-cream maker and freeze according to the manufacturer's instructions. Put a 2-quart container in the freezer to chill. Transfer the ice cream to the chilled container and stir in the reserved prunes. Store the ice cream in the freezer until hard enough to scoop, about 30 minutes.

MAKE IT AHEAD
The prunes need to soak in the Armagnac at least a day in advance so that they soften and absorb the liquid. At the same time, you can make the ice-cream base, cool it and chill it in the refrigerator overnight. The next day, all you have to do is churn the ice cream and stir in the prunes. You can keep the finished ice cream

in the freezer for up to a week before serving. Check the ice cream twenty minutes before serving. If it's too hard, let it sit at room temperature until softened slightly, about fifteen minutes.

THE VANILLA BEAN

Vanilla adds a seductive note to desserts, and no vanilla flavor is better than that from the bean itself. To extract that flavor, infuse a hot liquid, such as cream or milk, with the vanilla bean, either whole or split. If you opt to keep the bean whole, it can be used again. Simply remove it from the liquid after steeping, rinse it off, pat dry and store in the freezer for a second use. Or split the bean lengthwise, scrape the seeds into the liquid and drop the pod in. The flavor will be somewhat stronger, and the tiny black seeds will speckle the dish appealingly, but you won't be able to use the pod again.

CINNAMON ICE CREAM

Infused with cinnamon sticks, this ice cream is great on its own, with cookies, or served with one of our other desserts such as Italian Plum Cake, page 243, or Apple Orange Crisp with Pecan Topping, page 245.

MAKES ABOUT 1½ QUARTS

- 3 cups milk
- 2 cups heavy cream
- 1 cup sugar
- 5 cinnamon sticks
- 10 large egg yolks

1. In a large saucepan, combine the milk, cream, ½ cup of the sugar and the cinnamon sticks. Cook over moderate heat, stirring frequently with a wooden spoon, until the sugar dissolves and the mixture is hot, 6 to 8 minutes. Remove from the heat, cover and let infuse for 10 minutes.

2. In a large bowl, whisk the egg yolks with the remaining ½ cup sugar until pale yellow, about 3 minutes. Bring the milk mixture to a simmer, uncovered, stirring frequently.

3. Pour the hot milk into the yolks in a thin stream, whisking. Pour the mixture back into the pan and cook over moderately low heat, stirring constantly, until it is just thick enough to coat a spoon, 3 to 5 minutes. Do not let the custard boil or it may curdle. Strain into a bowl and let cool. Cover and refrigerate until very cold, about 4 hours.

4. Pour the cold custard into an ice-cream maker and freeze according to the manufacturer's instructions. Put a 2-quart container in the freezer to chill. Transfer the ice cream to the chilled container. Store the ice cream in the freezer until hard enough to scoop, about 30 minutes.

MAKE IT AHEAD
Prepare the ice-cream base and chill it in the refrigerator overnight. The next day, you just have to churn it. While it's best right out of the ice-cream maker, you can freeze the finished ice cream for up to a week before serving. Check it twenty minutes before serving. If it's too hard, soften slightly at room temperature for about fifteen minutes.

VARIATION

GINGER ICE CREAM WITH CRYSTALLIZED GINGER

You can make ginger ice cream with the same custard base. Simply use ¼ cup grated fresh ginger in place of the cinnamon sticks and top the finished ice cream with ¼ cup finely chopped crystallized ginger.

CANTALOUPE AND PORT SORBET

Cantaloupe and port is a classic summertime combination that makes a delicious and refreshing sorbet. It's one of the easiest sorbets we know; just puree cantaloupe in a blender or food processor, add a little sugar, lemon juice and a splash of port, and freeze the mixture in an ice-cream maker.

MAKES ABOUT 1 1/2 QUARTS

6¾ pounds cantaloupe (about 3), peeled, seeded and chopped

5 tablespoons lemon juice (from about 2 lemons)

¾ cup plus 2 tablespoons super-fine sugar

5 tablespoons port

1. In a blender or food processor, puree the cantaloupe with the lemon juice, sugar and port in batches.

2. Pour the mixture into an ice-cream maker and freeze according to the manufacturer's instructions. Put a 2-quart container in the freezer to chill. Transfer the sorbet to the chilled container and store in the freezer until hard enough to scoop, about 30 minutes. Serve in chilled bowls or glasses.

MAKE IT AHEAD
All homemade sorbet is best served soon after it is churned, but you can make the sorbet up to twelve hours ahead. Store it in the freezer and check it about twenty minutes before serving. If it's very hard, let it soften slightly at room temperature.

WHAT'S SUPER-FINE SUGAR?

Super-fine sugar, also known as *bar sugar*, is just finely ground granulated sugar. It dissolves in a flash, making it ideal for sorbets. Not only is using it easier than adding sugar the traditional way by first making sugar syrup, but it doesn't dilute the flavor the way the water in syrup can. Most supermarkets stock super-fine sugar.

GREEN-GRAPE AND GRAPPA SORBET

Because they're loaded with juice and have plenty of natural sweetness, green grapes make a delicious, pastel sorbet. Grappa, the Italian brandy made from the grape skins, seeds and stems left after winemaking, is added just before freezing to heighten the flavor and maintain the smoothness of the sorbet. Frosted grapes carry out the theme for an attractive and tasty finishing touch.

MAKES ABOUT 1 1/2 QUARTS

5 pounds seedless green grapes, stems removed

7 tablespoons super-fine sugar

3¾ teaspoons lemon juice

3 tablespoons grappa

Frosted Grapes, recipe follows (optional)

1. In a food processor, puree the grapes in batches. Strain into a large bowl and press the grape skins to get all the juice. Discard the skins. Add the sugar, lemon juice and grappa and stir until the sugar dissolves.

2. Pour the mixture into an ice-cream maker and freeze according to the manufacturer's instructions. Put a 2-quart container in the freezer to chill. Transfer the sorbet to the chilled container and store in the freezer until hard enough to scoop, about 30 minutes. Serve in chilled bowls or glasses and garnish with the frosted grapes, if using.

MAKE IT AHEAD
You can, of course, make any frozen dessert well ahead of time, but the sooner you serve sorbet after churning, the smoother it will be. After about twelve hours, even those with alcohol tend to get icy. If you make sorbet in advance, check it about twenty minutes before serving. If it's very hard, let it sit at room temperature to soften slightly. While you can serve the frosted grapes after one hour, they're best made up to eight hours ahead and left to dry at room temperature. The sugary crust becomes even crisper—a pleasant contrast to the juicy interior.

FROSTED GRAPES

MAKES GARNISH FOR 8

¾ pound seedless green or red grapes

2 egg whites, beaten to mix

½ cup granulated sugar, more if needed

1. Wash the grapes and let dry completely on paper towels. Cut small bunches, 5 to 10 grapes to a bunch.

2. With a pastry brush, coat the grapes with a thin layer of egg white. Sprinkle with the sugar. Let the grapes dry at room temperature for at least 1 hour.

ALMOND TUILES

Their elegant curved shape, like that of roof tiles, gives these traditional European cookies their name. Thin and crisp, they add the perfect touch to any dessert but go especially well with ice cream and sorbet.

MAKES ABOUT 3 DOZEN

¾ cup slivered almonds

½ cup sugar

¼ cup flour

1 large egg, at room temperature

1 large egg white, at room temperature

½ teaspoon vanilla extract

1. Heat the oven to 350°. In a food processor or blender, chop the almonds into small pieces and put them in a medium bowl. Add the sugar and flour and whisk to blend. In a small bowl, whisk the egg, egg white and vanilla just to mix. Add the eggs to the almond mixture and whisk until smooth.

2. Generously butter a baking sheet. Spoon 1½-teaspoon mounds of the batter about 2 inches apart on the baking sheet. Flatten the mounds with a fork.

3. Bake the cookies in the middle of the oven for 8 minutes. Remove and let cool for 5 minutes. Put the cookies back in the oven until golden brown, about another 4 minutes. (Baking them twice ensures even coloring.) Working quickly, lift each cookie from the pan with a metal spatula and curve it around a thin (French) rolling pin. Leave until set. If the cookies on the pan harden before you've shaped them all, pop the pan back in the oven for a few seconds to soften them. Repeat with the remaining cookie batter, allowing the cookie sheet to cool before starting the next batch. Cool the tuiles completely and store in an airtight container.

MAKE IT AHEAD
You can make the tuiles a day or two ahead and keep them in an airtight container. In humid weather, it's especially important to store the cookies carefully, or they'll quickly go limp and lose their shape.

Press the cookies around a French rolling pin. Leave until set. Put the pin on a towel so that it won't roll.

MOLASSES SPICE COOKIES

Spicy and slightly chewy, with a lovely cracked, sugary surface, these cookies are a tradition at *Food & Wine*'s annual holiday party. Quick and easy, they're great any time of year and go especially well with fruit desserts such as our Cold Orange Zabaglione with Raspberries, page 261.

MAKES ABOUT 4 DOZEN

  6 ounces unsalted butter
¼ cup molasses
  1 teaspoon vanilla extract
  2 cups flour
1⅓ cups sugar
  2 teaspoons baking soda
  2 teaspoons ground ginger
  2 teaspoons cinnamon
¼ teaspoon ground nutmeg
¼ teaspoon ground cloves
¼ teaspoon salt
  1 large egg

1. Heat the oven to 375°. In a small saucepan, melt the butter over low heat. Remove from the heat and add the molasses and vanilla. Set aside to cool.

2. In a medium bowl, whisk together the flour, 1 cup of the sugar, the baking soda, spices and salt.

3. Add the egg to the butter mixture and whisk to mix. With a wooden spoon, stir the butter mixture into the dry ingredients. Cover with plastic wrap and chill until firm, about 15 minutes.

4. Put the remaining ⅓ cup sugar in a small bowl. Shape the dough into 1-inch balls. Toss the balls in the sugar to coat completely and put them on an ungreased baking sheet, about 2 inches apart.

5. Bake the cookies in the middle of the oven until the bottoms begin to brown, about 10 minutes. Let the cookies cool on the baking sheet for 5 minutes, then transfer to a rack to cool. Repeat with the remaining cookie dough, allowing the cookie sheet to cool before starting the next batch.

—PEGGY CULLEN

MAKE IT AHEAD
You can make these cookies several days in advance and keep them in an airtight container.

LEMON CIAMBELLE

Ciambelle are slices of an Italian butter cake that comes in many flavors and shapes. Here it's lemony, with a sugary crust. The dough is shaped into logs, baked and then sliced. The end product is more like a cookie than cake. These slices are great with sorbets, with fruit compotes or with fresh fruit and a dessert wine, such as vin santo.

MAKES ABOUT 4 DOZEN

2 cups flour

1 cup sugar

1 tablespoon baking powder

Pinch salt

3 tablespoons unsalted butter, at room temperature

2 large eggs, at room temperature

1 large egg white, at room temperature

4 tablespoons milk

1 tablespoon lemon juice

1 tablespoon grated lemon zest (from about 2 lemons)

1. Heat the oven to 350°. In a medium bowl, whisk together the flour, 3/4 cup plus 2 tablespoons of the sugar, the baking powder and salt. Rub in the butter until the mixture is the texture of fine meal.

2. In a medium bowl, whisk together the eggs, egg white, 2 tablespoons of the milk, the lemon juice and zest. Add to the dry ingredients and stir just until mixed.

3. On a lightly floured surface, shape the dough into two logs, about 1 1/2 inches in diameter. Put them about 5 inches apart on a baking sheet lined with parchment paper, or on a buttered and lightly floured baking sheet. Brush the tops with the remaining 2 tablespoons milk and sprinkle with the remaining 2 tablespoons sugar.

4. Bake in the middle of the oven until the logs begin to brown and they spring back when pressed with a finger, about 20 minutes. Do not overbake or the cookies will be dry. Cool 10 minutes on the baking sheet and then peel off the parchment paper. Transfer to a rack and cool completely. Using a serrated knife, cut crosswise into 1/2-inch slices.

MAKE IT AHEAD
Ciambelle keep well in an airtight container; in fact, the lemon flavor is stronger the day after they're baked. If the slices do get dry, toast them in the oven and serve warm. Or turn the ciambelle into crisp biscotti by letting them air-dry for two days or by baking them in a 325° oven until beginning to brown, about fifteen minutes.

🍇 SERVING WINE WITH DESSERT

A small glass of gorgeously sweet, unctuous dessert wine such as a French Sauternes, Barsac or Sélection de Grains Nobles (from Alsace), a German *auslese* or *beerenauslese*, or an American late-harvest wine can add a luxurious coda to a fine meal. Unfortunately, it may not do much for your dessert, and vice versa. The flavor of even very sweet wines may at best be neutralized by very sweet desserts. Less sweet dessert-type wines, such as French Muscat de Beaumes-de-Venise, Italian vin santo, Spanish oloroso sherry or various countries' muscat or moscato wines, will taste even worse, sour or pallid, with a sweet dessert.

If you have an elegant or complex wine to feature, the best idea is to serve the wine by itself after dessert, or with fruit, fruit tarts like the Blueberry Crostata, page 239, or not-too-sweet cookies, such as the Almond Tuiles, page 268. Certain other combinations, such as semi-sweet chocolate preparations, like the Molten Chocolate Cakes, page 223, as well as caramel desserts or medium-sweet sorbets can also work with the sweeter wines. These wines can be wonderful with the milder blue cheeses, too.

There are worse ways to end a meal than with a toast of Champagne, but be aware that the common brut style of sparkling wine is relatively dry and will taste sour with most desserts. Look for an "Extra Dry" (perversely, it's extra sweet), a "Demi-Sec" or, for something more casual, an Asti Spumante from Italy.

Port (or Porto) is most classically matched with salty foods, such as aged Stilton or cheddar or a dish of walnuts. There is a contingent that loves sweet port and chocolate, though this can be too much of a good thing. A sweeter Madeira, such as a bual (or boal) or malmsey, is not only a novelty to serve in this day and age but a wonderful accompaniment to medium-sweet cakes, like the Lemon Pound Cake, page 250.

—RICHARD NALLEY

271

BASICS

CLASSIC VINAIGRETTE

A vinaigrette is the classic French combination of vinegar, oil, salt and pepper. Mustard is often added, and lemon or lime juice can replace the vinegar. We suggest two variations, but feel free to experiment further. Try raspberry, tarragon or balsamic vinegar. A spoonful of walnut or hazelnut oil adds a surprising amount of flavor, and chopped fresh herbs, shallot or garlic is a pleasant addition. Olive oil is hardly traditional (French chefs, except those in Provence, find the flavor too strong for greens), but by all means use it for all or part of the oil, if you like.

MAKES ABOUT 1/2 CUP

- 2 tablespoons red-wine vinegar
- 1/2 teaspoon Dijon mustard
- 1/2 teaspoon salt
- 1/8 teaspoon fresh-ground black pepper
- 1/3 cup cooking oil, such as peanut, corn or safflower

In a small bowl, whisk together the vinegar, mustard, salt and pepper. Add the oil slowly, whisking.

MAKE IT AHEAD
A vinaigrette will last indefinitely in the refrigerator; so it's convenient to make extra. Store any leftover dressing in a glass jar with a tight lid so that you can shake the vinaigrette to re-emulsify it. Don't add fresh herbs, shallot, scallion or garlic more than a day ahead, or the herbs will lose their vibrant color and the other flavorings will taste stale.

VARIATIONS

SHERRY SCALLION VINAIGRETTE

Sherry vinegar has a strong flavor; you don't need much. Make as at left with these ingredients and add the scallion at the end.

- 2 teaspoons sherry vinegar
- 1/2 teaspoon salt
- 1/8 teaspoon fresh-ground black pepper
- 1/3 cup cooking oil
- 2 teaspoons minced scallion

■ ■ ■

LEMON PEPPER VINAIGRETTE

Make as at left with these ingredients.

- 2 tablespoons lemon juice
- 1/2 teaspoon salt
- 3/4 teaspoon fresh-ground black pepper
- 1/3 cup olive oil

PESTO ALLA GENOVESE

Don't limit this pungent Northern Italian basil sauce to pasta. Try something less conventional and spoon it onto miniature squares of polenta, page 19, for an appealing hors d'oeuvre.

MAKES ABOUT 1 CUP

   2   cloves garlic, chopped

1½   cups lightly packed fresh basil leaves

 ¾   teaspoon salt

 ½   cup olive oil

 ¼   cup pine nuts

 ½   cup grated Parmesan cheese

   1   tablespoon butter, at room temperature

1. In a blender or food processor, mince the garlic and basil with the salt.

2. With the machine on, add the oil in a thin stream. Add the pine nuts, Parmesan and butter and whir just until the nuts are chopped.

MAKE IT AHEAD
Pesto will last in the refrigerator for about a week, or it can be frozen.

CHICKEN STOCK

Make plenty of chicken stock while you're at it. It's a great all-purpose stock that you can use in fish and meat dishes as well as chicken recipes. Boil it down to half or even less, freeze in small containers and reconstitute as needed.

MAKES ABOUT 1¹/₂ QUARTS

4   pounds chicken carcasses, backs, wings and/or necks, plus gizzards (optional)

2   onions, quartered

2   carrots, quartered

2   ribs celery, quartered

8   parsley stems

5   peppercorns

2   quarts water

1. Put all the ingredients in a large pot. Bring to a boil and skim the foam that rises to the surface. Reduce the heat and simmer, partially covered, for 2 hours.

2. Strain. Press the bones and vegetables firmly to get all the liquid. Skim the fat from the surface if using immediately. If not, refrigerate for up to a week or freeze. Scrape off the fat before using.

MAKE IT AHEAD
You can keep the stock in the refrigerator for up to a week or freeze it almost indefinitely.

BEEF STOCK

While this stock takes a bit more than five hours from start to finish, the actual preparation time is minimal—less than twenty minutes. And what a difference from canned beef broth.

MAKES ABOUT 1 QUART

- 2 pounds beef bones, cut into pieces
- 1 onion, quartered
- 2 carrots, quartered
- 2 ribs celery, quartered
- 2½ quarts water
- 1 14-ounce can (about 1¾ cups) tomatoes, drained
- 8 parsley stems
- 4 sprigs fresh thyme, or ¾ teaspoon dried
- 1 bay leaf
- 4 peppercorns

1. Heat the oven to 450°. Put the bones in a large roasting pan. Brown in the oven for 40 minutes, stirring once or twice. Add the onion, carrots and celery and continue cooking until the bones and vegetables are well browned, about 20 minutes longer.

2. Put the bones and vegetables in a large pot. Pour off all the fat in the roasting pan and add 1 cup of the water. Bring to a boil, scraping the bottom of the pan to dislodge any brown bits. Add to the pot with the remaining 9 cups water, the tomatoes, parsley stems, thyme, bay leaf and peppercorns. Bring to a boil and skim the foam that rises to the surface. Reduce the heat and simmer the stock, partially covered, for 4 hours.

3. Strain. Press the bones and vegetables firmly to get all the liquid. Skim the fat from the surface if using immediately. If not, refrigerate for up to a week or freeze. Scrape off the fat before using.

MAKE IT AHEAD
See Chicken Stock, previous page.

VARIATION

VEAL STOCK

Milder in flavor than beef stock, veal stock is made in exactly the same way, with veal bones in place of beef. Make either a light-colored stock, by omitting the first step, or a dark one.

CROSTINI

An Italian country loaf is ideal for crostini, but any good bread will do. The number of slices you'll need will vary depending on the size of the loaf. For our recipes, you'll want the finished crostini to measure about three inches by two-and-a-half inches.

MAKES 24 CROSTINI

- 3 tablespoons olive oil
- 1 clove garlic, lightly crushed
- 6 ½-inch slices country bread
- ¼ teaspoon salt
- ¼ teaspoon fresh-ground black pepper

1. In a small bowl, combine the oil and garlic and leave to sit at least 10 minutes. Heat the broiler. Put the bread on a baking sheet and broil, turning once, until crisp and brown on the outside but still slightly soft in the center, about 3 minutes.

2. Brush one side of the bread with the garlic oil and sprinkle with the salt and pepper. Cut each slice of bread into quarters. Serve warm.

MAKE IT AHEAD The garlic oil can be made hours in advance. Or you can go ahead and finish the crostini. They'll stay crisp for several hours. If you want to serve them warm, reheat them in a 350° oven for a few minutes just before adding the topping.

Peppered Toast

Of course you can omit the pepper and make plain toast, but we particularly like this piquant version, especially when topped with Fresh-Cod Brandade, page 29. A French baguette makes small attractive slices, but any good bread will work just fine.

MAKES 24 TOASTS

24 ¼-inch slices French baguette, or an equal quantity of halved or quartered slices from a larger loaf

3 tablespoons cooking oil

½ teaspoon salt

¾ teaspoon fresh-ground black pepper

1. Heat the oven to 350°. Brush both sides of the bread with the oil and put the slices on a baking sheet.

2. Bake the bread, turning it once, until crisp, about 10 minutes. Sprinkle with the salt and pepper. Serve warm or at room temperature.

MAKE IT AHEAD The toast comes out of the oven crisp, and except on a humid day, it will stay that way for several hours. Or you can keep it in an airtight container for a couple of days.

WHIPPED CREAM

Don't consider this a hard-and-fast recipe. You can use more or less sugar. It can be added in the midst of whipping, and so you can adjust it to your taste. Use vanilla or not, or try another flavoring such as coffee, cognac or a liqueur. The half-teaspoon quantity we suggest for vanilla is fine for extracts, which are concentrated, but you'll need a little more of other flavorings. Taste and add.

MAKES ABOUT 3 CUPS

1½ cups heavy cream

2 tablespoons sugar

½ teaspoon vanilla extract (optional)

In a large bowl, whip the cream, sugar and vanilla, if using, just until the cream holds firm peaks when the beaters are lifted.

MAKE IT AHEAD
You can whip cream up to three hours in advance. Keep it covered in the refrigerator. Just before serving you may need to whisk the cream for half a minute if it has softened.

CHILL THE BOWL

You'll be surprised how much faster you can whip cream in a chilled bowl with chilled beaters, especially if the weather's warm. The easiest way is to pour the cream into the bowl, stick the beaters in, too, and chill the whole thing for about five minutes or until you're ready to beat the cream.

WHITE-CHOCOLATE SAUCE

If you can boil water, you can make this luscious ivory-colored chocolate sauce. White chocolate tastes so sweet, you don't need any additional sugar.

MAKES ABOUT 2 CUPS

1½ cups heavy cream

6 ounces white chocolate, chopped

1½ teaspoons cognac or other brandy (optional)

1. In a medium saucepan, bring the cream to a boil over moderately high heat, stirring occasionally. Put the chocolate into a medium bowl. Pour the boiling cream over the chocolate and let sit for 5 minutes. Whisk until smooth.

2. Let the sauce cool and then stir in the cognac, if using. Chill for at least 30 minutes.

MAKE IT AHEAD
You can prepare the sauce ahead and keep it, refrigerated, for several days.

WHITE CHOCOLATE

Technically, white chocolate is not chocolate at all. It's made from the cocoa butter that is removed to leave the pure chocolate liquor (which carries the distinctive color and flavor of chocolate). If you don't see cocoa butter in the ingredient list, what you have is an artificial white chocolate. We don't recommend it, because it's usually cloyingly sweet and unappealingly waxy. While you don't need a top-of-the-line brand of white chocolate to make a sauce, as you would for making chocolate candies, you'll want the real thing. Lindt, Ghirardelli, Callebaut and Baker's are all excellent choices.

DARK-CHOCOLATE SAUCE

Unsweetened cocoa powder is used in place of chocolate to give this sauce its deep-brown color. Try the version on the opposite page as well and decide for yourself which one you like best.

MAKES ABOUT 2¹/₂ CUPS

1 cup water

1¹/₂ cups sugar

1¹/₄ cups unsweetened cocoa powder

³/₄ cup heavy cream

1. In a medium saucepan, bring the water and sugar to a boil over moderately high heat, stirring occasionally. Add the cocoa and bring back to a boil, whisking.

2. Add the cream and bring back to a boil, still whisking. Serve warm, at room temperature or chilled.

MAKE IT AHEAD
You can make the sauce several days in advance. Keep it in the refrigerator.

COCOA POWDER

When you're decorating desserts or making sauces with cocoa powder, we recommend Dutch-process cocoa, which is made with chocolate that has been treated with an alkali to neutralize the acid. It's darker with a milder, smoother flavor than regular unsweetened cocoa, and it gives your dessert or sauce a richer look. Most European cocoa powders are Dutch-process. A common brand in this country is Dröste. Also, Hershey's has introduced a Dutch-process cocoa.

CHOCOLATE SAUCE

The heat of the boiling cream melts the chocolate into a smooth sauce in minutes. Don't add the cognac until the sauce has cooled a bit, or the flavor of the brandy will not be strong enough.

MAKES ABOUT 2 CUPS

1¾ cups heavy cream

4 ounces semisweet chocolate, chopped

1 teaspoon cognac or other brandy

1. In a medium saucepan, bring the cream to a boil over moderately high heat, stirring occasionally. Put the chocolate into a medium bowl and pour the boiling cream over the chocolate. Let sit for 5 minutes. Whisk until smooth.

2. Let the sauce cool somewhat and then stir in the cognac. Serve warm, room temperature or chilled.

 **MAKE IT AHEAD**
See Dark-Chocolate Sauce, opposite.

ESPRESSO SAUCE

We suggest serving this coffee-flavored sauce to accompany Mocha Truffle Cake, page 229. You might also want to try it in place of the White-Chocolate Sauce in the Warm Chocolate Hazelnut Polenta Cakes, page 221.

MAKES 2 CUPS

¾ cup espresso beans, or 1 tablespoon instant espresso powder

2 cups heavy cream

Crush the beans, if using, with a rolling pin or in a mortar with a pestle. In a medium saucepan, bring the cream to a simmer over moderately high heat, stirring occasionally. Add the crushed espresso beans. Remove the pot from the heat, cover and let infuse 10 minutes. Strain. If using instant espresso, simply stir it into the hot cream until dissolved. Let the sauce cool. Chill for at least 30 minutes.

MAKE IT AHEAD
See Dark-Chocolate Sauce, opposite.

MENUS

THE AMERICAN CULINARY REPERTOIRE grows daily. We welcome dishes from more and more cuisines, and we make up our own recipes that reflect influences from all over. The increasing multiplicity of ethnic sources and the rise of eclectic recipes present cooks with an exciting, but potentially unruly, grab bag of flavors to tame into harmonious menus. It's not always an easy task. Herewith some suggestions that we hope will work for you, either as they are or as starting points for your own tasteful combinations.

■ ■ ■

■ ■ ■

Skewered Shrimp Marinated in
Lime-and-Basil Vinaigrette, page 33

Caviar and Crème Fraîche
on Puff-Pastry Squares, page 43

———

Wild-Mushroom Risotto, page 76

———

Salmon in Scallion Broth, page 99

French bread

———

Molten Chocolate Cakes, page 223

■ ■ ■

Mushrooms Filled with
Boursin Cheese, page 16

Peppered Cashews, page 37

———

Carrot Flans on Mixed Greens, page 79

———

Salmon Tandoori with
Cucumber Raita, page 100

Roasted Asparagus with
Brown Butter, page 180

Grilled naan or pita

———

Cold Orange Zabaglione with
Raspberries, page 261

■ ■ ■

■ ■ ■

Shrimp and Guacamole in
Mini-Pitas, page 35

———

Fennel-and-Mushroom Salad with
Shaved Parmesan, page 60

———

Black-Pepper Seared Tuna with
Corn Couscous, page 101

Spicy Green Beans with
Garlic and Ginger, page 179

———

Almond Cake with
Strawberries in Balsamic Vinegar, page 255,
or a variation, page 256

■ ■ ■

Buttered Pecans, page 37

Mussels on the Half-Shell with
Cilantro, page 39

———

Antipasto with Marinated Carrots, page 69

———

Whole Cod with Parsley Sauce, page 102

New Potatoes with Herb Oil, page 193

Roasted Beets with
Basil and Pine Nuts, page 204

———

Warm Lemon Mousse with
Raspberries and Vanilla Ice Cream, page 251

■ ■ ■

■ ■ ■

Chicken Kabobs with
Spicy Mango Sauce, page 49

Baked Radicchio and
Goat-Cheese Parcels, page 70

Poached Halibut with
Cilantro Lime Mayonnaise, page 105

Cold green beans
Classic Vinaigrette, page 274

Sliced fresh tomatoes

Crusty bread

Cinnamon Ice Cream, page 264
Chocolate Sauce, page 283

■ ■ ■

Black Olives with
Fennel Seeds and Fresh Fennel, page 25

Provençal Vegetable Terrines with
Chèvre, page 66

Herb-Stuffed Trout with Pancetta, page 107

Fresh-Corn Pudding, page 187

Country bread

Italian Plum Cake with
Cinnamon Plum Compote, page 243

■ ■ ■

■ ■ ■

Roquefort Walnut Biscuits, page 21

Black and green olives

Corn Chowder with
Roasted Poblanos and Crab, page 58

Broiled Swordfish Steaks with
Pineapple-and-Chile Salsa, page 108

Warm Eggplant Salad, page 201

Texmati rice

Mixed-Berry Cobbler, page 237

■ ■ ■

**Almond Cake with Strawberries
in Balsamic Vinegar, page 255**

■ ■ ■

Roasted-Eggplant and
Manchego-Cheese Crostini, page 45

Prosciutto-and-Herb Crostini, page 47

———

Fettuccine with
Walnut and Mascarpone Sauce, page 71

———

Roasted Monkfish with
French-Lentil Salad, page 110

———

Poached Pears in Cassis with
Kir Sorbet and Lemon Pound Cake, page 249

■ ■ ■

Tomato and Black-Olive Crostini, page 44

———

Thai Beef Salad, page 94

———

Boiled Lobster with Ginger Butter, page 111

Corn on the cob

———

Assorted goat cheeses

———

Blueberry Crostata, page 239

■ ■ ■

Spicy Shrimp Boil, page 113

■ ■ ■

Bocconcini Marinated in
Spiced Olive Oil, page 17

Feta and Black-Olive Wedges, page 24

———

Spicy Shrimp Boil, page 113

Green salad

Crusty bread

———

Peach Shortcake with
Citrus Sugar, page 241

■ ■ ■

■■■

Pork Satay with
Spicy Peanut Dipping Sauce, page 51

———

Warm Portobello and Basil Salad, page 61

———

Indonesian Rice with
Grilled Shrimp, page 114

Sautéed zucchini

———

Almond Cake with
Pineapple and Litchis in Kirsch, page 256

■■■

Cheddar Pecan Biscuits, page 21

Black olives

———

Ranch-Style Shrimp, page 116

Mexican Black-Bean Salad, page 205

Steamed rice

———

Bitter-Chocolate Mousse with
White-Chocolate Sauce, page 224

■■■

■■■

Tuna Tartare, page 36

Romesco Dip, page 40
Fresh vegetables

———

Spaghetti with Parmesan and
Mixed Spicy Greens, page 73

———

Polenta-Stuffed Cornish Hens, page 117

Sautéed Cucumbers with
Prosciutto and Cream, page 183

———

Blueberry Crostata, page 239

■■■

Peppered Cashews, page 37

———

Warm Scallop Salad with
Shiitake Mushrooms and Pine Nuts, page 81

———

Indian-Spiced Cornish Hens and
Red Lentils, page 118

Cucumber Raita, page 184

———

Ginger Ice Cream with
Crystallized Ginger, page 264

Almond Tuiles, page 268

■■■

■ ■ ■

Parmesan, Black-Pepper and
Pine-Nut Biscuits, page 20

———

Smoked Trout with
Jicama-and-Carrot Salad, page 89

———

Grilled Chicken Breasts with
Green-Olive Tapenade, page 119

Roasted Mediterranean Vegetables, page 177

———

Espresso-and-Rum Crème Caramel, page 257

■ ■ ■

Smoked Salmon with
Herbs and Crème Fraîche, page 23

———

Quail Wrapped in Prosciutto, page 121

Broccoli Rabe with
Oven-Dried Tomatoes and
Pine Nuts, page 181

Cheese Polenta, page 200

———

Vanilla Semifreddo with
Amaretti and Dark Chocolate, page 234

■ ■ ■

■ ■ ■

Vietnamese Spring Rolls with
Shrimp and Avocado, page 31

———

Asparagus Soup with
Salmon Caviar, page 57

———

Roasted Cured Chicken, page 122

Potato and Leek Gratin, page 196

Steamed spinach

———

Prune and Armagnac Ice Cream, page 262

Molasses Spice Cookies, page 269

■ ■ ■

Romesco Dip, page 40
Fresh vegetables

———

Chicken and Shrimp Paella, page 124

Crusty rolls

———

Manchego cheese

———

Hot Apple Tart with
Thyme Syrup, page 246

■ ■ ■

■ ■ ■

Cheddar Pecan Biscuits, page 21

Skewered Shrimp Marinated in
Sherry-Vinegar, Scallion and
Soy Vinaigrette, page 33

———

Smoked Salmon with
Watercress and Sugar-Snap Salad, page 92

———

Chicken Biryani, page 126

Cucumber Raita, page 184

———

Ginger Crème Brûlée, page 258

■ ■ ■

**Vietnamese Spring Rolls with
Shrimp and Avocado, page 31**

■ ■ ■

Belgian Endive Leaves with
Herbed Chèvre, page 15

Cheddar Lace, page 23

———

Caribbean Shrimp with Chile Aioli and
Mango Papaya Salad, page 83

———

Roast Capon with Leeks,
Apples and Pine Nuts, page 129

Bacon Mashed Potatoes, page 194

Brussels sprouts

———

Bitter-Chocolate Mousse with
White-Chocolate Sauce, page 224

■ ■ ■

Buttered Pecans, page 37

Crostini with White-Bean Salad, page 46

———

Mixed green salad

———

Duck-and-Shrimp Gumbo, page 131,
or Chicken-and-Shrimp Gumbo, page 132

Corn bread

———

Bread Pudding with Dried Cherries and
Bourbon Sauce, page 252

■ ■ ■

■ ■ ■

Black Olives with
Fennel Seeds and Fresh Fennel, page 25

Fresh-Cod Brandade, page 29

Peppered Cashews, page 37

——

Artichoke Salad with
Caper Vinaigrette, page 64

——

Roast Veal with Sage, page 133

Broccoli Rabe with
Oven-Dried Tomatoes and
Pine Nuts, page 181

Garlic and Rosemary
Mashed Potatoes, page 194

——

Gorgonzola, Parmigiano-Reggiano,
Fontina, Taleggio

——

Green-Grape and Grappa Sorbet, page 267

Lemon Ciambelle, page 270

■ ■ ■

■ ■ ■

Polenta Squares with Pesto, page 19

Peppered Cashews, page 37

——

Mussels with
Pancetta and Rosemary, page 85

——

Loin of Veal with Thyme Cream, page 134,
or a variation, page 135

Herbed Mashed Potatoes, page 194

Steamed broccoli

——

Mocha Truffle Cake with
Espresso Sauce, page 229

■ ■ ■

Tomato and Black-Olive Crostini, page 44

——

Artichoke Salad with
Caper Vinaigrette, page 64

——

Loin of Veal with Thyme Jus, page 135

Baked Polenta with
Wild-Mushroom Topping, page 200

Buttered green beans

——

Cold Orange Zabaglione with
Raspberries, page 261

■ ■ ■

292

■ ■ ■

Anchoïade Provençale, page 41
Fresh vegetables

———

Classic Cheese Risotto, page 77

———

Veal Chops with Mushrooms and
Roasted Garlic, page 137

Sautéed red bell peppers

Italian bread

———

Frozen Cappuccino Soufflé, page 231

■ ■ ■

Tuna Tartare, page 36

Prosciutto-and-Herb Crostini, page 47

———

Warm Portobello and Basil Salad, page 61

———

Ossobuco with
Balsamic Vinegar and Rosemary, page 139

Classic Cheese Risotto, page 77

Broccoli Rabe with
Oven-Dried Tomatoes and
Pine Nuts, page 181

———

Hazelnut Semifreddo with
Dark-Chocolate Sauce, page 232

■ ■ ■

■ ■ ■

Belgian Endive Leaves with
Roquefort and Walnuts, page 15

———

Creamy Broiled Oysters with Bacon, page 80

———

Wasabi-Marinated Strip Steaks, page 141

New Potatoes with Herb Oil, page 193

Sautéed Japanese Eggplant with
Soy, Mirin and Sesame-Oil Sauce, page 203

———

Poached Pears in Cassis with
Kir Sorbet and Lemon Pound Cake, page 249

■ ■ ■

Black Olives with
Fennel Seeds and Fresh Fennel, page 25

Shrimp and Guacamole in
Mini-Pitas, page 35

Buttered Pecans, page 37

———

Green-Bean Salad with
Shiitake Mushrooms, page 63

———

Sirloin with Chimichurri Sauce, page 143

Pommes Anna, page 197

———

Mimolette, Camembert, Comté,
Sells-sur-Cher, Roquefort

———

Warm Chocolate Hazelnut Polenta Cakes
with White-Chocolate Sauce, page 221

■ ■ ■

■ ■ ■

Chicken Kabobs with
Spicy Mango Sauce, page 49

———

Green-Bean Salad with
Shiitake Mushrooms, page 63

———

Standing Rib Roast with
Chile-Pepper Spice Rub, page 144

Southwestern Succotash, page 186

Baby carrots

———

Aged mimolette, Bleu d'Auvergne, Chèvre

———

Chocolate-and-Toffee Gâteau with
a Butter-Pecan Crust, page 227

■ ■ ■

Cheddar Pecan Biscuits, page 21

———

Carrot Flans on Mixed Greens, page 79

———

Braised Oxtails with Red Wine and
Portobello Mushrooms, page 146

Wild Rice with
Currants and Sautéed Apples, page 192

Brussels sprouts

———

Tiramisu, page 235

■ ■ ■

■ ■ ■

Roquefort Walnut Biscuits, page 21

———

Smoked Trout with
Jicama-and-Carrot Salad, page 89

———

Chipotle-Chile Beef Stew
with Butternut Squash, page 149

Corn bread

———

Pear and Dried-Cherry Crisp, page 245

■ ■ ■

Crostini with White-Bean Salad, page 46

Black olives

———

Green-Bean Salad with
Shiitake Mushrooms, page 63

———

Beef Tenderloin with
Peppercorn and Mustard-Seed Crust,
page 151

Orzo with Pesto and Lemon, page 199

Spinach

———

Dry Jack cheese

———

Chocolate and Mint-Tea
Pots de Crème, page 225

■ ■ ■

■ ■ ■

Polenta Squares with Pesto, page 19

———

Mussels with
Pancetta and Rosemary, page 85

———

Roast Loin of Pork
with Green-Olive Filling, page 152

Parmesan Potato Wedges, page 195

Roasted red bell peppers

———

Italian Plum Cake with
Cinnamon Plum Compote, page 243

■ ■ ■

Acorn-Squash Rings, page 191

■ ■ ■

Crostini with White-Bean Salad, page 46

———

Gravlax with Grainy-Mustard Sauce, page 91

Black and green olives

———

Fresh Ham with
Balsamic-Caramelized Onions, page 155

Sautéed Greens with
Peppers and Lime, page 185

Pommes Anna, page 197

———

Aged Gouda, Reblochon

———

Frozen Cappuccino Soufflé, page 231

■ ■ ■

Vietnamese Spring Rolls with
Shrimp and Avocado, page 31

———

Wine-Braised Ham with
Spiced Peach Chutney, page 156

Acorn-Squash Rings, page 191

Wild Rice with
Currants and Sautéed Apples, page 192

———

Baked Radicchio and
Goat-Cheese Parcels, page 70

———

Prune and Armagnac Ice Cream, page 262

Molasses Spice Cookies, page 269

■ ■ ■

■■■

Anchoïade Provençale, page 41
Fresh vegetables

———

Crab Cakes with Chile Remoulade, page 87

———

Pork Tenderloin with
Pomegranate Sauce, page 158

Corn Couscous, page 188

———

Camembert

———

Cantaloupe and Port Sorbet, page 265

Lemon Ciambelle, page 270

■■■

Black Olives with
Fennel Seeds and Fresh Fennel, page 25

Prosciutto-and-Herb Crostini, page 47

———

Grilled Quail with
Cucumber Relish, page 93

———

Polenta Lasagne, page 161

Green salad

———

Green-Grape and Grappa Sorbet, page 267

Almond Tuiles, page 268

■■■

■■■

Grilled Scallops with Salsa Verde, page 27

———

Grits with Wild-Mushroom Ragout, page 74

———

Garlic-Rubbed Rack of Lamb, page 163

Acorn-Squash Rings, page 191

Cipollini in Marsala Glaze, page 207

———

Mocha Truffle Cake with
Espresso Sauce, page 229

■■■

Mushrooms Filled with
Boursin Cheese, page 16

Pistachios

———

Caribbean Shrimp with Chile Aioli and
Mango Papaya Salad, page 83

———

Braised Lamb Shanks with
Caramelized Onions and Mint, page 164

Bacon Mashed Potatoes, page 194

Sautéed Greens with
Peppers and Lime, page 185

———

Ginger Crème Brûlée, page 258

■■■

■ ■ ■

Mussels on the Half-Shell with
Cilantro, page 39

———

Smoked Salmon with
Watercress and Sugar-Snap Salad, page 92

———

Boneless Leg of Lamb with Pommery
Mustard, Garlic and Rosemary, page 166

Italian Eggplant Salad, page 201

Steamed asparagus

Country bread

———

Stilton, Gruyère, Farmhouse cheddar,
Swiss Sbrinz

———

Warm Chocolate Hazelnut Polenta Cakes
with White-Chocolate Sauce, page 221

■ ■ ■

Sesame Soy Tuna Tartare, page 36

———

Artichoke Salad with
Caper Vinaigrette, page 64

———

Moroccan Lamb with
Vegetable Couscous, page 169

———

Apple Orange Crisp with
Pecan Topping, page 245

■ ■ ■

■ ■ ■

Spicy Scallop Salsa in
Cucumber Cups, page 28

———

Warm Portobello and Basil Salad, page 61

———

Venison Stew with
Parsnips and Rosemary, page 170

Bacon Mashed Potatoes, page 194

———

Aged Gouda, Pont l'Evêque, Chèvre,
Maytag Blue

———

Molten Chocolate Cakes, page 223

■ ■ ■

Black Olives with
Fennel Seeds and Fresh Fennel, page 25

Peppered Cashews, page 37

Soy and Lime Marinated Chicken, page 50

———

Wild-Mushroom and
Goat-Cheese Lasagne, page 172

Green salad

Crusty bread

———

Mixed-Berry Cobbler, page 237

■ ■ ■

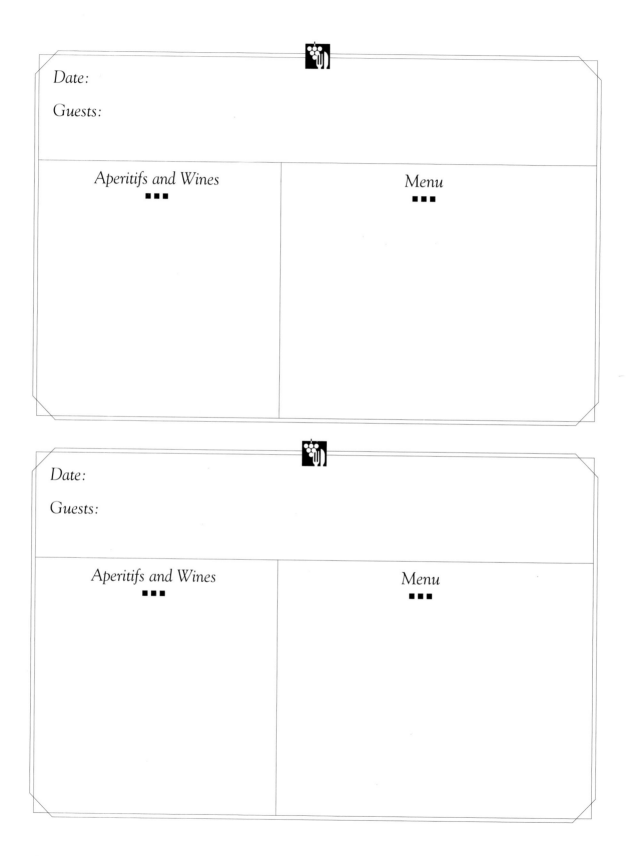

Date:

Guests:

Aperitifs and Wines ∎∎∎	*Menu* ∎∎∎

Date:

Guests:

Aperitifs and Wines ∎∎∎	*Menu* ∎∎∎

Date:

Guests:

Aperitifs and Wines
■ ■ ■

Menu
■ ■ ■

Date:

Guests:

Aperitifs and Wines
■ ■ ■

Menu
■ ■ ■

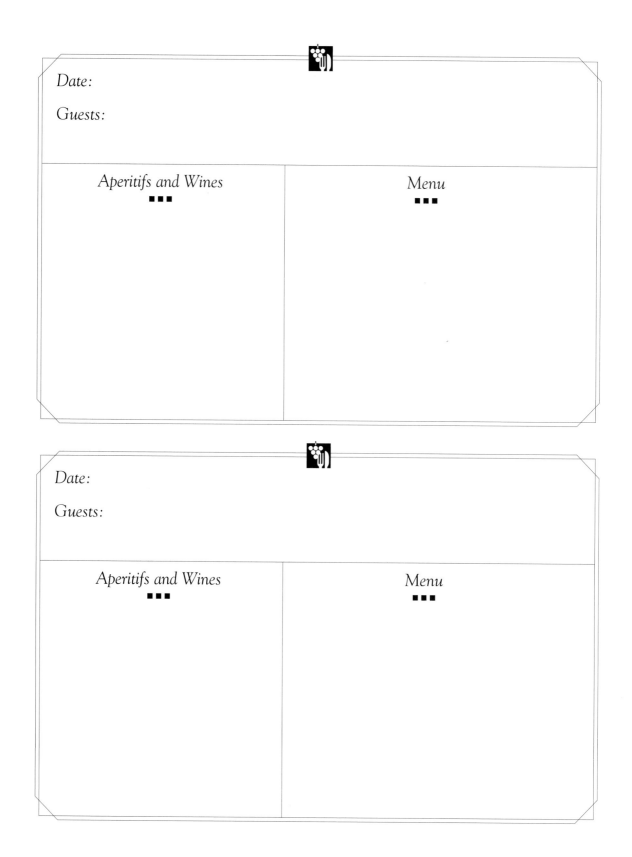

Date:

Guests:

Aperitifs and Wines
■■■

Menu
■■■

Date:

Guests:

Aperitifs and Wines
■■■

Menu
■■■

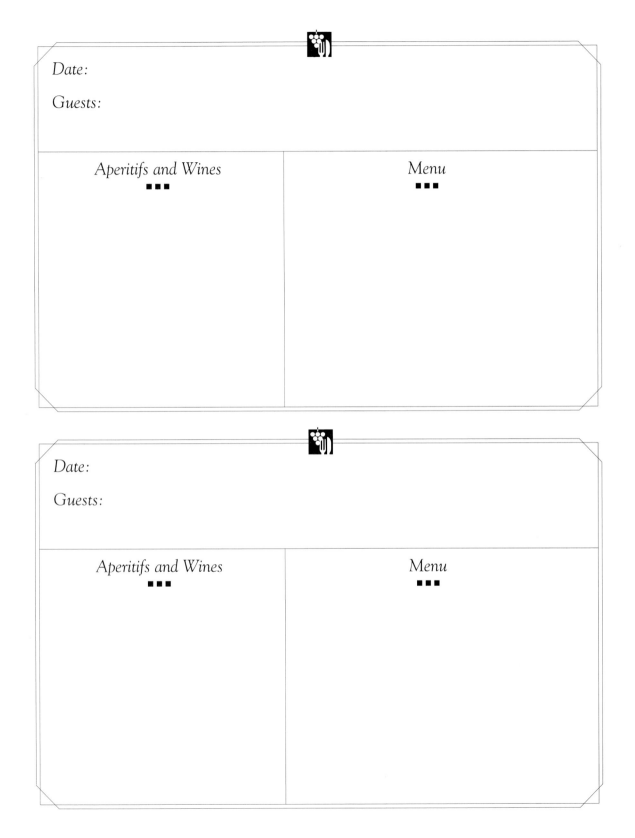

Date:

Guests:

Aperitifs and Wines
■ ■ ■

Menu
■ ■ ■

Date:

Guests:

Aperitifs and Wines
■ ■ ■

Menu
■ ■ ■

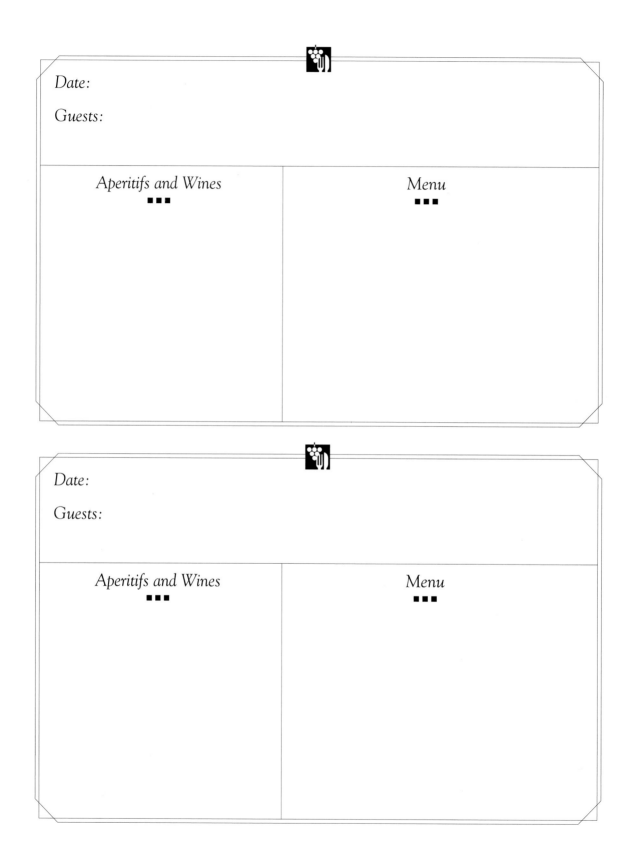

Date:

Guests:

Aperitifs and Wines	Menu
■ ■ ■	■ ■ ■

Date:

Guests:

Aperitifs and Wines	Menu
■ ■ ■	■ ■ ■

Date:

Guests:

Aperitifs and Wines	Menu
■ ■ ■	■ ■ ■

Date:

Guests:

Aperitifs and Wines	Menu
■ ■ ■	■ ■ ■

INDEX

C

M

Q

R

S

V

W

Z

CONTRIBUTORS

KATHERINE ALFORD is a food writer and cooking instructor in New York City.

KEVIN CAULDWELL is the pastry chef at San Domenico NY.

BOB CHAMBERS is the executive chef for Lancôme/L'Oreal Inc. He is also a food writer and food stylist.

PEGGY CULLEN is a baker, candy maker and food writer who lives in New York City.

ERICA DE MANE is a chef and food writer in New York City who specializes in Italian cooking and the history of Italian food.

JIM FLINT is an avid home cook specializing in Italian cuisine.

STEPHEN KALT is a restaurant consultant and chef/co-owner of Spartina in New York City

STEPHANIE LYNESS is a food writer and recipe developer. She has just completed a translation of Jacques Manière's cookbook, *Cuisine à la Vapeur: The Art of Cooking with Steam* (Morrow).

NICKY MAJOR is the owner of the catering firm Major the Gourmet and the restaurant MTG Cafe to Go in Vancouver, British Columbia.

ZARELA MARTINEZ is the chef/owner of Zarela in New York City.

RICHARD NALLEY, responsible for all the wine recommendations in this book, is a nationally syndicated wine columnist. His articles have appeared in numerous publications including *Food & Wine* and *The New York Times*.

GRACE PARISI is a chef, food writer and food stylist in New York City.

ALVIO RENZINI is a professor at the University of Bologna and an avid Italian cook.

MICHAEL RICH, an astronomer by day, is an enthusiastic cook in his off hours.

RICK SPINELL is the chef/owner of Spinell's Litchfield Food Company in Litchfield, Connecticut.

JEAN-GEORGES VONGERICHTEN is the chef/owner of three restaurants, Vong, Jo Jo and Lipstick Cafe, all in New York City. He is the author of *Simple Cuisine* (Simon & Schuster) and is working on a new cookbook on Thai cuisine.

ARI WEINZWEIG is the co-owner of Zingerman's Delicatessen, Markadia (a specialty-produce market) and Zingerman's Bakehouse, all in Ann Arbor, Michigan. He is a former president of the American Cheese Society and travels extensively, buying well over one hundred varieties of cheese from traditional makers throughout Europe and the U.S.